Atheism and Secularity

Atheism and Secularity

Volume 2
Global Expressions

Edited by
Phil Zuckerman

Praeger Perspectives

PRAEGER
An Imprint of ABC-CLIO, LLC

A B C ☰ C L I O

Santa Barbara, California • Denver, Colorado • Oxford, England

Library of Congress Cataloging-in-Publication Data

Atheism and secularity / Phil Zuckerman, editor.
   p. cm.
   Includes bibliographical references and index.
   ISBN 978-0-313-35181-5 (hard copy : alk. paper) — ISBN 978-0-313-35182-2 (ebook) — ISBN 978-0-313-35183-9 (hard copy vol. 1 : alk. paper) — ISBN 978-0-313-35184-6 (ebook vol. 1) — ISBN 978-0-313-35185-3 (hard copy vol. 2 : alk. paper) — ISBN 978-0-313-35186-0 (ebook vol. 2) 1. Irreligion and sociology. 2. Atheism. 3. Secularism. I. Zuckerman, Phil.
   BL2747.A85 2010
   211'.6—dc22   2009036682

ISBN: 978-0-313-35181-5
EISBN: 978-0-313-35182-2

14 13 12 11 10   1 2 3 4 5

This book is also available on the World Wide Web as an eBook.
Visit www.abc-clio.com for details.

Praeger
An Imprint of ABC-CLIO, LLC

ABC-CLIO, LLC
130 Cremona Drive, P.O. Box 1911
Santa Barbara, California 93116-1911

This book is printed on acid-free paper (∞)

Manufactured in the United States of America

Contents

Introduction:
The Social Scientific Study
of Atheism and Secularity

Phil Zuckerman

In 1972, almost forty years ago, Colin Campbell, then a lecturer at the University of York, published a book titled *Toward a Sociology of Irreligion.*[1] The inside jacket cover dubbed it "the first serious study of the social phenomenon of the rejection of religion." In this groundbreaking treatise, Campbell observed that sociologists have "entirely ignored irreligion."[2] He sought to vigorously address this major lacuna by calling for a new focus of study within sociology, that is, the study of people who live their lives indifferent to, without, or in opposition to religion. Campbell began his work by pondering why it is that sociologists have ignored secularity over the years, and he then went on to broach a variety of significant topics ripe for inquiry and attention: the role antireligious and/or humanist movements play in spreading secularization within society; the various forms and definitions of irreligion; irreligion and morality; irreligion and politics; the social functions of irreligion, and so on. Campbell's work remains significant for its insights, its thoughtfulness, and its incontrovertible prescience. But what is perhaps most striking about the work is this: it fell on deaf ears. Campbell's call for a widespread sociological analysis of irreligion went largely unheeded.

The publication of this two-volume set seeks to redress that regrettable outcome, to hear and to heed Campbell's call, and to finally take seriously the social scientific task of exploring, investigating, documenting, and analyzing various aspects of atheism and secularity. The authors of the chapters contained in this collection have attempted to do just that and thereby offer studies of irreligiosity with the same level of interest and rigor that social scientists have devoted to studying the topic of religiosity for well over a century.

While bemoaning the dearth of scholarship on atheism, irreligion, and secularity that has typified the social sciences,[3] it must also be acknowledged that a significant amount of academic writing and scholarship has in fact been devoted to the topic of *secularization*—the historical process whereby religion weakens, fades, or loses its hegemonic dominance or public significance. A plethora of scholars have been aggressively debating secularization for years.[4] Despite the impressive amount that has been published on secularization, nearly all of it—at least that I am aware of—is generally theoretical, typological, or broadly historical in nature, and doesn't actually deal with secular life or atheism as they are actually lived, expressed, or experienced by irreligious men and women in the here and now. Nor does the cottage industry of scholarship on or about secularization entail a direct focus on the social, anthropological, and/or psychological particulars of how secularity actually manifests itself or "plays itself out" in the contemporary world.

As with work on secularization, when it comes to the advocacy of atheism—or the debunking of religion—there's also a lot out there, to be sure. Thousands of books, essays, and articles have been published since the days of David Hume (1711–1776) and Baron D'Holbach (1723–1789), which argue against theism, critique the Bible, deride religion, harangue clergy, and/or promote naturalism, materialism, agnosticism, humanism, freethought, and so on. Most recently, a spate of best sellers have been published in this formidable vein, including *The End of Faith: Religion, Terror, and the Future of Reason* (2004) by Sam Harris,[5] *God Is Not Great: How Religion Poisons Everything* (2007) by Christopher Hitchens,[6] and *The God Delusion* (2006) by Richard Dawkins[7]—the last of which has sold over 1.5 million copies as of this writing. These books, however, are not studies of atheists and/or secular people, per se. They are distinctly polemical works with the expressed goal of convincing people that theism is false and/or that religion is a bad or harmful thing. Such endeavors, however thought provoking, are not social science. Nor are they meant to be. Lest the reader be confused, this point bears stressing: the advocacy of atheism and/or the urging of secularity are not to be mistaken for the social-scientific study of atheism and secularity—just as one wouldn't confuse works that advocate faith and religion with those that seek to study, explain, or analyze faith and religion. And as stated above, when it comes to the advocacy of atheism and secularity, one finds a rich, diverse, and undeniably copious corpus of work. But when it comes to the study and analysis of atheism and secularity, one doesn't find much. As William Sims Bainbridge recently lamented, "we know surprisingly little about Atheism from a social-scientific perspective."[8]

That said, for one to suggest that absolutely *no* social science has been undertaken devoted to the study of atheism or secularity since Campbell's call would be untrue. In fact, several years just prior to the publication of Campbell's book, N. J. Demerath wrote what may very well be the first sociological investigations of irreligion ever published in academic journals; one, coauthored with Victor Thiessen and published in 1966, was an article on the Freie Gemeinde, a small freethought movement in Wisconsin and the other, published in 1969, was an article on the Society for Ethical Culture and the American Rationalist Federation.[9] Also in 1969, Armand Mauss published an article on religious defection among Mormons.[10] And one year prior to the publication of Campbell's book, Rocco Caporale and Antonio Gumelli edited a volume titled *The Culture of Unbelief*, which was an assemblage of papers delivered at a symposium held in Rome on the very topic of the lack of religious belief in the contemporary world. Most of the papers in this publication, however, tended to be highly tentative and/or speculative, for as one contributor noted, there is an "appalling lack of empirical data on unbelief" and "we do not know enough about the phenomenon of unbelief to formulate even a minimum inventory of validated propositions that may constitute the basis of further analysis."[11] While a slew of studies emerged in the 1970s and 1980s with a focus on apostasy,[12] aside from these and a few additional disparate books and articles,[13] in the words of Talal Asad, "social scientists ... have paid scarcely any attention to the idea of the secular."[14]

That sociologists, anthropologists, and psychologists have largely neglected the study of secularity is truly remarkable, especially given the fact that secular, irreligious, nonreligious, and antireligious men and women have always existed.[15] Even Rodney Stark and Roger Finke can admit that atheism is "probably as old as religion."[16] Today, we know that atheists and secular folk represent a large slice of humanity; one recent (and conservative) estimate of nonbelievers in God places the number somewhere between 500 million and 750 million people worldwide.[17] And if the category were to be widened to include those who self-identify as simply "nonreligious" or "unreligious," these numbers would no doubt increase dramatically. The fact is, the portion of humans who reject, have no interest in, or are indifferent to belief in God and/or religion is not limited to some miniscule batch of angry deviants or disgruntled "village atheists." On the contrary, for if our estimates are correct, nonbelievers in God as a worldwide group come in fourth place after Christianity, Islam, and Hinduism in terms of the global ranking of commonly held belief systems. Put another way, there are 58 times as many nonbelievers in God as there are Mormons, 35 times as many nonbelievers in God as there are Sikhs, and twice as many nonbelievers in God as there are Buddhists.

Granted, in most nations, the irreligious may represent but a small minority.[18] However, in many other nations—such as Sweden, the Czech Republic, and Japan—the nonreligious or irreligious most likely constitute a majority of the population.[19] In the United States, over 15 percent of Americans (approximately 35 million people) claim "None" as their religion when asked by pollsters; of those 35 million, one study reports that 4 percent self-identify as atheists and another 6 percent as agnostics, with most of the remaining people simply saying that they have "no religion."[20] Some estimates of irreligious Americans are even slightly higher; according to the 2008 U.S Religious Landscape Survey carried out by the Pew Forum on Religion and Public Life, more than 16 percent of Americans identify as "unaffiliated."[21] This is quite an increase in irreligiosity, for back in the 1950s only 3 percent of Americans claimed "none" as their religion.[22] Thus, the percentage today (15 or 16 percent) represents a quadrupling of "none's" in one generation. And just to give readers some perspective, these percentages mean that there are more unaffiliated or "none's" in the United States than there are African Americans. When it comes to God-belief specifically, a recent Harris poll from 2008 found that 10 percent of Americans do not believe in God, with an additional 9 percent who said "not sure."[23] That means that nearly one American in five is either an atheist or possible agnostic. We're talking about 60 million Americans who are nontheists. These numbers and percentages render any suggestion that secular folk are atypically unhappy, alienated, elitist, or otherwise unwell or unnatural manifestly untenable, if not downright quaint.

Whether atheists and secular folk represent a very small minority of a nation's population (as in the case of, say, Ghana or Zimbabwe), or a very large percentage (as in the case of, say, the Netherlands or France), the bottom line is that, in the succinct and understated words of Darren Sherkat, "not everyone desires religious goods."[24] Such irreligious women and men—their identities, worldviews, associations, and experiences—deserve to be studied. Of particular interest for social scientists is how atheism, and/or secularity, intersects with, is influenced by, and in turn influences other aspects of the social world.

Fortunately, it appears as though a new day is dawning for the social-scientific study of atheism and secularity. In addition to the founding in 2005 of the Institute for the Study of Secularism in Society and Culture—the first of its kind to be established in North America—a growing body of research and scholarship has begun to emerge that focuses specifically on the irreligious. Some of the more noteworthy, pioneering efforts include *Atheists: A Groundbreaking Study of America's Nonbelievers* by Hunsberger and Altemeyer,[25] *Secularism and Secularity: Contemporary International Perspectives* edited by Kosmin and Keysar,[26] *The Cambridge Companion to Atheism* edited by Michael Martin,[27] my own *Society Without God: What the Least Religious Nations Can Tell Us about*

Contentment,[28] and finally, this publication. The essays in this two-volume set have been assembled and published in a concerted effort to not only begin filling a major lacuna within the social sciences, but more hopefully, to inspire further social-scientific research on irreligiosity in all its numerous dimensions and varied manifestations.

NOTES

1. Colin Campbell, *Toward a Sociology of Irreligion* (New York: Heider and Heider, 1972).

2. Ibid., 8.

3. In the words of Benjamin Beit-Hallhami: "Those who shaped the modern human sciences have been preoccupied with explaining the phenomena of religion and religiosity. Accounting for the absence of religious faith has never been of much concern to them." Benjamin Beit-Hallahmi, "Atheists: A Psychological Profile," in *The Cambridge Companion to Atheism,* ed. Michael Martin (Cambridge: Cambridge University Press, 2007), 300.

4. For some major works on secularization, see Karel Dobbelaere, *Secularization: An Analysis at Three Levels* (Bruxelles: P.I.E.-Peter Lang, 2002); William Swatos and Daniel Olson, *The Secularization Debate* (Lanham, MD: Rowman and Littlefield, 2000); Steve Bruce, *God is Dead: Secularization in the West* (Oxford, UK: Blackwell Publishing, 2002); Peter Berger, ed., *The Desecularization of the World: Resurgent Religion and World Politics* (Grand Rapids, MI: William B. Eerdmans, 1999); David Martin, *A General Theory of Secularization* (New York: Harper and Row, 1978); Peter Glasner, *The Sociology of Secularization: A Critique of a Concept.* (London: Routledge of Kegan Paul, 1977); Peter Berger, *The Sacred Canopy* (New York: Anchor, 1967).

5. Sam Harris, *The End of Faith: Religion, Terror, and the Future of Reason* (New York; W.W. Norton, 2004).

6. Christopher Hitchens, *God is Not Great: How Religion Poisons Everything* (New York: Twelve, 2007).

7. Richard Dawkins, *The God Delusion* (Boston: Houghton Mifflin, 2006).

8. William Sims Bainbridge, "Atheism," *Interdisciplinary Journal of Research on Religion* 1 (2005): 3.

9. N. J. Demerath and Victor Theissen, "On Spitting against the Wind: Organizational Precariousness and American Irreligion," *The American Journal of Sociology* 7, no. 6 (1966): 674–87; N. J. Demerath, "A-Religion, and the Rise of the Religion-less Church: Two Case Studies in Organizational Convergence," *Sociological Analysis* 30, no. 4 (Winter 1969): 191–203.

10. Armand Mauss, "Dimensions of Religious Defection," *Review of Religious Research* 10, no. 3 (1969): 128–35.

11. Rocco Carorale and Antonio Grumelli, eds., *The Culture of Un-Belief* (Berkeley, CA: University of California Press, 1971), 3–4.

12. Including David G. Bromley, ed., *Falling From the Faith: The Causes and Consequences of Religious Apostasy* (Newbury Park, CA: Sage Publications, 1988); David Caplovitz and Fred Sherrow, *The Religious Drop-Outs: Apostasy among College Graduates* (Beverly Hills, CA: Sage Publications, 1977); Roger Louis

Dudley, "Alienation from Religion in Adolescents from Fundamentalist Religious Homes," *Journal for the Scientific Study of Religion* 17, no. 4 (Dec. 1978): 389–98; Bruce Hunsberger, "Apostasy: A Social-Learning Perspective," *Review of Religious Research* 25 (1983): 21–38; Bruce Hunsberger, "A Re-examination of the Antecedents of Apostasy," *Review of Religious Research* 21 (1980): 158–70.

13. J. Russell Hale, *The Unchurched* (San Francisco, CA: Harper and Row, 1980); W. Feigelman, B. S. Gorman, and J. A. Varacalli, "Americans Who Give up Religion," *Sociology and Social Research* 76 (1992): 138–44; Bon Altemeyer and Bruce Hunsberger, *Amazing Conversions: Why Some Turn to Faith and Others Abandon Religion* (Amherst, NY: Prometheus Books, 1997); Michael Hout and Claude S. Fischer, "Why More Americans Have No Religious Preference: Politics and Generations," *American Sociological Review* 67 (2002): 165–90.

14. Talal Asad, *Formations of the Secular: Christianity, Islam, and Modernity* (Palo Alto, CA: Stanford University Press, 2003), 17.

15. Jennifer Michael Hecht, *Doubt: A History* (New York: Harper Collins, 2003); James Thrower, *Western Atheism: A Short History* (Amherst, NY: Prometheus Books, 2000).

16. Rodney Stark and Roger Finke, *Acts of Faith* (Berkeley, CA: University of California Press, 2000), 13.

17. Phil Zuckerman, "Atheism: Contemporary Numbers and Patterns," in *The Cambridge Companion to Atheism*, ed. Michael Martin (Cambridge: Cambridge University Press, 2007).

18. Pippa Norris and Ronald Inglehart, *Sacred and Secular: Religion and Politics Worldwide* (New York: Cambrdige University Press, 2004).

19. Phil Zuckerman, "Atheism: Contemporary Numbers and Patterns," in *The Cambridge Companion to Atheism*, ed. Michael Martin (Cambridge: Cambridge University Press, 2007).

20. http://www.trincoll.edu/secularisminstitute/.

21. http://religions.pewforum.org/affiliations/.

22. C. Kirk Hadaway and Wade Clark Roof, "Apostasy in American Churches: Evidence from National Survey Data," in *Falling From the Faith: The Causes and Consequences of Religious Apostasy*, ed. David G. Bromley (Newbury Park, CA: Sage Publications, 1988).

23. http://www.harrisinteractive.com/harris_poll/index.asp?PID=982/.

24. Darren E. Sherkat, "Beyond Belief: Atheism, Agnosticism, and Theistic Certainty in the United States," *Sociological Spectrum* 28 (2008), 438.

25. Bruce E. Hunsberger and Bob Altemeyer, *Atheists: A Groundbreaking Study of America's Nonbelievers* (Amherst, NY: Prometheus Books, 2006).

26. Barry A. Kosmin and Ariela Keysar, eds., *Secularism and Secularity: Contemporary International Perspectives* (Hartford, CT: Institute for the Study of Secularism in Society and Culture, 2007).

27. Michael Martin, ed., *The Cambridge Companion to Atheism* (New York: Cambridge University Press, 2007).

28. Phil Zuckerman, *Society without God: What the Least Religious Nations Can Tell Us about Contentment* (New York: New York University Press, 2008).

Chapter 1

Atheism and Secularity in North America

Bob Altemeyer

How many Americans do not believe in God? Not very many, according to the polls. The 2006 General Social Survey (GSS) found that 2.2 percent of its respondents declared they "do not believe in God," and 4.3 percent stated they did not know if God exists. A 2008 Pew Research Center survey reported that atheists accounted for only 1.6 percent of the sample and agnostics 2.4 percent. So nonbelievers embody but a little of the American population. Furthermore, the masses are hardly swarming to their ranks. In 1988–1991, when the GSS first asked the question, 1.9 percent said they did not believe in God, compared to 2.2 percent 15 years later, and 4.1 percent were agnostics, compared with 4.3 percent in 2006.

Secularism, the disregarding of religious concerns whatever one's belief about the supernatural, runs a bit thicker, with 6.3 percent of the PEW sample saying they had no religion at all and could care less. Another 5.8 percent also had no affiliation but stated they were religious in some way. And the number of unaffiliated "Nones" *has* been growing over time. Five percent of first GSS, conducted in 1972, said they were Nones. In 2006 the figure topped 16 percent. This tripling of people stiff-arming organized religion signals a noteworthy shift in American religious attitudes.

Furthermore, some of the "religiously *affiliated*"—by far the largest group in the polls—affiliate in name only. Many people call themselves "Protestant," "Catholic," or "Jew" for cultural or family reasons, but scrupulously avoid going to church, showing up for only the most important religious holidays and for marrying and burying. The 2006 GSS found that most Americans (53 percent) seldom or never attend religious services. In counterpoint, only about a third (31 percent) say they attend regularly (and some of them must be varnishing the truth, since studies find churches rather emptier than these numbers indicate).

But for all of the current disconnect with organized religion, the vast majority of American adults do believe in God and probably in the traditional Judeo-Christian God. In fact, 63 percent of the 2006 GSS sample said they had "no doubts" whatsoever about God's existence. People are not leaving churches because of theological misgivings, but for other reasons that we shall discuss later.

After centuries of religious preeminence, Canada has morphed into a largely secular society in just two generations. In the 1950s Canadian churches were packed fuller than American ones. Now, according to a 2006 Ipsos-Reid Survey, only 17 percent of Canadians attend religious services every week—about half the figure for the United States. In turn, the number of nonbelievers has multiplied. A 2008 Harris-Decima Survey found 23 percent of Canadian adults do not believe in God, many times the level of disbelief in America. As in the United States, the Nones are growing faster than any other "religious group."

Correspondingly, evangelical Christians make up only 10 percent of the Canadian population, compared with about 30 percent of Americans. And Canadians attach relatively little stigma to atheism, although in some parts of the U.S. atheists have to hide their religious views for fear of social retribution. Indeed, a 2007 Gallup Poll found Americans would rather have a black, Jewish, female, Hispanic, Mormon, Muslim, or gay president than an atheist. In fact most (53 percent) of the sample said they would vote against an atheist. In Canada, only 32 percent said they would not want an atheist prime minister.

DEMOGRAPHIC TENDENCIES AMONG NONBELIEVERS

Studies almost universally find that nonbelievers tend to be men rather than women: the flip side of the oft-noted tendency of women to be more religious. Atheists and agnostics also tend to be better educated than believers, have higher socioeconomic status, are more likely to live in urban than in rural communities, and strongly prefer liberal political parties. They also tend to be younger than the general population. Does this mean disbelief is a "phase" young people go through before accepting their parents' ways? Or does it merely show that secularism is becoming more common as generations move on? Let us consider how people become nonbelievers.

THE ORIGINS OF NONBELIEF AND THE PERSONALITIES OF NONBELIEVERS: ACTIVE AMERICAN ATHEISTS

National polls tell us how many atheists and agnostics walk among us and a few things about them. But polls are not usually designed to yield much psychological insight into nonbelievers' minds, and how they got that way. So we now turn to research that digs deeper—albeit into less representative samples—to figure such things out.

One study sent a long questionnaire to members of cooperating atheist clubs in the San Francisco Bay area in 2002 and then followed that up with a similar survey of Alabama and Idaho atheists. The 281 participants obviously do not represent the several million atheists in the United States. They belonged to the sort of atheist organizations that launch court cases about mentioning God in the Pledge of Allegiance, but their answers can tell us what such "hard core" atheists are like.

Were They Really Atheists?

Some of the respondents disliked the name "atheist" and called themselves "humanists." But the survey asked them in seven ways if they believed in a supernatural power, a deity:

1. That is a thinking, self-aware being, not just some physical force like the "Big Bang"?
2. That is almighty: that can do anything it decides to do?
3. That is eternal: that always was and always will be?
4. That intentionally created the universe for its own purposes?
5. That is constantly aware of our individual lives and hears our prayers?
6. That is all-loving and all-good?
7. That will judge us after we die, sending some to Heaven and others to Hell?

Virtually all (99.5 percent) of the answers came back "No."

Then the survey directly asked about belief in the traditional concept of God in our culture. Three answers were provided:

1. "I am an atheist. I do not believe in the existence of this traditional God. I believe it does *not* exist."
2. "I am an agnostic. I do not believe in the existence of this traditional God, *nor* do I disbelieve in it."
3. "I am a theist, a believer. I believe in the existence of this traditional God."

All of the 281 respondents said they were atheists.

Going yet further, the survey asked, "If you do not believe in the 'traditional' God, is there any sense in which you do believe in 'God'? If so, would you please describe what kind of God or supernatural being or supernatural force you DO believe in? Does this being play an active role in human lives (If so, how?)?" Only 6 percent of the atheists said they believed in any kind of supernatural power, and their names for it (e.g., "Nature," "Life Force," "Laws of the Universe") imply that even these are not *super*natural entities in the usual sense. Thus the active American atheists denied the existence of any sort of divine being.

Origins of Their Atheism

Like most atheists, these were predominantly male (68 percent) and well-educated (with 17 years of schooling on the average), and they overwhelmingly preferred the Democratic Party over the Republicans. But they averaged nearly 60 years of age—much older than the atheists found in American polls. So young atheists do not appear to be joining atheist clubs.

The great majority of the active atheists, about 75 percent, came from nonreligious backgrounds. Does this mean their parents were atheists? No, only 30 percent had an atheist or agnostic mom or dad. Instead, the parents usually believed in God, but otherwise had no interest in religion. If you (correctly) believe that very religious offspring tend to come from very religious upbringings, you can see why a nonreligious background can lead to nonbelief. Socialization usually works.

But what about the 25 percent who became atheists despite religious (and occasionally very religious) childhoods? They not only failed to follow in their parents' footsteps, they went to the opposite extreme. They did not just backslide into a lax association with the faith of their fathers, they did not just become "unaffiliated seculars," and they did not "just" become atheists. They became the kind of atheist who challenges religious practice in court and mocks it in public events like the Bible-throwing Contest held on the summer solstice in San Francisco's Golden Gate Park. How on earth did socialization in very religious homes produce that?

The researchers asked the atheists to describe their journey to disbelief. Surprisingly the solid majority, from both nonreligious and religious backgrounds, had believed in God at some point in their lives. After all, it is natural to wonder where *everything* came from, and religions give answers that can permeate a culture. The respondents with *non*religious parents said they picked up their belief in the traditional God from peers, grandparents, teachers, and so on. Moreover, the nonreligious parents did not mind. They were not hostile toward religion, just uninterested. So belief sprung up in some rather unlikely, unintended, and untended soil.

But challenges to God and the Bible also crop up in our culture. An awful lot rides on how the believer deals with those challenges. Studies of Canadian university students reveal that, just as almost everyone believes in God at some point in her life, almost everyone begins to wonder about God's existence too. Typically the doubts arise in the middle-teen years. Some students then make a very one-sided search of the issues. They take their questions to their parents, to their religious friends, and to their minister. They pray for guidance and read the Bible. Not surprisingly, almost all their doubts are allayed—if not directly answered.

Other students take a more two-sided approach to the issue. They too seek out believers, but they also talk to disbelieving peers and teachers, and they read up on scientific findings and Bertram Russell. Most of all, they seem determined to hammer out a real decision, to make up their own minds on the matter, whereas the "one-siders" appear mostly searching for reassurance so they will *not* have to confront the issue. When all is said and done, many two-siders continue to believe in God. But some do not. Almost all the students who became nonbelievers had made two-sided searches.

Amazing Apostates

Why do some "two-side searchers" stop believing in God? We can get insight from interviews of "Amazing Apostate" Canadian students. Like some of the active American atheists we are trying to understand, they had come from very religious backgrounds, and yet they had rejected the family faith and become nonbelievers by the time they entered college. The decision had often cost them plenty, even shunning and disownment by their families, losing their best friends, and becoming social pariahs in their communities. Why on earth then did they do it?

Over and over again, these students said they *wanted* to believe what their families believed, but they could not make themselves do it because "It's too unbelievable!" What made it so unbelievable then? After all, almost everyone else accepts it!

The disbeliefs basically arose "internally" from the student's knowledge of his religion. The Bible seemed to overflow with contradictions— sometimes in successive verses. It hardly smacked of a competent editor, much less a supreme being. Furthermore the classic arguments for the existence of God crumbled when given a good shake. The reasoning behind the Uncaused Cause, for example, turned out to be circular, self-contradictory, and incapable of demonstrating even a conscious god, much less a benign one. The "argument from order" assumed that because some things obviously had a conscious builder, all things must, and so on. Furthermore, so much of the religion's teachings flew in the face of scientific discovery.

When the Amazing Apostates brought these concerns to their parents, teachers, or ministers, they were given unsatisfying stock answers. Or the elders told them to have faith, that unquestioning faith was the highest virtue. Or the grown-ups chastened them for even having the thoughts. It was wrong to ask questions; Satan was obviously working on them. They must not let others know they had wondered about such things.

The problem was that they had usually been told their religion topped all others because it was the *true* religion. Their teachers had made quite a point of that; everything they taught was so deeply, so totally, so fundamentally true, they said. So truth was the bottom line, not the teachings. In these students such instruction had, it seemed, sparked a desire for the truth that became more important, ultimately, than all the pressures to have faith. When their religion failed by the criterion it had itself established, these students felt almost helpless to do anything but reject it. In short, the Amazing Apostates had taken their religion too seriously, been influenced by it too much, to continue believing in it. Socialization had trumped itself.

What was different about the Amazing Apostates?

The interesting question then emerges, why do most people believe in God if the evidence is so flawed? Several things stood out about the Amazing Apostates. First, they had usually been devout members of their religion, following its rules and practicing its rituals more faithfully than their peers. They had thus been praised for their integrity, and that drive for personal consistency put them between a rock and a hard place when religion failed the test. They could not simply settle for reassurance and go with the flow. Attending church, saying prayers, pretending to believe when they did not—these things ate away at them.

Second, the Amazing Apostates were usually highly intelligent and had typically been "A" students in high school. They could spot the problem with the Bible saying Cain worried that anyone might kill him as he wandered the earth. They would do the background reading in biology that verified evolution. They were not afraid to read books by philosophers. They had been rewarded all their lives for getting the "right answer" to questions and consequently may have been less willing than most to settle for something that, upon examination, did not seem right.

Third, when asked why their siblings had not also become nonbelievers, they commonly answered their brothers and sisters might have their doubts too, but they were too afraid to take the next step— not just because of their parents, but because the next step took one off a cliff, into the Unknown. Believing intensely in a religion brings an enormous number of rewards. You know who you are, you know what life is about, you know what you are supposed to do, you know you will have friends all of your life, you know you will never really die, and you know you will rejoin all the loved ones who die before and after you. It is all laid out for you. In contrast, most of the Amazing Apostate students did not have a clue what to "believe in" now, only that it would have to make sense. They usually felt alone and misunderstood, facing the abyss people warned them would be there if they turned their backs on God. They also were hounded by the thought, deeply planted in them, that if they abandoned God they would burn forever in the hottest flames of Hell. So they said they would love to return to the bosom of Abraham, but they just could not make themselves do it. It takes an uncommon amount of courage to take that stand, and that is probably another reason why disbelief is so rare.

(Incidentally, this study also investigated "Amazing Believers": students with no religious background who nonetheless became very fervent Christians. In contrast to the Amazing Apostates, the Amazing Believers typically joined a religion to meet emotional needs. For example, they became terrified of death or became depressed over the mess they had made of their lives. Also unlike the apostates, who typically worked things out alone in their own minds, the Amazing Believers were usually "brought to God" by peers who belonged to church youth groups. The feeling of acceptance, love, and community support led them to join the religion, not a voice from above, Pascal's Wager, or an airtight syllogism. Indeed, often they did not know much about what the religion taught and had to learn what they now believed.)

Comparing Loss of Faith by the Amazing Apostates and the Active Atheists

Few of the Amazing Apostates will ever become active in atheist causes. Canadian nonbelievers have comparatively little to protest about. But one can find parallels to their lives in the much older active American atheists. Almost all of the latter's doubts arose, they reported, over cerebral issues: religion versus science, inconsistencies in the Bible, and teachings that made no sense. Their atheism did not have emotional roots, such as the death of a loved one. Anger, fear, lust, and unhappiness did not trigger their quest, but rather (like the Amazing Apostates) the intellectual basis of their faith collapsed when poked and probed.

Also like the Amazing Apostates, the active atheists had usually worked things out on their own, doing a lot of reading and thinking, determined to discover the truth. And ultimately they found what they held unholdable, and they dropped it. As one wrote, "My mother believes with all her heart that Satan turned me away, but it was the Bible. Nobody brainwashed me or led me into a cult. I studied my church's teachings and that's what made me stop believing."

The final decision to become an atheist took a long time: six years on the average in the San Francisco sample, and fourteen years in Alabama and Idaho, where atheism could prove hazardous to one's social standing and bank account. And most of the active atheists reported that being a nonbeliever had produced difficulties in their lives—even in San Francisco. When asked why they then had chosen to join a vilified group, they gave the Amazing Apostates' answer: they had no other choice; they could not believe what was so unbelievable.

The Personalities of Active Atheists

Dogmatism

The San Francisco, Alabama, and Idaho study also provided data on various aspects of the active atheists' personalities. For example, dogmatism was measured in three different ways. These active atheists scored rather highly on a dogmatism scale that has items such as, "Anyone who is honestly and truly seeking the truth will end up believing what I believe," and "I am absolutely certain that my ideas about the fundamental issues in life are correct." In a second test they were asked how they would react to the hypothetical discovery of a scientifically verified "Roman file" on Jesus' life that closely supported the Gospels, including his death and resurrection. Two-thirds of the atheists said this would make no difference at all in their strong (dis)-belief that Jesus was the son of God. Finally, about half (51 percent) of the respondents also said they could not think of anything that could happen which would lead them to believe in the traditional God. So some of the active atheists appeared to be rather dogmatic.

Zealotry

Active atheists might also be very zealous, attempting to convince others there is no God. Indeed, their opponents commonly speak of "the atheist agenda," perceiving challenges to school prayer and so on as part of a vast, long-range effort to destroy religion in the United States. So the survey had three measures of missionary zeal. In one, the atheist was asked what he would do if a Christian teenager experiencing religious doubts came to him for advice. Most (62 percent) responded they would have thumped the drum for atheism—some softly ("I would have told her why I became an atheist"), some loudly ("I'd tell her religion was ridiculous."). Most (51 percent) would have wanted the teen to become an atheist, but a smaller number (42 percent) said they would actually try to convert the teen to atheism.

The second measure of zealotry simply asked the atheists what they had taught their own children regarding religion. About 20 percent said they had directly tried to pass on their disbelief in God. The rest said they wanted their children to make up their own minds, not just copy them. So here the atheists looked positively nonzealous.

The third measure of zealotry involved school prayer in which the atheists were asked to react to the following proposition. "Suppose a law were passed requiring strenuous teaching in public schools against belief in God and religion. Beginning in kindergarten, all children would be taught that belief in God is unsupported by logic and science and that traditional religions are based on unreliable scriptures and outdated principles. All children would eventually be encouraged to become atheists or agnostics. How would you react to such a law?"

This proposal would seem to be the centerpiece of an atheist agenda. Yet 76 percent of the active atheists said this would be a bad law. Most of these committed atheists thought it would be just as wrong for schools to teach their opinions as it would be to teach Christianity. The people who launch court cases against public prayer do not want their views crammed down other people's throats instead.

All in all, the three measures indicate active atheists have little "missionary zeal."

Religious ethnocentrism

The active American atheists were also asked to rate various religious groups on a 0–100 scale. Not surprisingly, they gave their highest marks (90) to atheists and their second-highest (60) to agnostics. On the other hand, they give very, very low ratings (0–10) to religious fundamentalists, be they Christians, Jews, or Muslims. The data reveal a strong streak of "Us versus Them" ethnocentrism in the active atheists, which is hardly amazing given how often they battle fundamentalists over various issues.

Happiness, joy, and comfort

Studies of the parents of Canadian university students have found that traditional religious beliefs bring far more happiness, joy, and comfort to people than logic and science do. Very religious people, in fact, said they get almost nothing from logic and science. Perhaps the active atheists would.

Accordingly the San Francisco atheists were asked to say, in sixteen different ways, how much happiness, joy, and comfort they derived from logic and science. Generally speaking, they highly endorsed these approaches. They especially agreed with, "[Logic and science] provide the surest path we have to the truth," "They enable me to search for the truth, instead of just memorizing what others say," and "They give me the satisfaction of knowing that my beliefs are based upon objective facts and logic, not an act of faith." But overall the active atheists did *not* derive nearly the joy and happiness from this approach to life that highly religious people did from their beliefs, who endorsed to the max statements such as, "[My religion] reveals how I can spend all of eternity in heaven with God," "It brings me the joy of God's love," "It tells me I shall rejoin my loved ones after we die," and "It has brought the forgiveness of my sins."

However, this cannot be too surprising, given the findings we reviewed earlier. Logic and science are not intended to satisfy one emotionally. They are "cold" endeavors, cerebral and intellectual, that one should pursue dispassionately. And ultimately science may show us the universe is a purposeless accident that will eventually become a very big cloud of low-level energy pockmarked here and there with dead stars. That is not the sort of thing that gets people jumping out of bed in the morning, compared to promises of salvation and eternal bliss. Yet nonbelievers are willing to chuck all the good stuff because they believe it is a fairy tale and take instead the poor bargain of logic and science because their quest for the truth matters more.

MORE ORDINARY NONBELIEVERS

"Ordinary" Atheists

So far we have been talking about Americans who belong to atheist organizations. Although they command one's interest, they comprise only a small part of the atheist population in North America. What are more ordinary atheists like?

The most comprehensive answer comes from studies of *parents* of university students in central Canada. Such parents provide powerful data because they have lived most of their lives and most have made their final decisions about religion. Furthermore, studying parents will not only tell us about more ordinary atheists, but also allow comparisons with agnostics and with theists of varying commitment (from inactive believers to very active fundamentalists) who answered the same survey.[1] We shall spend the rest of this chapter considering these results, getting a better picture of why people end up believing what they do about God, and how certain aspects of personality vary with how religious people are.

Origins of Ordinary Atheists

Comprising but 5–6 percent of the parent samples—about the same figure found in national polls in Canada, the atheistic parents were largely (61 percent) male and (like all the other subgroups in these studies) averaged about 48 years of age. But the atheists had more extensive educations than the other groups, with a median of 15 years. All said they were atheists, and like the active American atheists, 99 percent of their answers to the "Seven Attributes of God" questions were "No."

Compared to the other parents, the atheists had received the least religious upbringings. But they were not usually reared by nonbeliever parents; only 12 percent said they had been raised in "no religion." Nevertheless, like the active American atheists, they had usually received little religious instruction from their theistic parents and had minimal experience in church. Only 6 percent of the atheists came from highly religious backgrounds and could be called Amazing Apostates.

The parent atheists scored as highly on the Religious Doubts scale as the active American atheists had, displaying a thunderous rejection of religious faith. They too castigated religion on cerebral grounds: There is no proof that God exists; religious accounts of creation do not square with scientific evidence; the Bible hardly seems to be the work of a supernatural being; teachings do not make sense. Emotional reasons played little or no role at all.

Personalities of parent atheists

Being an authoritarian follower.   The parents answered a personality test that measures one's tendency to be an authoritarian follower. Persons who score highly on this scale tend to submit extensively to established authority, aggress in the name of that authority, and insist that others live by the social conventions their authorities endorse. Authoritarian followers tend to be fearful and to memorize the beliefs of the powerful people in their lives rather than think things out for themselves. They consequently have disorganized, unintegrated minds packed with stereotypes, logical inconsistencies, and double standards. They often act in hypocritical ways, but are highly defensive and blind to themselves. Authoritarian followers tend to accept uncritically false ideas that come from trusted sources and reject out of hand true facts that come from "outsiders."

How do you think atheists would score on this measure of authoritarianism? Atheistic parents scored very low, lower than any other group in the sample.

Hostility toward homosexuals.   The measure of authoritarianism predicts many other things about a person's beliefs and behavior. For example, because of their conventionality authoritarian followers often attack persons who violate their notions of respectable behavior, such as homosexuals. Because atheists are very *un*like authoritarian followers, we would expect them to be more accepting of homosexuals than most people. And indeed the atheists in the parent sample scored lowest of all the groups on a measure of hostility toward homosexuals that asked for reactions to statements such as, "Homosexuals should be locked up to protect society" and "Homosexuals should never be given positions of trust in caring for children."

Ethnic and racial prejudice.   Authoritarian followers, like the leaders they obey, tend to be highly prejudiced against many minorities. So again we expect atheists to be less prejudiced and more accepting of diverse ethnic/racial groups than most people are. And once again the data support this, with atheists scoring lower than any other subgroup among the parents on a scale that contains items such as, "Certain races of people clearly do not have the natural intelligence and 'get up and go' of the white race," and "Black people as a rule are, by their nature, more violent than white people are."

Religious ethnocentrism. People are also sometimes prejudiced against others based on their religious affiliations. We saw earlier that active American atheists gave fundamentalists a very low rating and their own group, "atheists," a very high one on the 0–100 scale. But the parent atheists responded quite differently to this question, showing only a small preference for atheists (50) over fundamentalists (30)—amounting to the second-smallest preference of all the groups in the study. This reinforces the findings above that ordinary atheists, however rejecting they may be of various ideas, are relatively accepting of other people.

The parents also answered a scale that measures religion-versus-religion prejudice. It contains items such as "Our country should always be a Christian country, and other beliefs should be ignored in our public institutions," and "All people may be entitled to their own religious beliefs, but I don't want to associate with people whose views are quite different from mine." The scale focuses on Christianity versus other faiths, and atheists would have little reason to favor one religion over another. But atheists also posted low numbers on items about wanting to avoid people with "other" religious beliefs, whatever they were. Overall, atheists had lower scores on this measure than any other group, so again they appear to be relatively tolerant of others.

Dogmatism. The parents also answered the three measures of dogmatism used in the American survey. They scored much lower than the active atheists on the dogmatism scale. Like the Americans, 64 percent said they would be unmoved by a scientifically verified "Roman file" that confirmed the Gospels. And more of them (57 versus 51 percent) said they could not think of anything that would lead them to believe in the traditional God. So the parent atheists appear about as dogmatic overall as the active American atheists. But among the parents as a whole, the atheists usually had the second-lowest group scores on these measures.

Zealotry. Almost none (8 percent) of the atheist parents indicated they would tell a questioning Christian teen that his parents' beliefs were wrong. Only about a third (35 percent) stated they would want the teen to have their beliefs. And only a sixth (16 percent) said they would try to convert the teen to atheism. Correspondingly, only one in seven (14 percent) reported that they had tried to raise their children to be atheists; instead they had emphasized making up one's own mind. In all of these measures, the atheists slid under the rather low totals posted by the American atheists and had the second-lowest proselytizing scores in the whole sample.

Parent atheists were also asked if they would like to see nonbelief taught in public schools. *None* of them said he would. And the parents also answered a Zealotry scale, which asks people how much they promote their basic outlook on life through items such as, "I try to explain my outlook to others at every opportunity," and "I think every sensible person should agree with this outlook, once it has been explained." Atheists had the second-lowest score in the sample.

Group cohesiveness. People vary in how much they want to belong to groups and to conform to a group's standards and insist that others conform too. This was measured by a Group Cohesiveness scale, which contains such items as "For any group to succeed, all its members have to give it their complete loyalty," and "There is nothing lower than a person who betrays his group or stirs up disagreement within it." Atheists had the second-lowest average of all the religious groupings in this study. They pretty much take a pass at being a "good team member."

Belief in a dangerous world. Authoritarian followers post big numbers on a scale that measures fear that the world is becoming so dangerous and degenerate that civilization will soon be destroyed. Some of the items say God will do the destroying. But other statements make no mention of a divinity, such as "It seems that every year there are fewer and fewer truly respectable people, and more and more persons with no morals at all who threaten everyone else." Atheists scored second-lowest of all the subgroups in the sample.

Willingness to revoke Canada's "Bill of Rights." Being easily frightened, authoritarian followers look for someone to "take charge" and "stomp out the rot" that they think is ruining society. They are not inclined to let something like constitutional guarantees of individual freedoms get in the way. Thus they support the revocation of the Bill of Rights in the United States and the Charter of Rights and Freedoms in Canada. When parents in the present study were presented with arguments for abolishing this Charter, some agreed and most disagreed. Atheists showed very little inclination to agree and had the second-lowest score in the study.

Giving to charity. The Canadian parents were also asked what percent of their income they gave to charities. (The question said not to count gifts to one's church or to church activities such as tuition to church schools or support of missionary work—but they could count gifts to religion-sponsored aid programs.) According to their reports, atheists gave the *least* (1.7 percent of their income) to social charities of all the groups in the study.

Happiness.   Finally, parents were asked how happy they were in general, on a 0–6 scale. Atheists had the *lowest* self-rating of happiness of all the groups (3.6, between "moderately" and "pretty" happy.)

Summary.   One cannot assume that these results would apply to perfectly ordinary middle-aged Canadian atheists, much less American ones. But they do provide a point of comparison for the findings on active American atheists. The atheist parents seem as dogmatic as the active Americans. They showed even less inclination to proselytize, and the parents proved much less religiously ethnocentric. Within the Canadian parent sample, the atheists scored low on all these measures.

The parent studies used a broader range of measures than the American survey and suggest what atheists in general might be like. First they are very uninclined—as most people would surmise—to follow the established authorities in society. Compared with others, atheists show little prejudice against traditional targets of discrimination. They do not see the world as a scary place and cannot be easily panicked into supporting the destruction of constitutional freedoms. They (obviously) have little inclination to conform to group norms. In many respects, they seem to be good democratic citizens. But in two ways at least they do not shine: they are not very charitable, and (as was suggested in the studies of the active American atheists and Amazing Apostates), they are not particularly happy.

Ordinary Agnostics

Many agnostics appeared in the Canadian parent samples—more than three times the number of atheists, which again corresponds to the results obtained in national polls. How did they become agnostics, and what are they like?

Origins of agnosticism

Agnostics, like atheists, tended to be guys (54 percent), and they had 14 years of education compared with the atheists' 15. When asked, they declared they were agnostics rather than atheists or theists. Their 85 percent "no" answers to the Seven Attributes of God questions show they clearly do not believe in the traditional God; but the residual 15 percent "yes" answers show they maintain a little wiggle room on the issue.

Only 11 percent of the agnostic parents had come from nonreligious homes, and overall they had experienced only slightly more religious upbringings than the future atheists had. So the agnostics, like the atheists, usually had theistic parents who seldom went to church, prayed as a family, and so on. But more than twice as many agnostics as atheists (16 versus 6 percent) had *highly* religious backgrounds.

Persons leaving a strong religious tradition may well find agnosticism a more comfortable landing place than atheism.

Predictably, agnostics did not doubt the existence of God as strenuously on the Doubts scale as the atheists did. Nor did they doubt the divine origin of the Bible quite as much, nor were they as troubled by inconsistencies in the Bible and religious teachings. They were less put off than the atheists by the bad things religions had done in the past, by the intolerance of some religious people, and by "the way faith made people blind." They *did* have significant doubts about all these counts, but did not see things as strongly black-and-white as the atheists did.

Personalities of agnostics

In general, agnostic and atheistic parents mustered very similar scores on the personality tests. On all of the measures described earlier, when the atheists came in lowest on a trait, the agnostics finished second lowest. When the atheists scored second lowest, it was the agnostics who beat them out. Usually the differences were trivial and not "statistically significant." Recall, for example, that 0 percent of the atheist parents wanted nonbelief taught in public schools. Well, only 1 percent of the agnostics did. You cannot get a more trivial difference than that.

Bigger gaps existed however and should be noted. Atheists scored significantly lower in being authoritarian followers than agnostics did. This makes sense, because atheists take a bigger step away from the established, authority-blessed norm than agnostics do. Atheists also notched significantly lower scores on prejudice against homosexuals and ethnic/racial minorities. Agnostics in turn proved significantly less dogmatic than atheists on all the measures used. For example, although 64 percent of the atheists said they would be unmoved by ancient scrolls supporting the Gospels, only 38 percent of the agnostics said this. This also makes sense, as agnostics have not declared there is no God. And although parent atheists appeared markedly nonzealous, the agnostics predictably wound up even lower. One does not find many "Agnostics Clubs."

Agnostics, like atheists, reported giving 1.7 percent of their income to social charities. They also appeared a little happier, with an average of 4.0 ("Pretty happy") on the 0–6 percent scale.

Summary. Atheists and agnostics differ in their certainty that God does not exist, which may jointly flow from atheists' lesser authoritarianism and agnostics' lesser dogmatism. But when one examines their backgrounds and personalities, the two groups have a great deal in common, as evidenced by their consistent 1 to 2 standings on almost all the measures used. But how isolated are these dissenting camps in a culture where the vast majority believes in God?

THEISTS

Inactive Theists

Origins of believing in God yet being "unchurched"

Inactive theists, who say they believe in God but almost never go to church, made up the largest group in the parent sample—again reflecting a result found in national polls. In fact, if you throw in the 20–25 percent who were atheists or agnostics, you have accounted for about 60 percent of the survey. Thus most of the parents were nonbelievers or believers who for most purposes might as well be nonbelievers. Nonbelievers do not stand nearly as isolated as one might think.

Most (57 percent) of the inactive theists were females, and they went to school for 12 years on the average. They said they believed in the traditional God, with 74 percent of their answers to the Seven Attributes questions being yes, compared with only 15 percent for the agnostics and 1 percent for the atheists. What was their biggest hesitation about the deity? Nearly half did not think God would judge them after they died, which may have helped them sleep in on Sundays.

The inactive theists had notably more religious upbringings than the atheists or agnostics. A sizeable number of them (27 percent) even came from highly religious homes. So why did they end up Nones or at best names on the parish roll who would not even get a participation award?

The "inactives" almost never went to church—which they made clear on the Doubts scale—because of the people they encountered there. Some lay persons and clergy members pressured others to believe what they believed and often seemed to be hypocrites and prejudiced. Religion thus did not appear to make people better; if anything, it seemed to provide springboards for being worse. The church experience itself drove these members out of the congregation.

These disclosures by the inactives reinforce the results of an earlier study that focused on parents who decided *not* to raise their children in the family religion—and thus to break a tradition that usually went back many generations. Most of these religious dropouts said they quit because of problems with their churches, not because doubts arose about God. Most of all, they spotted too much hypocrisy in the church community. People talked a good game on Sunday and put on a pious display, but then they acted otherwise the rest of the week—sometimes before they even exited the church parking lot. Also, many parishioners and some of the clergy were intolerant of others on racial, ethnic, religious, and sexual orientation grounds, as well services became boring, it seemed the church was always asking for money, the social norm of going to church every week was fading away, and so on.

The dropouts' dissatisfaction with the religious experience had usually begun in their teen years. Obviously they had *not* just been going through a youthful "phase," for now in their late forties, they seldom darkened a church door. Most of them doubted they would ever become religious again. And of course, as a direct consequence of their loss of interest, nearly all of their children had secular upbringings: the rich seedbed for agnosticism and atheism.

The personalities of inactive believers

We saw that the atheists and agnostics had the lowest scores on all of the traits measured in these studies. The inactive believers almost always logged the next lowest ones, which made them the least authoritarian, the least antigay, the least racially prejudiced, the least dogmatic, the least proselytizing, the least group-cohesive, and the least religiously ethnocentric subgroup among the theists. Continuing another trend, they gave a bit more to charity (1.8 percent) and were slightly happier (4.1 percent) than the agnostics.

Modestly Active Theists

Some of the parents who believed in God said they attended church up to twice a month. Mainly female (56 percent), they had 13 years of education on the average. They had a more traditional view of God than the inactive believers we just considered, with 82 percent of their answers to the Seven Attributes questions being Yes.

The parents who attended services now and then came from more religious backgrounds than the inactives, with 30 percent of them having a very religious upbringing. They had spotted a little less hypocrisy and intolerance in the pews than the inactives did, and overall they had slightly fewer doubts about religion. Their stronger beliefs presumably led them to church on a regularly irregular basis.

The data from the personality tests continued the trend. On almost every measure the infrequent church-goers had the fourth highest scores, after the atheists or agnostics and then the inactive theists. They gave 2 percent of their income to charity and were "Pretty happy" (4.0 percent).

Regular Church-Goers

Origins

A little over a quarter of the parents said they attended religious services at least three times per week, qualifying as regular church goers. Again 56 percent were women, and the regularly attending parents had gone to school for 13 years on the average. They had the most traditional view of God, with 88 percent of their answers to the

Seven Attributes questions being Yes. They came from more religious backgrounds, by far, than any other group in the sample. Most of them (58 percent) had very religious upbringings. They also had the fewest doubts of any of the subgroups.

Personalities of regular church-goers

Without exception the regular church-goers piled up the highest scores on all of the personality measures in the survey. They had more authoritarian followers than any other group, and they were the most dogmatic on all the tests used, the most zealous on all the measures, the most religiously ethnocentric, the most hostile toward homosexuals, and the most prejudiced against racial and ethnic minorities. Many of them accordingly matched the description of the intolerant hypocrites who had driven other members of their congregation away. However, they gave the most (3.1 percent) to charity and posted the highest happiness score (4.5 percent, halfway between "Pretty happy" and "Very happy").

A Comparison of Atheists Parents with Very High Fundamentalist Parents

The data block out a remarkable progression, do they not? As one moves from nonbelieving parents to believing ones, and as one moves through the ranks of believers from the religiously inactive to regular church goers, the scores on our various personality assessments march up and up, step by step, almost without exception. The more "religious" the parents were, the more authoritarian, dogmatic, prejudiced, and so on they tended to be. This generalization, of course, has many individual exceptions. One can find some bigoted atheists, for example, and some breathtakingly tolerant regular church goers. But the course of the overall numbers can hardly be missed.

One can grasp the disparity that results by comparing the groups on the extreme ends of the religiosity dimension. Fifty-one atheists served in the biggest parent study, and their answers can be compared to the 51 parents who chalked up the highest scores on a measure of religious fundamentalism. These groups have very opposite opinions about religion. How similar, or different, might they be as people?

Authoritarianism

Scores on the scale that measures a tendency to be an authoritarian follower can range from 20 to 180. The atheists averaged 51, and the fundamentalists placed over twice as high at 135.

Prejudice against minorities could also vary from 20 to 180. A smaller difference emerged between the two groups here, 64 versus 84—but an unflattering one for fundamentalists. Hostility toward homosexuals could go from 12 to 108. The atheists averaged 23, and the fundamentalists 70.

The dogmatism scale runs from 20 to 180. The atheists posted a 65, and the fundamentalists 126. Both groups were asked to respond to hypothetical "ancient scrolls" that challenged their beliefs. Sixty-four percent of the atheists indicated they would be unmoved by scientifically validated evidence that supported the Gospels. But 93 percent of the fundamentalists said a validated scroll showing the Gospels had originally been part of a Greek myth that predated Jesus by 200 years would have no impact whatsoever on their belief in the divinity of Jesus. Fifty-seven percent of the atheists indicated nothing could change their belief that God does *not* exist; 100 percent of the fundamentalists said nothing could change their belief that God does exist.

Only 8 percent of the atheist parents said they would tell a questioning Christian teen that his parents' religious beliefs were wrong; 88 percent of the fundamentalist parents replied that they would tell a questioning atheist teen that his parents' beliefs were wrong. Would these groups *like* the teen to adopt their views? Thirty-five percent of the atheists stated they would, compared with 96 percent of the fundamentalists. Would the two sets of parents try to convert the teen? Only 16 percent of the atheists said they would, whereas 98 percent of the fundamentalists would try to change him.

In a follow-up to this study, Canadian students were asked if would be morally wrong for an atheist to try to convert a questioning teen who had been raised in a strongly Christian family. Most atheists (64 percent) declared it *would* be wrong, as did most (75 percent) fundamentalists. Other students responded to the mirror-image situation of a questioning atheist who seeks advice from a highly religious Christian. Again, most atheists (75 percent) said it would be wrong for the Christian to try to convert the atheist, but 85 percent of the fundamentalists asserted there would be nothing wrong with it—a huge double standard.

Only 14 percent of the atheist parents reported that they had tried to raise their children to be nonbelievers; the other 86 percent said they wanted their children to make up their own minds. Ninety-four percent of the fundamentalists wrote that they had raised their sons and daughters to believe what they believed. Only 6 percent wanted their children to investigate and decide.

The religious ethnocentrism scale can produce scores from 16 to 144. The atheists averaged 38, and the fundamentalists 103.

When asked to rate various religious groups on a 0–100 scale, the atheists gave "Atheists" a rating of 50 and "Christian fundamentalists" a score of 30—a 20-point gap. The fundamentalists rated "Christian fundamentalists" at 90, and "Atheists" at 30—a 60-point gap showing three times as much ethnocentrism.

When atheist parents were asked if they wanted atheism taught in the public schools, none of them (0 percent) said yes. They thought it was wrong for any religious beliefs, including their own, to be taught in tax-supported institutions. When the fundamentalist parents were asked if they favored teaching *their* beliefs in public school, 84 percent answered yes.

(It had previously been established that most Christian fundamentalist parents supported a proposed law that would require Christian prayer and readings from the Bible in public schools, as part of an effort to get students to eventually accept Jesus Christ as their personal savior. Their main argument went, "The majority rules. This is a Christian country, and its beliefs should be taught in public schools." But when presented with a parallel situation of Christian children in an Arab country, or Israel, being indoctrinated in Islam or Judaism in the public schools, most Christian fundamentalists opposed the idea, arguing that minority rights must be protected.)

The fundamentalists reported giving substantially more to charity (3.8 percent of their income) than the atheists did (1.7 percent) and were markedly happier (4.7 versus 3.6 percent).

Summary

The data make it clear that, within this population at least, atheists and strong fundamentalists are cut from very different cloth. As well, do not the findings challenge the common notion that belief in God is necessary for moral behavior? True, the fundamentalists did give more to charity, and while nonbelievers can probably live with the realization that they would be happier if they became deeply religious, it would be interesting to see how they explain the difference in charitable giving. But on the other hand, one might be interested in seeing how fundamentalists deal with the fact that, when tested, atheists showed more integrity, open-mindedness, acceptance of others, independence, and so on than fundamentalists did, who showed instead double standards, closed-mindedness, prejudice, and authoritarianism.

OUTLOOK FOR THE FUTURE

What does the future hold for disbelief in God and secularism in North America? Growth, it would seem. More and more adults in the United States and Canada are becoming religiously inactive, ending up as unaffiliated Nones, or church members in name only. They do not usually become atheists or agnostics, but they likely adopt a secular outlook on life. Their children in turn will very likely end up secular theists as well, or even disbelievers. These predictions are based on the simple fact, long recognized by religions themselves, that if the parents do not raise their children to be religious, the children will probably not become active members of the church.

Even when parents emphasize the family religion, the effort often fails. Looking at the Canadian parents whose family religion was emphasized *to them*, by the grandparents, less than half (47 percent) were attending services regularly by the time they were in their late forties. Fifteen percent attended occasionally, and twenty-six percent had lapsed into inactive status. Eleven percent had settled for agnosticism, and 1 percent had become atheists. A lot of the apples fell surprisingly far from the tree, given that we are talking about adults who had a solid religious childhood. Religions do gain some active members who had nonreligious backgrounds, but in general North American faiths are working against a strong outgoing tide nowadays that is carrying their members away and seriously threatening their relevance.

One can imagine events that would reverse the trend. If a planet-destroying asteroid came hurtling toward Earth, the churches might fill up again. A pandemic might bring lost sheep running back to the flock. So might major changes in the behavior of various "religious" people, but barring such dramatic developments, secularism seems the future.

NOTES

1. Several studies are involved. Most of the findings reported in this chapter came from a 2002 survey answered by 836 parents of introductory psychology students at the University of Manitoba. These results are summarized on page 127 of *Atheists*, by Bruce Hunsberger and Bob Altemeyer. A second study involved 638 similar parents who answered a booklet in 2005. It included the Zealotry Scale, the Group Cohesiveness Scale, the Dangerous World Scale, support for abolishing the Charter of Rights and Liberties, and the measures of giving to charity and happiness. As well, a 1999 study of 634 parents provided the data on religious dropouts reported toward the end of the chapter.

REFERENCES

Altemeyer, Bob, and Bruce Hunsberger. 1997. *Amazing conversions: Why some turn to faith & others abandon religion*. Amherst, NY: Prometheus Books.

General Social Survey (GSS). 2006. National Opinion Research Center (NORC), University of Chicago. http://www.norc.org/GSS+Website/ (accessed August 27, 2009).

Hunsberger, Bruce, and Bob Altemyer. 2006. *Atheists: A Groundbreaking Study of America's Nonbelievers*. Amherst, NY: Prometheus Books.

Pew Research Center for People & the Press. 2008. Pew Forum on Religion and the Public Life. http://religions.pewforum.org/ (accessed August 27, 2009).

Chapter 2

Atheism and Secularity in Modern Japan

Michael K. Roemer

In 2003 I interviewed a Japanese woman in her 60s who described herself as "nonreligious" (*shu kyo wa nai*). During our conversation she got up to prepare some offerings for her home Shintō shrine (*kamidana*) and ancestor altar (*butsudan*). Meanwhile, she proceeded to tell me that she does not do anything religious. When I asked her whether what she was doing was "religious," she paused. "I never thought of it that way. You're right, you're right," she replied. "Well, I guess I'm Buddhist," she continued, "because I believe in that [pointing to the ancestor altar] but not that [referring to the shrine]." I asked her why she makes offerings to the *kami* (briefly, Shinto gods, spirits, deities) of the shrine if she does not believe in kami. "Oh!" she laughed, "I don't believe in the kami, but I'm scared that if I don't make these offerings the kami will punish me."

In Japan, scenarios such as these are not uncommon. Most identify themselves as nonreligious but make a point of carrying out a variety of private and public rituals that connect them with kami, buddhas, or ancestors. Secularity and atheism on some levels are, therefore, difficult to research. In this chapter, I examine processes of secularization and examples of atheism in modern Japan. Both topics have received relatively little academic attention in Japan. Overall, I argue that secularization at the macro level is relatively obvious and clearcut. Evaluating secularity at the cultural or individual levels, however, is more complicated. Nonetheless, it is evident that certain beliefs and practices remain quite common and that atheism—the belief that supernatural or mystical beings do not exist—is rare.

Although few scholars adhere to the fatalist interpretation that modernization will inevitably bring an end to religion, even very recent publications reveal that in many of the most modern and industrialized nations, religion appears to have less influence than before at the macro, mezzo, and micro levels (e.g., Bruce 1996; Norris and Inglehart 2004). Today, Japan is one of the world's leading societies and since the 1980s, has become globally influential economically, politically, and (to a lesser—but important—extent) militarily. Like other advanced societies, in recent decades religious organizations in Japan have lost a great deal of authority over the government and the people. As is the case elsewhere, though, we cannot conclude from this that Japan is becoming a "secular" nation.

I begin this chapter by explaining how recent differentiation processes have led to a weaker presence of religious organizations in Japanese society. This approach allows us to compare the secularization process in Japan with that of other nations. The next section offers an introduction to atheism in contemporary Japan. There are very few studies on atheism, and there is less to report. This dearth of research is, no doubt, a result of cultural differences concerning "religion" and "atheism" in Japan versus the United States, most of Europe, and elsewhere and because of a lack of social and academic interest in the topic. In Japan, there is an abundance of gods, spirits, and deities that have been incorporated into their mythological history and mainstream culture. Unlike societies that are dominated by monotheistic religious traditions—where one is either a believer in one God or not and there is very little room for vacillation—Japanese have always had a choice concerning which God, god, or gods they acknowledge. Moreover, there is less social concern over whether one "believes in" the existence or efficacy of one or more gods. So, first it is unlikely that one disavows the existence of *all* supernatural beings, and second it is simply not very important to most Japanese. Consequently, few scholars have addressed atheism in Japan.

My analysis of both subjects is based on a combination of qualitative research and international, domestic, and regional survey data. The quantitative data allow us to explore trends over time with large samples. The qualitative data are historical and ethnographic, and they fill in some of the blanks missing in survey research.

JAPANESE RELIGIOUSNESS

Though this is not the place for a detailed description of contemporary Japanese religiousness, we cannot discuss atheism or secularity without mentioning some of the core characteristics of what it means to be religious in Japan.

For many scholars of religion in Japan, the most common aspects include (1) a focus on practices and rites over doctrines, theology, or meaning (Reader 2001); (2) concern for this-worldly benefits, particularly individual and collective well-being (Reader and Tanabe 1998; Traphagan 2004); (3) ancestor veneration (Klass 2005); and (4) beliefs in the existence and efficacy of a pantheon of abstract kami and buddhas (Kawano 2005). Japanese religiousness is a syncretistic blend of, mainly, Buddhist, Shinto, and folk traditions, practices, and beliefs. It is important to recognize, however, that despite the multitude of sacred beings, they are not the focus of attention for most Japanese. Often, religiousness is more about the *doing* and the *act* of worship than the meaning behind the rituals or the specific objects of veneration or consideration.

Another important aspect of religiousness is the lack of individual religious affiliation. Most Japanese describe themselves as "not religious" (*mushūkyō*), and though religious organizations remain influential in mainstream culture (e.g., weddings and funeral ceremonies, local festivals, and certain taboos and beliefs), few claim to be Buddhist, Shinto, Christian, or a member of a "New Religion."[1] Elsewhere I described this phenomenon in detail (Roemer 2009), and despite misleading figures published by the Japanese government that indicate that the number of religious adherents is more than the total population, it is more likely that approximately 10 percent claims to be individual affiliates of a religious organization.

This statistic is highly relevant here because to identify as "not religious" in Japan does not mean the same thing as being an "atheist." These individuals are also *un*likely to refer to themselves as "spiritual"— a term that has even less meaning for the average Japanese. The word "religion" (*shūkyō*) is still viewed negatively by many Japanese. Christianity and more indigenous religions such as Shinto, Japanese Buddhism, and New Religions have all suffered from social stigmas in the past century because of their associations with repressive governments, excessive recruitment strategies, or social violence or because of their foreignness (Tamaru and Reid 1996). For these reasons, many Japanese think of religion as something to be feared (*"kowai shūkyō,"* Ōmura 1996).

In Japan religious institutions most commonly affect individuals via religious traditions that are used to mark important life cycle events. For example, it is not uncommon for a child to be purified at a Shinto shrine soon after its birth, later get married in a Christian church, and then be buried with a Buddhist funeral ceremony (Reader 1991). Other important folk and Taoist traditions, such as ancestor veneration and special ceremonies during an individual's "unlucky" years (*yakudoshi*), are also typical. Annual festivals get locals involved as well, and major urban festivals can attract crowds of hundreds of thousands. Still, it is not the religious organization that matters for many—or even the religious nature of the event (Roemer 2006). Indeed, it is arguable that many religious beliefs and practices have become so engrained in the mainstream culture that it can be difficult to separate the religious from the not religious, or the sacred from the profane. For example, many describe acts such as ancestor veneration and visits to Shinto shrines or Buddhist temples as "traditions" or "customs" (Fitzgerald 2003; Ōmura 1996), so it is difficult to categorize them as religious or not. As expected, this confounds the study of secularity and atheism in Japan, and I address these concerns throughout the chapter.

SECULARITY IN MODERN JAPAN

Previous Research

As in the West, the few scholars who have examined secularism in Japan are divided: some insist that Japan is very secular and others are unwilling to commit to that conclusion. For example, noted Japan scholar Edwin Reischauer claimed that secularism in Japan extends over 300 years, and he writes, "Clearly religion in contemporary Japan is not central to society and culture" (1988, 215). Similarly, Bryan Wilson asserts that religion is a "remnant" in modernity because of the breakdown of communities, and he extends this assumption to all modern nations, including Japan (1976, 266). Max Eger admits that, though certain religious practices and beliefs remain important socially, they no longer have any "inner meaning" for many Japanese (1980, 21).

Others see Japanese religion as having secular characteristics, though not as being "secular" per se. Shinto, Buddhism, New Religions, and many indigenous Christian denominations in Japan focus on this-worldly goods; thus many scholars have interpreted them as secular (e.g., Koizumi 1979). As Reader and Tanabe point out Buddhism and Shinto have been criticized heavily for such "superstitious" characteristics (1998, 3). Still, these secular aspects are by no means new to the religions of Japan, so their presence today does not indicate a process of secularization.

In one of the first extensive English language examinations of this topic, Jan Swyngedouw (1976) interprets secularization as the extent of differentiation on multiple levels and argues that religions have less authority in modern Japan than in the past. However, as I discuss below, he also limits this differentiation to the organizational level, not the cultural or individual ones. Ultimately, he concludes that Japan is undergoing religious changes—at all levels—that are inevitable because of modern challenges to traditional values (also Earhart 1974).

More recently, Hitoshi Miyake (2001) claims that folk religion remains highly influential in the lives of contemporary Japanese via worldviews and ritual practices. In fact, he argues that many "feel insecure" without these practices, indicating strongly the persistent and important social function of religion in Japan today (176). Susumu Shimazono (2006) discusses Japan's increase in animistic beliefs, "spirituality," and certain rites such as *mizuko kuyō*, or Buddhist cere-monies for the unborn. Recent economic, political, legal, and cultural changes have yielded increased attention to and participation in certain traditional beliefs and rituals and the development of new expressions of religion (organized and subjective).

In his book on religion in contemporary Japan, Winston Davis (1992) concludes that although certain aspects of Japanese religiousness—namely religious institutional influences and beliefs—have declined in recent decades, Japan is *not* a secular nation. He provides a number of examples in the Japanese context in which secularization has occurred, such as in community festivals and ties between communities and their local shrines and temples, yet he cites Itō Makiharu as claiming that complete secularization is not possible in Japan (p. 247). He discusses Itō's "logic of relative contrasts," an interpretation that means that de-spite changes that could be interpreted as secular, the "implicit" or underlying motivations and reasons for the adaptations (such as parties instead of shrine visits at New Years) remain the same: out with the old (impure or *ke*), in with the new (pure or *hare*, 247). The concern with this argument, as Davis aptly notes, is that it requires a reinter-pretation of how we define and (more importantly) measure seculariza-tion. Based on the logic of relative contrasts, simple statistics of decline do not address the unspoken nonsecular meanings and motivations that may remain. It begs the question: is this religion in another guise (*change*) or is it a form of decline (*secularization*)? To answer this ques-tion I first turn to historical data.

Political Secularity: Early Modern Japan

Most recent influential studies concerning secularization have focused on the process of differentiation. Differentiation in this literature refers to a decrease in the involvement and authority of religious institutions in mainstream society, including other institutions (e.g., political, eco-nomic, and cultural) and individuals (e.g., beliefs and practices; Chaves 1994; Gorski 2000; Marwell and Demerath 2003). In Japan, this was most apparent in two historic periods: during the modernization period of the late 1800s and during the Allied Occupation after World War II.

In 1868, Japan ended its isolationist shogunate and began major social, political, and economic reforms. Ultimately, the goals were to modernize (which meant "Westernize") and strengthen the nation mili-tarily and economically. In the 1870s, the government decided to emu-late many European nations and the United States and officially separate religion from its state. It did so in three primary overlapping steps: (1) the government replaced support for Buddhism with support for Shinto, (2) Shinto and Buddhism were officially separated, (3) and State Shinto was created to become a "nonreligious" patriotic practice.

From the early 1600s until 1868, the government favored Buddhism over Shinto in terms of political connections and economic support. Shinto, on the other hand, remained important for the (then politically powerless) imperial family. When Emperor Meiji was given control of Japan from a rather weak shogun in 1867, he and his advisors decided to support Shinto instead of Buddhism. Shinto myths and legends provided support for the emperor's right to rule by tracing his ancestry to Japan's alleged first emperor in 660 BCE and more importantly to the Sun Goddess, Amaterasu no Ō kami. Buddhism, on the other hand, was imported from Korea and China, and though it had been widely accepted by the people and supported by governments past, it did not offer the same kinds of nationalistic support that Shinto could provide.

This was also the first time that Shinto and Buddhism were officially separated. For centuries, the two religious traditions were practiced concurrently. Kami were considered guardians or were seen as manifestations of Buddhist deities at Buddhist temples, and Shinto shrines conducted Buddhist rituals for buddhas alongside worship of kami. Thus, when the Meiji government decided to favor Shinto over Buddhism, it forced the temples and shrines to choose one or the other as their "official" religion.

A third major change of this period was the creation of State Shinto. The purpose of this move was to allow the government to use the support of Shinto for nationalistic purposes while still maintaining a separation of church and state. By officially developing a "nonreligious" branch of Shinto, the government created a secular means by which the people could show their patriotism to the country and their loyalty to the emperor. In reality, as some have argued, this secularization process was not wholly successful, and Shinto—its priests and shrines—benefited very little from and even disapproved of this type of political support (Breen and Teeuwen 2000; Earhart 1974; Shimazono 2006). Shinto priests were not always the main players in the creation of State Shinto, and Sect Shinto (the "religious" branch of Shinto) ranked lower in support and influence. To make matters worse, the early Meiji period saw serious division between several Shinto sects, and they were unable to assert themselves as a unified voice (Murakami 1983).

Overall, these changes led to significant losses in religious authority for both Buddhism and Shinto, and no other religious groups replaced their influence. When Buddhism lost political and financial support, thousands of temples were closed, priests lost their livelihoods, and Buddhism became less socially influential. There were even attempts to eradicate Buddhism and its teachings (Sharf 1995). Additionally, without forced registration at temples,[2] Buddhism lost community support, financial and otherwise.

Shinto did not fair much better. On the surface, the creation of State Shinto added to Shinto's authority in Japan; however, its restructuring as nonreligious was not well accepted by many priests, and tens of thousands of shrines were destroyed (Sakamoto 2000, 278). Moreover, there were not enough Shinto priests at the time to meet this newfound social support from converts from Buddhism (Hardacre 2002). Though bureaucratic, political, and (to a lesser degree) social influence of Shinto increased, its religious authority did not. Buddhism and Shinto maintained some importance, but their authority declined significantly at the macro level of society. Modernizing Japan meant separating religion from state—at least officially, and this resulted in the country's first major differentiation process in modern history.

Political Secularity: Post–World War II Japan

After Japan's surrender in World War II, the U.S.-led occupation forces designed a new constitution for Japan, which included new laws concerning religion. According to one noteworthy historian of Japan, "Among all the changes brought about by the occupation forces, the most radical and far-reaching steps were those relating to the religious foundation of the Japanese nation" (Kitagawa 1987, 280). Robert Bellah claimed that the new constitution "theoretically completed the process of secularization [in Japan]" (1958, 5). These developments not only changed the way the government and religious institutions could interact, they also altered individuals' impressions of religious meanings and practices. The 1947 Japanese constitution disestablished State Shinto, outlawed governmental support of any kind to any religion, and gave individuals freedom of religion, among other changes.

The dissolving of State Shinto and increase in religious freedoms had mixed effects on Shinto in general. On the one hand, changes from the new constitution meant that Shinto lost the political and economic privileges it especially had grown to rely on since the late 1800s. Further, the separation of religion from politics ran counter to the ancient understanding that religion and government were united (*saisei-itchi*). Because of its ties to the militant government, Shinto also suffered from a "loss of the people's sympathy" (Earhart 1974, 121; also Morioka 1975). Despite declines in community support in postwar Japan, Shinto has remained a relatively stable force for society at large in the past half century.

Buddhism was already suffering economically from changes that took place in the Meiji period. The new constitution made matters worse because religious freedoms divided Buddhism into about three times more subgroups, thus weakening the overall influence of Japanese Buddhism (Kitagawa 1987). Other new laws enacted just after the war (e.g., the land reform of 1945–1946 and the Civil Code in 1947) also had pejorative effects on Buddhist temples. Land reforms meant significant income losses, and new family laws in the Civil Code allowed individuals to more easily sever ties with temples—often ties that had been held for centuries

(Noriyoshi 1996). For the past 60 years especially, the main interaction between Japanese individuals and Buddhist priests has been limited to funeral and postfuneral services (Covell 2005; Earhart 1974; Tamaru 2000).

Since the seventh century, Shinto and Buddhism had supported and were supported by the court, state, and aristocracy (Takayama 1998). Japan's modernization period has seen a distinct separation of religion and politics, and it is clear that differentiation has occurred, particularly in the past 140 years. Coupled with intense urbanization that began in the 1960s and 1970s, these two major religions are still struggling— particularly in rural areas across the country where temples and shrines have been abandoned (Ishii 1996). Additionally, Christianity and New Religions have not replaced Shinto or Buddhism in terms of political influence. At the macro level, Japan has secularized significantly.

Having said that, it is worth noting a few important exceptions to this general trend. For instance, one political party that has strong— albeit "unofficial"—ties with a religious organization is the New Kōmeito.[3] This party is affiliated with Sōka Gakkai, a New Religion that grew tremendously in the 1960s. In the 2009 elections, the New Kōmeito remained the third most powerful political party in terms of Lower and Upper Diet seats (out of seven established parties). Argu- ably, Japan is moving closer to a two-party system, though (Govella and Vogel 2008), and the New Kōmeito has not gained the kinds of governmental ties that Shinto and Buddhism once experienced.

Another prominent exception is the recurrent link between Yasukuni Shrine and official support from elected politicians. Yasukuni is a Shinto shrine dedicated to war dead, including war criminals from World War II. Thus, governmental support is interpreted by many as both a violation of the separation of church and state mandated by the Japanese constitution and a political offense to Koreans, Chinese, and other nationals who suffered under Japanese control during the war. Since 1956 various nationalist groups have been encouraging govern- ment leaders and the emperor to rekindle their (financial and political) ties with Yasukuni—with varying degrees of success (Hardacre 1989). Recently, this issue returned to prominence when Japan's Prime Minis- ter Junichiro Koizumi (April 2001 to September 2006) made repeated visits to the site. Though he is only one of many prime ministers who have visited the shrine since the 1970s (Nelson 2003), Koizumi's visits served as a very contemporary reminder that religious organizations continue to garner support from elected officials (also Deans 2007).

By no means are these examples exhaustive. As Hardacre (2005) has shown, religious organizations have also been influential in very recent attempts to make constitutional revisions. Still, these links are some- what sporadic and almost always met with trepidation by the general population. Distrust of religious organizations has not waned signifi- cantly since the end of the war, and many Japanese are outwardly concerned with official ties between religions and the government. For these reasons, the differentiation process has been rather sweeping in contemporary Japan at the macro level.

Social Secularity in Japan: A Qualitative Analysis

At the cultural level there are a number of rituals practiced that are rooted in religious traditions. The most obvious examples are weddings, funerals, and New Years and All Souls (*Obon*) celebrations (Miyake 2001). Shinto and more recently Christian-style weddings are extremely popular, and most funerals are conducted by Buddhist priests. Priests also perform rituals in people's homes and at temples that days, months, and years later commemorate the dead. A recent *New York Times* article revealed an increase in the number of secular companies that are offering funeral services at prices lower than most temples (Onishi 2008). Nonetheless, this is a relatively recent phenomenon, and it is not certain yet whether these groups will replace this important function that has been served predominantly by Buddhist priests for several centuries (Covell 2005; Tamaru 2000).

Both Buddhism and Shinto also remain influential in the realm of household rituals. Ancestor veneration, for instance, dates back to the 1500s and 1600s (Miyake 2001) and is regularly practiced by Japanese today (e.g., Klass 2005; Traphagan 2004). This includes rituals in the home at ancestor or Buddhist altars (*butsudan*) and at Buddhist temples (Morioka 1975). According to a recent study on household Shinto altars (*kamidana*), approximately half of most national samples maintain these altars in their homes and most make offerings several times a month at least (Ishii 2004). Though there appears to be a slight decline since the 1950s, household rituals remain important parts of the culture.

Shrine and temple grounds remain significant as well. Undeniably, rural areas have seen a decline in the number of temples and shrines as a result of depopulation. Still, annual festivals and close and long distance visits to these sacred spaces are frequent. Indeed, Reischauer—who as mentioned previously does not view Japan as religious—maintains that shrine festivals are what keep Shinto "most alive today" (1988, 210). Festivals achieve a number of social functions, especially uniting community members with each other and with kami (Ashkenazi 1993; Roemer 2007). Additionally, Japanese continue to make pilgrimages (Reader 2005; Shimazono 2006) and make shorter visits to local and far-off shrines and temples for a variety of reasons (Reader and Tanabe 1998). Many of these visits are for others, and people offer prayers and buy amulets (*omamori*) or prayer tablets (*ema*) as expressions of concern (Traphagan 2004).

At certain holidays, such as New Years and All Souls (*Obon*) in August, millions of Japanese flock to temples and shrines to usher in the New Year safely and wipe their slates clean and to pay respects to their ancestors and the recently departed. A 1984 survey revealed that 81 percent of the sample visited a shrine or temple at New Years, and 89 percent made pilgrimages to their ancestral tombs in August (Okada 1994, 606). Other events such as Shinto rituals for the purification and safe development of seven-, five-, and three-year-olds (*shichi-go-san*) and purification rites for adults who are in particularly inauspicious years of their lives (*yakudoshi*) are also popular.

Presently, data are not available to examine long-term trends concerning whether or not these shrine- and temple-related activities have declined or escalated in recent decades. The fact that they remain common, though, is a strong indicator that Japanese religious practices, values, and beliefs remain influential in society and for the individual. Though religious organizations do not maintain the amount of political sway they once enjoyed, they retain influence at the cultural and individual levels.

Social Secularity in Japan: A Quantitative Analysis

In this section, I rely on several data sets to explore more specific aspects of social or cultural secularization to add empirical support for the more general claims above. Do people apply religion to their lives outside of these special events? To what extent do they believe in the efficacy of mystical beings, such as kami, buddhas, or ancestors—and are frequencies of religious belief changing in Japan?

One measure of individual religiousness is affiliation. Figure 2.1 illustrates the percentage of religious adherents (Shinto, Buddhist, Christian, and other—including New Religions) in Japan from 1950 to 2005 based on surveys by Japan's Ministry of Internal Affairs and Communications. Despite the initial postwar losses for Buddhism and Shinto I addressed previously, the number of religious adherents has soared since the data was first collected in 1948. As the figures below indicate, adherence has been relatively stable in recent decades, though the number of Buddhists has declined from 95,420,000 in 2000 to 91,260,000 in 2005. Those claimed as "Other" has also dropped from 10,221,000 in 2000 to 9,918,000 five years later (Statistics Bureau 2008, 747). Individuals reported as Shinto or Christian changed little in that five-year period, and over the long run the numbers have generally increased.

These statistics must be interpreted cautiously, however, because they are reported by shrine, temple, and church organizations and not by individuals. Over-reporting and multiple-reporting (i.e., the claiming of the same individual by more than one religious organization) are likely in Japan because temples and shrines often claim all residents who live in their precincts as parishioners and precincts can overlap. Multiple reporting also occurs because Japanese are free to

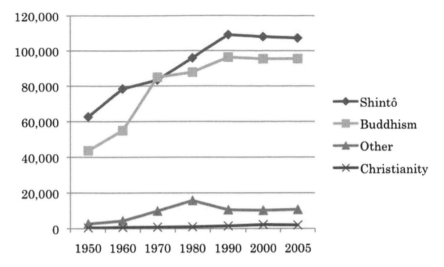

Figure 2.1. Religious Adherents in Japan (1950–2005)
Source: Statistics Bureau of Japan (2008, 747)
Note: Y-axis in millions

make donations that may be recorded at a number of places of worship, regardless of the religion (Roemer 2009).

Other data sets that measure religious affiliation are the Japanese General Social Surveys (JGSS).[4] The shortcoming is that they only look at very recent history (2000–2003, 2005; the survey was not administered in 2004). The advantage is that responses are based on individuals who *claim* religious affiliation ("belief"—*shinkō*—in a religious organization) rather than being *claimed by* organizations—as in the Statistics Bureau data above. Again, the basic trend in these five years of data is stability with slight, nonlinear fluctuations (Table 2.1). The overall average for the five years of data is 10.66 percent who claim to believe in a religion, and most (around 70 percent) identified

Table 2.1
Religious affiliation, 2000–2003 and 2005

	2000	2001	2002	2003	2005	Average
Personal Religion	9.5%	10%	9.7%	11.8%	12.3%	**10.66%**
Buddhist	76%	71.9%	70.9%	67.2%	70.6%	**71.32%**
Shinto	2.7%	2%	0.9%	0.8%	1.6%	**1.6%**
New Religion	9.8%	10.7%	14.2%	13.3%	10.7%	**11.74%**
Christian	2%	3.3%	3.1%	4.7%	3.2%	**3.26%**

Source: Nihonban General Social Surveys (2000–2003, 2005)

themselves as "Buddhist" or a Buddhist sect member (e.g., Jōdo Shin, Nichiren, Zen, etc.). The data from the Statistics Bureau and the JGSS reveal that religious adherence has been steady overall since its initial growth period following the war; however, the JGSS data support what most qualitative studies have shown, that few Japanese personally identify with one or more religious organizations officially.

Another way to assess secularity at the individual level is by examining specific beliefs and practices that are more common in the Japanese context. The 2001 Asian Values Survey (AVS) includes a nationwide probability sample of 1,000 Japanese adults (Kisala 2001 for details). The 2007 Health and Faith (H&F) survey was a survey I designed and administered using a random sample of Japanese adults living in Kyoto Prefecture (for details see Roemer 2008). Although both surveys capture only one point in time, they include a number of questions on religion that are specific to Japan. Table 2.2 summarizes some of the findings from these two surveys. Percentages in the first seven rows represent a combination of those who selected "agree" or "agree

Table 2.2
Recent statistics on religious beliefs and practices

	AVS	H&F
	N=1000	N=333
1. There's a mysterious power in Nature	—	71.99%
2. It is important to respect ancestors	—	87.86%
3. There is something like fate that goes beyond human powers	—	71.64%
4. Kami/hotoke[‡] protect me	—	40.59%
5. Kami/hotoke[‡] help me when I am troubled	—	28.55%
6. Kami/hotoke[‡] curse me	—	24.82%
7. When I pray, I am purified and at peace	—	56.70%
8. I get comfort from religion	73.70%[*]	25.27%
9. Kami/hotoke[‡] exist	62.60%[*]	47.48%
10. There is an afterlife	46.54%[*]	—
11. Souls/spirits (tamashii) exist	64.02%[*]	
12. I own a kamidana (Shinto shrine)	—	70.90%[*]
13. I own a butsudan (ancestral/Buddhist altar)	—	39.70%[*]
14. I pray, meditate, or contemplate	27.87%[*]	53.74%

Notes: These percentages do not include missing data. Due to nonresponse, sample sizes vary somewhat per question. Percentages for the H & F are weighted to reflect true population and age ranges of Kyoto Prefecture residents in 2005.
[‡]Kami are loosely translated as god(s), deities, or spirits; hotoke can be translated as ancestors or buddhas.
[*]Indicates that response categories are Yes or No; otherwise, they are combined percentages of Agree and Agree somewhat. Though kami and hotoke are not identical, it is common for surveys in Japan to ask about both simultaneously rather than in separate questions.

somewhat." An asterisk indicates that the answer categories were dichotomous: "yes" or "no."

For the most part, respondents answered these statements positively. A majority of these samples agree that supernatural beings or superhuman powers exist, but fewer believe in the efficacy of kami and hotoke specifically (Table 2.2, rows 4–6). One particularly noteworthy statistic is row 9: 47.48 percent of the H&F sample agreed that kami and *hotoke* (buddhas or ancestors) exist (*sonzai suru*), and 62.60 percent of the AVS sampled agreed. This slight difference may be attributable to the answer categories (Yes or No in the AVS versus Agree to Disagree scale in the H&F). Previous studies that have asked about "belief" (*shinkō*) in the supernatural have reported much lower frequencies (e.g., Davis 1992, 233; Mullins, Shimazono, and Swanson 1993, 52), so these more recent findings are important (Roemer 2006). As Table 2.2 reveals, ownership of household altars such as kamidana and butsudan (rows 12 and 13) remains fairly common (Ishii 2004; Kawano 2005), though only a small percentage pray, meditate, or contemplate (row 14).

By analyzing four years of data from the World Values Survey (WVS)— a multiyear, multinational survey, it is apparent that some of these beliefs have declined in recent decades (for details visit www.worldvaluessurvey. org). Table 2.3 illustrates frequencies (after deleting responses of "don't know" and missing data) in 1981, 1990, 1995, and 2000. In all four belief measures, the percentages have declined, and this is particularly noteworthy with belief in kami and with those who responded positively that they get comfort and strength from religion. Frequencies dropped by almost 10 percent in both cases. Granted, this is not a panel study so we can only interpret these as general trends across society: trends that may be influenced by changes in social interpretations of "religion," kami, the afterlife, and the relevance or importance of praying.

Based on these data, certain religious beliefs appear to have declined since Japan has become the second largest economy in the world. These findings raise several important questions, however. Have these beliefs actually declined or are the lower frequency rates a sign of changes in how Japanese interpret these ideas? And, have these beliefs

Table 2.3
Changes in beliefs over time (WVS 1981–2000)

	1981	1990	1995	2000
	N = 1204	N = 1011	N = 1054	N = 1362
Comfort/strength from religion	46.85%	41.61%	31.61%	35.05%
I believe in *kami*	62.47%	64.53%	57.39%	52.59%
I believe in an afterlife	55.60%	53.99%	48.51%	50.83%
I take moments for prayer, etc.	—	41.27%	—	37.72%

and behaviors been replaced with other, more outwardly secular worldviews and practices? By addressing these questions, future studies will be able to present a more comprehensive interpretation of the secularization process in modern Japan.

ATHEISM IN CONTEMPORARY JAPAN

The Zen Atheist

In July 2007, I interviewed an 83-year-old man who was introduced to me as someone who often attends lectures on Buddhist philosophy. During the course of our two-hour conversation, it became clear that his interest in these topics has very little to do with personal spiritual or religious interests. Although he identified himself as "Zen," much of our conversation revolved around his lack of beliefs in any supernatural beings and his distaste for organized religions in general.

In Japan, this seemingly dichotomous identification (a Zen atheist) is not unusual. Mr. Suzuki (a pseudonym) only identifies himself as "Zen" because of his family ties to a local temple. For twenty generations, his ancestors have been buried at a local Zen temple, and twice a year he, his wife, and his older brother visit these graves to clean them with purified water and make offerings of flowers and incense. Otherwise, he has nothing to do with the temple. (In fact, the temple where he has attended Buddhist lectures is not Zen.) His "religious" connection has everything to do with his obligation to his ancestors—an obligation he carries out with great pride and gratitude, not aversion or disdain—and very little to do with the *religion* itself. Still, when his eldest son decided he wanted to join Sōka Gakkai, Mr. Suzuki forbade it because joining this new religion would mean "cutting his ties with his relatives," as he explained to me, and his household would no longer be Zen. As the eldest son, it is his responsibility to carry on such family traditions, and Mr. Suzuki forbade his son to sever these long-established ties with their ancestors and with the temple.

Mr. Suzuki's atheist tendencies stem from a lifelong series of events that began before the violence he experienced as a World War II fighter pilot. During the war, as he described, he saw dozens of men die, and these constant deaths made him even more skeptical that kami or buddhas exist. A few more recent examples he gave were the damage to shrines and temples after the major earthquake of central Japan that killed over 5,000 people in 1995. He could not understand why the kami and buddhas of these supposedly holy grounds would allow such destruction and losses of life.

Mr. Suzuki's absolute disbelief in the existence or influence of supernatural beings is atypical in Japan. As previously explained, though few Japanese identify themselves as religious and most maintain that they have no

Table 2.4
Religious identification

	AVS	WVS	H&F
I am religious	27.39%	26.48%	6.04%
I am somewhat religious	—	—	15.94%
I am not religious, but I pray and make offerings	—	—	48.46%
I am not religious	57.37%	59.70%	16.75%
I am an atheist	15.25%	13.83%	12.62%

religion, many Japanese conduct certain household rituals regularly and are willing to admit the possibility that kami and buddhas exist.

Japanese Atheists in Statistics

Table 2.4 illustrates how Japanese identify themselves religiously. Here we see important distinctions between the 2001 AVS, 2000 WVS, and the 2007 H&F datasets that are a result of answer categories. All three surveys include three main answer categories: religious, not religious, and atheist. The H&F survey includes three other options to better reflect some of the nuances of Japanese religious identification. So, if we add the religious and somewhat religious categories of the H&F survey, there is little difference between the "religious" in the AVS, WVS, and H&F samples (27.39, 26.48, and 21.98 percent, respectively). The greatest discrepancy lies in the more secular categories. In the AVS, 57.37 and 15.25 percent claimed to be not religious and atheist, respectively, and 59.70 and 13.83 percent in the WVS sample, but only 16.75 and 12.62 percent in the H&F data. This is very likely due to the additional category I added to the H&F survey. After conducting in-depth interviews, focus groups, and pretests of the survey I added a middle category ("I am not religious, but I do rituals"), and as it turned out, this response was selected most frequently (48.46 percent). As previously discussed, ritual participation is often interpreted as "traditions" or "cultural" and not explicitly as "religious." Thus, I feel that the H&F survey categories likely reveal a more accurate portrayal of religious identity in contemporary Japan. Concerning atheists, we can see that approximately 13 to 15 percent of these sample populations identified as atheists.

Frankly, we know very little about what it means to be an atheist in Japan. It is a topic that has received scant attention from the academic community. Table 2.5 presents results from binary logistic regression analysis to explore sociodemographic characteristics of individuals who identified themselves as atheist in the AVS, WVS, and H&F data sets. Interestingly, there are some important distinctions in the results of these three data sets. There are also some noteworthy similarities.

In these models, the age category includes individuals 20 years old and older (18 and older in the WVS), and I created two dummied controls for whether respondents are married (1 = married and 0 = divorced, single, widowed, etc.) and whether they live in urban areas (1 = largest cities/other cities, 0 = towns or villages). Education in the AVS is measured by age ranges (14 and younger, 15–18, 19–22, and 23 years and older) at which respondents completed their formal educations (range = 1–4, mean = 2.43), and the other data sets report the highest levels of education achieved (WVS range = 1–9, mean = 6.79; H&F range = 1–5, mean = 2.59). Income measures total household income and is also coded differently for the datasets (AVS range = 1–11, mean = 5.31; WVS range = 1–10, mean = 4.98; H&F range = 1–9, mean = 5.08). There was substantial nonresponse for this question in the AVS (25.30 percent), so I created a new income variable that includes the mean of the original income to replace the missing data. An Income_miss variable is included in the AVS model to account for this change. Except for the income in the AVS, missing values were deleted using list-wise deletion, and the WVS and H&F models include standardized weights.

As Table 2.5 illustrates, Japanese atheists are much more likely to be men than women and more likely to be young than old. Based on the odds ratios, men are 1.67 (AVS), 2.25 (WVS), or 2.54 (H&F) times more likely than women to identify as atheists. Also, with each unit increase in age, respondents are 18 percent *less* likely to be atheists in the AVS data and 4 percent less likely in the H&F data. Age is not significantly correlated with atheist identity for the WVS sample. Beyond that, none of the other AVS variables are significantly related. The H&F data, however, indicate that education is a positive predictor (OR = 1.74), and income (OR = 0.61), married (OR = 0.37), and urban (OR = 0.36) are negatively related. Interestingly, the urban category is *positively* linked to atheism in the WVS data (OR = 1.50).

Of these findings, perhaps the most surprising is that H&F respondents who live in urban areas are significantly less likely than those in smaller towns or villages to identify as atheists. Those in rural areas tend to be more traditional in thought and action, so this finding is counterintuitive. It is possible that the substantial decline in the number of religious institutions in rural areas explains this phenomenon in part. It is also not clear why this varies per dataset. One explanation might be that a majority of the WVS sample (53.88 percent) reported living in cities with over 150,000 people (coded as urban), whereas a smaller percentage (47.71) of the H&F sample live in urban areas.

Table 2.5
Binary logistic regression coefficients and odds ratios for predicting atheist identification in Japan

	AVS		WVS		H&F	
	b	OR	*b*	OR	*b*	OR
Intercept	−1.62***	—	−2.22***	—	1.08	—
	(.49)		(.53)		(1.32)	
Male	.51**	1.67	.81***	2.25	.93*	2.54
	(.19)		(.20)		(.43)	
Age	−.19**	.82	−.01	.99	−.04**	.96
	(.07)		(.01)		(.01)	
Education	.15	1.17	.04	1.04	.56*	1.74
	(.14)		(.06)		(.27)	
Income	−.01	.99	.03	1.03	−.49***	.61
	(.04)		(.03)		(.14)	
Inc_miss	.03	1.03	—	—	—	—
	(.22)					
Married	−.24	.79	−.34	.71	−1.00*	.37
	(.22)		(.23)		(.43)	
Urban	.15	1.16	.37*	1.45	−1.01*	.36
	(.22)	—	(.19)	—	(.52)	—
N	926	—	1051	—	296	—
Max-rescaled R²	.05		.06		.38	
LR χ²	26.28***	—	34.21***	—	69.50***	—
	(7)		(6)		(6)	
−2 Log Likelihood	777.42	—	779.39	—	165.13	—

b Unstandardized coefficient (standard error)
OR Odds Ratio
*p < .05, **p < .01, ***p < .001 (two-tailed test)
Sources: 2001 AVS, 2000 WVS, 2007 H&F

Because this is the first time multivariate analysis has been used to examine sociodemographic correlates of atheism in Japan, these results are important despite some of the conflicting statistics. Overall, we can see that atheists in Japan tend to be younger men, but it is not yet clear what other characteristics they might have. Much more research is needed on this topic before we can make more conclusive arguments.

CONCLUDING THOUGHTS

In this chapter I have presented historical, ethnographic, and quantitative data to provide a general overview of atheism and secularity in contemporary Japan. I argued that secular forces have been most visible at the macro level—especially since the late 1800s—but not as much on the mezzo or micro levels of society. As previous scholars have noted, secularization can be as fluid and susceptible to sociohistorical forces as religion. It is not static or absolute, and societies that begin the process of differentiation are not destined, necessarily, to continue on that path unchangingly. Religious organizations, their clergy, and their lay members have the ability to reverse these trends. In Japan, secularization at the mezzo and micro levels reversed course soon after World War II in what some have referred to as a religious boom (McFarland 1967). On the other hand, events such as the Aum Shinrikyō gas attacks on the Tokyo subway system in 1995 serve as a reminder to Japanese of how damaging religion can be, and they may fuel other secular waves.

I do not pretend to make predictions about the future of religion in Japan. I can say confidently, however, that presently Japan is not a wholly secular nation, despite differentiation processes that began over 140 years ago. Religious practices and beliefs remain important aspects of daily life through cultural norms and traditions.

Concerning atheism, in this chapter I reported on what little we know. What we can learn from secondary data analysis is that atheists in Japan makeup approximately 7–15 percent of the population and that men are more likely than women to claim an atheist identity. Additionally, age is inversely related with atheism.

Compared to the situation in the United States and much of Europe, for instance, there are some important distinctions concerning these topics. For example, though few Japanese claim religious affiliation, we cannot call them "spiritual but not religious" (e.g., Fuller 2001; Zinnbauer et al. 1997) because the word "spiritual" is not common in the Japanese vernacular. In some ways, Japan's religious context is more similar to Davie's (1994) notion of "believing without belonging" in England (for Japan see Yanagawa 1991). Few Japanese claim to belong to a religion. In fact, there are possibly more atheists in Japan than those who claim personal religious affiliation. Still, a combination of these two groups would only comprise less than one-third to 40 percent or so of the population. The majority falls into what scholars often identify as those who practice "religious" rituals and maintain "religious" beliefs (because of their connections to religious organizations, the supernatural, or the noncorporeal) but do not, necessarily, describe such behaviors and worldviews as "religious." Instead, Japanese often explain them as "traditional" or "customary."

If we are to translate these interpretations as examples of secularism in Japan, then Japan is and has been for centuries a very secular nation. On the other hand, to do so would be a misunderstanding of how the religious and the secular intermingle seamlessly in Japan. Such behaviors and beliefs may indeed be traditions, but they are not the same kinds of traditions as the ancient arts of flower arrangement or tea ceremony, for example. Most likely, the average Japanese would not equate ancestor veneration, festival involvement, or the belief in kami with the tea ceremony. They are all traditional and full of rituals, however, the former more obviously include the supernatural or are linked to religious organizations.

In Japan, belief and belonging are not absolutes, and underlying these "traditions" and "customs" are recognizably "religious" symbols, actions, and beliefs that continue to permeate (though often lie latent in) Japanese society. Secularity in Japan thus becomes muddled and difficult to research, and people like the woman I described at the beginning of this chapter and the Zen atheist are not unusual. In Japan, one can deny the existence of kami but fear their retribution or be an atheist by personal choice and Buddhist by ancestral ties. Ultimately, we should rely on how individuals label themselves—rather than place labels upon them, and in the future we should ask what they mean by "traditional" and "customary" to understand better the extent to which "religion" plays a part in these behaviors and beliefs.

NOTES

1. Japanese New Religions include those established in the past 150 years or so. Often, they include beliefs and practices taken from Buddhism, Shinto, and other traditions.

2. During the Tokugawa era (1603–1868), Japanese families were required to register with a local Buddhist temple. This served as a census and was used to reinforce the ban on Christianity because individuals had to step on an image of Jesus Christ (*fumie*) and renounce Christianity (e.g., Covell 2005).

3. There is also a subgroup within Japan's largest political party (the Liberal Democratic Party) that has close connections with the Association of Shinto Shrines, a secular entity that lobbies on behalf of Shinto and has been active since 1969 (e.g., Hardacre 2005, 241).

4. The Japanese General Social Surveys (JGSS) are designed and carried out at the Institute of Regional Studies at Osaka University of Commerce in collaboration with the Institute of Social Science at the University of Tokyo under the direction of Ichiro Tanioka, Michio Nitta, Hiroki Sato, and Noriko Iwai with Project Manager, Minae Osawa. The project is financially assisted by Gakujutsu Frontier Grant from the Japanese Ministry of Education, Culture, Sports, Science and Technology for 1999–2005 academic years, and the datasets are compiled with cooperation from the SSJ Data Archive, Information Center for Social Science Research on Japan, Institute of Social Science, the University of Tokyo.

REFERENCES

Ashkenazi, Michael. 1993. *Matsuri: Festivals of a Japanese town*. Honolulu: University of Hawaii Press.

Bellah, Robert N. 1958. Religious aspects of modernization in Turkey and Japan. *American Journal of Sociology* 64(1): 1–5.

Breen, John, and Mark Teeuwen, eds. 2000. *Shinto in History: Ways of the Kami.* Honolulu: University of Hawaii Press.

Bruce, Steve. 1996. *Religion in the modern world: From cathedrals to cults.* Oxford: Oxford University Press.

Chaves, Mark. 1994. Secularization as declining authority. *Social Forces* 72 (3): 749–774.

Covell, Stephen G. 2005. *Japanese Temple Buddhism: Worldliness in a Religion of Renunciation.* Honolulu: University of Hawaii Press.

Davie, Grace. 1994. *Religion in Britain since 1945: Believing without belonging.* Oxford: Blackwell.

Davis, Winston. 1992. *Japanese religion and society: Paradigms of structure and change.* Albany, NY: State University of New York Press.

Deans, Phil. 2007. Diminishing returns? Prime Minister Koizumi's visits to the Yasukuni Shrine in the context of East Asian nationalisms. *East Asia* 24: 269–294.

Earhart, H. Byron. 1974. *Japanese religion: Unity and diversity.* 2nd ed. Encino, CA: Dickenson Publishing.

Eger, Max. 1980. "Modernization" and "secularization" in Japan: A polemic essay. *Japanese Journal of Religious Studies* 7 (1): 7–24.

European and World Values Surveys four-wave integrated data file, 1981–2004, v.20060423, 2006. The European Values Study Foundation and World Values Survey Association. Aggregate File Producers: ASEP/JDS, Madrid, Spain/ Tilburg University, Tilburg, the Netherlands. Aggregate File Distributors: ASEP/JDS and ZA, Cologne, Germany.

Fitzgerald, Timothy. 2003. "Religion" and the "secular" in Japan. *Electronic Journal of Contemporary Japan* 10. http://www.japanesestudies.org.uk/ discussionpapers/Fitzgerald.html. (accessed 28 August 2009).

Fuller, Robert C. 2001. *Spiritual, but not religious: Understanding unchurched America.* Oxford: Oxford University Press.

Gorski, Philip S. 2000. Historicizing the secularization debate: Church, state, and society in late medieval and early modern Europe, CA. 1300 to 1700. *American Sociological Review* 65 (1): 138–167.

Govella, Kristi, and Steven Vogel. 2008. Japan in 2007: A divided government. *Asian Survey* 48 (1): 97–106.

Hardacre, Helen. 1989. *Shinto and the state: 1868–1989.* Princeton, NJ: Princeton University Press.

———. 2002. *Religion and society in nineteenth-century Japan: A study of the southern Kantō region, using late Edo and early Meiji gazetteers.* Ann Arbor, MI: Center for Japanese Studies, The University of Michigan.

———. 2005. Constitutional revision and Japanese religions. *Japanese Studies* 25 (3): 235–247.

Ishii, Kenji. 1996. Urbanization, depopulation, and religion. In *Religion in Japanese culture: where living traditions meet a changing world,* ed. Noriyoshi Tamaru and David Reid, 156–170. New York: Kodansha International.

———. 2004. *Kamidana saishi: Jingu tama no genzai no rikai ni mukete* [For a better understanding of household altars: *Kamidana* and the distribution of "*Jingu-tama*"]. In *Shinto honchō kyōgaku kenkyū kiyō daikyūgo* [*Bulletin of Shinto Education Institute,* vol. 9], ed. Kōji Itō, 23–40. Tokyo: Jinja Honcho Kengaku Kenkyusho.

Kawano, Satsuki. 2005. *Ritual practice in modern Japan: Ordering place, people, and action*. Honolulu: University of Hawaii Press.

Kisala, Robert. 2001. Asian values survey. Nanzan Institute for Religion and Culture. Nagoya: Nanzan University.

Kitagawa, Joseph M. 1987. *On understanding Japanese religion*. Princeton: Princeton University Press.

Klass, Dennis. 2005. The psychology of Japanese ancestor rituals. In *Dead but not lost: Grief narratives in religious traditions*, ed. Robert E. Goss and Dennis Klass, 19–72. Walnut Creek, CA: Alta Mira.

Koizumi, Tetsunori. 1979. The ways and means of the gods: An analysis of Japanese religions. *Journal of Cultural Economics* 3 (2): 75–88.

Marwell, Gerald and N. J. Demerath III. 2003. Comment: "Secularization" by any other name. *American Sociological Review* 68 (2): 314–316.

McFarland, Neill H. 1967. *Rush hour of the gods: A study of new religious movements in Japan*. New York: Macmillan.

Miyake, Hitoshi. 2001. *Shugendō: Essays on the structure of Japanese folk religion*. Ann Arbor, MI: University of Michigan.

Morioka, Kiyomi. 1975. *Religion in changing Japanese society*. Tokyo: University of Tokyo Press.

Mullins, Mark, Susumu Shimazono, and Paul L. Swanson, eds. 1993. *Religion and society in modern Japan*. Berkeley, CA: Asian Humanities Press.

Murakami, Shigeyoshi. Trans. by H. Byron Earhart. 1983. *Japanese religion in the modern century*. 2nd ed. Tokyo: University of Tokyo Press.

Nelson, John K. 2003. Social memory as ritual practice: Commemorating spirits of the military dead at Yasukuni Shinto Shrine. *Journal of Asian Studies* 62 (2): 443–467.

Nihonban General Social Surveys: Kiso shūkei-hyō, kōdo bukku JGSS ruiseki dēta 2000–2003 [Japanese General Social Surveys: Main Tables and Codebook, JGSS Accumulated Data 2000–2003]. 2006. Osaka: Osaka Commerce University.

Nihonban General Social Surveys: Kiso shūkei-hyō, kōdo bukku JGSS 2005 [Japanese General Social Surveys: Main Tables and Codebook, JGSS 2005]. 2007. Osaka: Osaka Commerce University.

Noriyoshi, Tamaru. 1996. Buddhism. In *Religion in Japanese culture: Where living traditions meet a changing world*, ed. Noriyoshi Tamaru and David Reid, 43–62. Tokyo: Kodansha International.

Norris, Pippa, and Ronald Inglehart. 2004. *Sacred and secular: Religion and politics worldwide*. Cambridge: Cambridge University Press.

Okada, Shigekiyo, ed. 1994. Nihon shūkyō he no shikaku [Approaches to Japanese religion]. Osaka: Toho Shuppan.

Ōmura, Eishō. 1996. *Gendai shakai to shūkyō: Shūkyō-ishiki no henyō*. [Contemporary society and religion: Transfigurations of religious consciousness]. Tokyo: Iwanami Shoten.

Onishi, Norimitsu. 2008. In Japan, Buddhism, long the religion of funerals, may itself be dying out. *New York Times*, July 14. International: A6.

Reader, Ian. 1991. *Religion in contemporary Japan*. Honolulu: University of Hawaii Press.

———. 2005. *Making pilgrimages*. Honolulu: University of Hawaii Press.

———, and George J. Tanabe, Jr. 1998. *Practically religious: Worldly benefits and the common religion of Japan*. Honolulu: University of Hawaii Press.

Reischauer, Edwin O. 1988. *The Japanese today*. Cambridge, MA: Belknap Press of Harvard University Press.

Roemer, Michael K. 2006. Religious tourism in contemporary Japan: Kyoto's Gion Festival. In *On the road to being there: Studies in pilgrimage and tourism in late modernity*, ed. William Swatos, H., Jr., 187–218. Boston: Brill Academic Publishers.

————. 2007. Ritual participation and social support in a major Japanese festival. *Journal for the Scientific Study of Religion* 46 (2): 185–200.

————. 2008. Religiosity and subjective and psychological well-being in contemporary Japan. Ph.D. dissertation, Austin: The University of Texas at Austin.

————. 2009. Religious affiliation in contemporary Japan: Untangling the enigma. *Review of Religious Research* 50 (3): 298-320.

Sakamoto, Koremaru. 2000. The structure of State Shinto: Its creation, development, and demise. In *Shinto in history: Ways of the Kami*, ed. John Breen and Mark Teeuwen, 272–294. Honolulu: University of Hawaii Press.

Sharf, Robert H. 1995. The Zen of nationalism. In *Curators of the Buddha: The study of Buddhism under colonialism*, ed. Donald S. Lopez, Jr., 107–160. Chicago: University of Chicago Press.

Shimazono, Susumu. 2006. Contemporary Japanese religions. In *Nanzan guide to Japanese religions*, ed Paul L. Swanson and Clark Chilson, 220–31. Honolulu: University of Hawaii Press.

Statistics Bureau, Ministry of Internal Affairs and Communications, Japan. 2008. *Japan Statistical Yearbook*. Hong Kong: International Publication Service.

Swyngedouw, Jan. 1976. Secularization in a Japanese context. *Japanese Journal of Religious Studies* 3/4: 283–306.

Takayama, K. Peter. 1998. Rationalization of state and society: A Weberian view of early Japan. *Sociology of Religion* 59: 65–88.

Tamaru, Noriyoshi, and David Reid, eds. 1996. *Religion in Japanese culture: Where living traditions meet a changing world*. Tokyo: Kodansha International.

Tamaru, Yoshiro. 2000. *Japanese Buddhism: A cultural history*. Tokyo: Kosei Publishing.

Traphagan, John W. 2004. *The practice of concern: Ritual, well-being, and aging in rural Japan*. Durham, NC: Carolina Academic Press.

Wilson, Bryan R. 1976. Aspects of secularization in the West. *Japanese Journal of Religious Studies* 3/4: 259–276.

Yanagawa, Kei'ichi. 1991. *Kindai nihonjin no shūkyō [Religion among the contemporary Japanese.]* Kyoto: Hozokan.

Zinnbauer, Brian J. et al. 1997. Religion and spirituality: Unfuzzying the fuzzy. *Journal for the Scientific Study of Religion* 36 (4): 549–564.

Chapter 3

Atheism and Secularity in the Former Soviet Union

Leontina M. Hormel

The study of atheism and secularism in the former Union of Soviet Socialist Republics (USSR) is a unique and complex case. At no other time in the history preceding the 1917 Bolshevik Revolution had a state officially endorsed and enforced the promotion of an irreligious society upon its citizens. The belief structure that was hoped to supersede that of the traditional religions of the Soviet territory (such as Orthodox, Islamic, Judaic, Catholic, and Lutheran faiths) was that of scientific atheism. According to Paul Froese[1] scientific atheism, "as the official term for the Communist Party's philosophical worldview, posited the ultimate purpose of human existence, a moral code of conduct, and created a collection of atheistic rituals and ceremonies that mimicked religious ones." From the outset of the USSR's creation, leaders and activists rigorously engaged in a variety of methods to create a society whose people no longer needed religion to explain everyday phenomena. However, efforts to strip people of religious beliefs proved complicated in a society comprising diverse cultures, and the techniques for changing the hearts and minds of people were often insensitive to local experiences. It is among these reasons that despite the commitment to establish the first atheist society in history, the number of people claiming to believe in God appeared to substantially increase across all former Soviet Republics after the system's collapse.

This chapter examines religious experiences across four regions: the Baltic (Estonia, Latvia, and Lithuania), Eastern Europe and Eurasia (Belarus, Moldova, Ukraine, and Russian Federation[2]), the Southern Caucasus (Armenia, Azerbaijan, and Georgia), and Central Asia

(Kazakhstan, Kyrgyzstan, Tajikistan, Turkmenistan, and Uzbekistan). These regions comprise such a wide variety of religious and cultural experiences that no single article can capture all of them adequately. Thus, this study is a modest effort to highlight the patterns of religious experience that are a result of these former Soviet societies sharing a history in which the state officially promoted atheism. This experience led to individuals following different strategies to preserve ways of life and identities in the midst of a Soviet campaign to standardize them and their relations to society. Although it was not fully successful in its mission, the Soviet-led antireligious campaign might have had some lasting effects, as the proportion of atheists and nonreligious in post-Soviet societies remains quite high even in the absence of scientific atheist propaganda and coercion.

HISTORY OF STATE IMPOSED ATHEISM

In the midst of gaining power, the Bolsheviks began an antireligious campaign seeking to disestablish influential religions like Eastern Orthodoxy,[3] to nationalize all church property, and to transfer responsibility in providing public services (such as birth, marriage, and death registration) from church to state organizations. Seeing religion as antithetical to the modern project of socialist political and economic development, revolutionary leaders thought it necessary to disentangle religious institutions from the state and to create conditions in which religion was deemed irrelevant to society's members.

The timing for an antireligious campaign seemed ripe in the late tsarist regime as an increasing portion of the population, especially in Russia, was disenchanted with the close role the Russian Orthodox Church bore with the state.[4] In the same year as the Bolshevik revolution of 1917, the Russian philosopher Berdyaev observed, "This emptiness [the rise of atheism and nihilism] is a result of slavery that lasted too long, of a process of regeneration of the old regime that went too far, of a paralysis of the Russian Church and moral degradation of the ecclesiastical authorities that lasted too long."[5]

Thus, even though the Soviet regime would be the first regime ever to devise a campaign promoting atheism, a general skepticism (at least with regard to the Russian Orthodox Church) was already present at the eve of the revolution.

Shortly following the Bolsheviks' rise to power in January 1918, V. I. Lenin crafted a decree for the Russian Soviet Federated Socialist Republic (RSFSR) Constitution that set official policy separating church and state. In the constitutional terms adopted in July 1918, religious clergy were classified along with merchants and capitalists as second-class citizens.[6] Seeking immediate separation, the newly established Bolshevik leaders provoked an antireligious campaign that often involved violent, coercive actions. This initial campaign was followed by a relatively calm period (although intimidation tactics and arrests of clerics continued), which focused on propaganda and socialization. "Cavalry raids" were common from 1917 to 1919 in Islamic regions. From 1919 to 1928, though, Islamic leaders were able to maintain authority even as Islamic cultural institutions were liquidated.[7] Conflicts with communities seeking to protect their churches and church valuables provoked harsh state reactions, such as Lenin's order for "the arrest and execution of as many clergy and active laity in Shuia [a town located northeast of Moscow] as possible."[8] The conflicts during the Civil War era, however, were eventually seen as counterproductive to the cause of establishing an atheist socialist society. Thus, most of the 1920s witnessed a shift from directly coercive measures to gradual measures to socialize citizens as atheists.

In 1925, the Party established the Soviet League of the Militant Godless (or, Militant Atheists) to organize a systematic program against religion. Organized in the same fashion as the Communist Party, the League broke itself down into cells. These cells were organized most simply at workplaces: at factory divisions, schools, and offices in urban areas and at collective farms, machine tractor stations, and reading huts in rural areas.[9] All cells were part of a network headquartered in Moscow. The League of the Militant Godless was conceived as an association of volunteers who were committed to promoting "scientific materialism" through educational activities like lectures, reading circles, and promotional materials. The League's creation symbolized the Bolshevik regime's attempts to shift the antireligious campaign away from coercion to socialization. However, this shift toward a more passive antireligious campaign was not supported unanimously.

By the late 1920s, the pendulum began to swing toward a more aggressive program. Lenin's original 1918 decree was further elaborated in 1929 when the RSFSR government adopted a comprehensive decree, "On Religious Associations," which remained in place over six decades. The decree established a model after which the fourteen other Soviet Republics would build their own constitutional approaches to religion. The 1929 law set out to establish strict boundaries within which religious organizations could conduct activities, making "all religious organization activity, except the most routine religious services and rituals within a State-registered place of worship, subject to State approval."[10] This law prohibited activities like charity work and church social events. However, the law remained vague enough in how it applied blanket prohibitions that room remained for arbitrary enforcement and antireligious activism.[11]

It is not clear the extent to which the 1929 law reflected the original intent of Lenin's 1918 decree (which may explain the inconsistency endemic to the antireligious campaign throughout the Soviet era). The ability to participate in cult practices remained possible; however, the right to disseminate religious propaganda was explicitly prohibited.[12] In contrast, the Constitution fully protected the ability to disseminate atheist propaganda using a variety of techniques.[13]

Reaching a consensus around the ways to promote atheism, though, was difficult. This chapter highlights two of the factors that complicated the strategies for promoting atheism through the antireligious campaign. One difficulty arose from early political debates concerning the role religion played in society, which meant different factions disagreed over the means for removing it.[14] Another reason the antireligious campaign was complicated was more obvious: the USSR's vast territory comprised diverse cultures and religions.[15] No single, standard plan could be applied to reach the desired effect. These two factors, among others, made it difficult for the Soviet state to impose atheism across the USSR uniformly and with a lasting impact.

Early Soviet Debates on Religion: Creating Homo Sovieticus

Even as the campaign against religion became more centralized under Stalin's cultural revolution (1928–1932), Daniel Peris's work finds that debates still ensued over the exact reasons for, and nature of, the antireligious campaign. A stenographic report of the June 14, 1929, Congress of the League of the Godless (*Soyuz bezbozhnikov*) documents the heated debates surrounding antireligious strategies. Peris illustrates how two factions—the "culturalists" and the "interventionists"—struggled with one another throughout the Congress' sessions. The culturalists, argued that instilling atheist philosophy and values throughout the various cultural institutions would gradually steer socialist citizens away from religious beliefs and would most effectively diminish resistance to atheism and Soviet modernization. Interventionists, on the other hand, saw religion and religious sentiments at all levels to be a direct threat to Soviet socialist development. In the arguments of the interventionists, people who remained committed to religious beliefs and practices were maintaining remnants of the old class system and were, thus, political enemies to Soviet modernization. Given the perceived threat of religious actors and groups to secularizing society, direct and swift action was considered necessary. According to Peris both positions, and those variations existing between the two, were difficult to support unequivocally as, "No unassailable source of wisdom in this regard existed because such a social transformation had never before been fully thought out or experienced."[16] As a consequence, a battle ensued over which position sat most squarely within Lenin's strategies—a task that could only be highly subjective since Lenin (and Marx, for that matter) had not mapped out an explicit outline of how to secularize society.[17] Rhetoric also reflected a desire to set concrete goals because "Many delegates referred to integrating antireligious activity into the five-year plan, to make antireligious achievements as much a part of the plan as steel production."[18]

In the end, the culturalists won the debates during the June 1929 Congress, but the long-run solution became one of direct action and coercion until World War II. From 1928 to 1941, anti-Islamic propaganda intensified, thousands of mosques were closed, and Muslim clerics and believers were victims of the Stalinist purges.[19] In 1930, the Ukrainian Autocephalous Orthodox Church was forced to declare its own liquidation, after which approximately half of its clergy was arrested. By the mid-1930s, the Russian Orthodox Church in Ukraine also saw its clergy arrested and deported, whereupon only 100 Orthodox priests were estimated to still reside in the Soviet republic by the end of the decade.[20] The Russian Orthodox Church in Russia was not decimated to the same extent; rather, Soviet authorities worked more toward co-opting the church hierarchy. This effort was most dramatically symbolized in Metropolitan Sergius' "The Declaration of Metropolitan Sergius" in 1927 that proclaimed to followers the Church's loyalty to the Soviet regime. The antireligious campaign was toned down during the Second World War in an attempt to build believers' trust and loyalty in the Soviet Union. During the same period, partly as a result of its failure in promoting scientific atheism, the League of the Militant Godless was dissolved.

The diminished fervor against religion as a response to WWII remained in place until Khrushchev reinvigorated the antireligious campaign from 1959 to 1964. During this period the number of places of worship and theological institutions in the Soviet Union was pared down by half.[21] Legal maneuvers were also used to strip societies of practices originating from religious teachings. For instance, Ro'i observes, "The attack on Islam . . . perhaps reached its peak in the 1962 *fatwa* (Islamic legal opinion) 'On Circumcision' put out by the Spiritual Board of Central Asia and Kazakhstan, which asserted that circumcision was not obligatory for Muslims since Islam had adopted this practice from Arabs of the pre-Islamic period."[22]

Under Brezhnev's leadership organized antireligious efforts relaxed. The less aggressive campaign remained in effect until Gorbachev's glasnost program, which marked official opening of Soviet societies to freedom of consciousness. The only exception to this relatively calm period arose in the early 1980s as a result of the Afghanistan conflict. The conflict heightened suspicion that Islamic movements would try to infiltrate Central Asian countries and Azerbaijan. As a consequence, a reactionary anti-Islamic campaign was reinstated. The constantly fluctuating waves throughout the Soviet period, waves undulating with more and less aggressive campaign tactics, reveal that consensus was never reached over the form and content of state-led programs promoting scientific atheism.

Religious and Cultural Diversity

Living in a social environment antagonistic to religion, atheist identity was, for some, a means to avoid scrutiny. For others, being atheist was a means to gain status through the Communist Party, which required its members to reject religion. These strategies' importance varied with one's situation, not least of which involved one's cultural background. The cultural diversity represented within the Soviet Union's extensive territory complicated how the state could impose a singular, atheist belief system (see Table 3.1).

Within historically Christian societies, national churches were capable of insulating themselves to some degree from the Soviet-led antireligious campaign.[23] As such, the presence of national churches served as a destabilizing entity. Although it was possible for churches to be co-opted by the Soviet state (as was apparently the case with the Russian Orthodox Church and the Moldovan Orthodox Church),[24] several incidents show churches were an instrumental force for dissent. Pedro Ramet includes the Catholic Church in Lithuania and Ukraine, the Lutheran Church in Estonia, and the Orthodox Church in Georgia as powerful entities in challenging the antireligious campaigns in these societies.[25] The most powerful role the churches played to weaken state ideology around atheism was to advocate the rights of ethnic minorities and national sovereignty. Being tightly woven into these societies' national histories, the national churches provided a lens from which Soviet citizens could critique the system.[26] Strong national churches, despite Soviet efforts to sanction their activities, were able to maintain public interest in national versus Soviet identities. This was done in various ways, such as churches "going underground" to continue religious rituals beyond the scope of state scrutiny and churches organizing underground dissemination of independent publications (samizdat).

Efforts to advance nationalist programs were organized by youth over the 1960s and 1970s throughout several of the republics historically linked to national churches. In Armenia, for which the Armenian Apostolic Church has been the key institution of Armenian identity, several demonstrations were organized in the 1960s and 1970s by nationalist youth organizations seeking recognition and independence. In Lithuania, where 70 percent of young people were Catholic members, Lithuanian youth organized investigations into the lost period of their country's independence from 1923 to 1940.[27] These activities demonstrate how religious identity remained part of national cultures, providing one way to separate individual identities from the drive to sovietize all people of the USSR.

Accounts in Islamic societies paint a picture of a different relationship between religious identity and Muslim identity in the midst of Soviet modernization. Muslims, while seemingly acquiescing to socialist modernization, still openly maintained their identities. Muslim

Table 3.1
**Ethnic composition and influential religion by country
in the former USSR**

	Ethnic Composition[*]	Influential Religion
Baltic		
Estonia	Estonian 67.9% Russian 25.6%	Lutheran
Latvia	Latvian 57.7% Russian 29.6%	Lutheran
Lithuania	Lithuanian 83.4% Polish 6.7% Russian 6.3%	Roman Catholic
Central Asia		
Kazakhstan	Kazakh (Qazaq) 53.4% Russian 30%	Islamic (Sunni)
Kyrgyzstan	Kyrgyz 64.9% Uzbek 13.8% Russian 12.5% other 5.7%	Islamic (Sunni)
Tajikistan	Tajik 79.9% Uzbek 15.3%	Islamic (Sunni)
Turkmenistan	Turkmen 85% Uzbek 5% other 6%	Islamic (Sunni)
Uzbekistan	Uzbek 80% Russian 5.5% Tajik 5%	Islamic (Sunni)
Eastern Europe & Eurasia		
Belarus	Belarusian 81.2% Russian 11.4%	Russian Orthodox
Moldova	Moldovan/Romanian 78.2% Ukrainian 8.4% Russian 5.8%	Russian Orthodox
Russian Federation	Russian 79.8% other 12.1%	Russian Orthodox
Ukraine	Ukrainian 77.8% Russian 17.3%	Ukrainian Orthodox (three competing divisions)
Southern Caucasus		
Armenia	Armenian 97.9%	Armenian Apostolic Church
Azerbaijan	Azeri 90.6%	Islamic (Shi'a)[1]
Georgia	Georgian 83.8% Azeri 6.5% Armenian 5.7%	Georgian Orthodox

[*]Source for ethnic composition data CIA World Factbook Web site. Groups comprising less than 5% of population are not included.
[1]Shortly following the U.S.S.R.'s collapse, it was estimated that 75 to 85 percent of Muslims in Azerbaijan were Shi'a. Shireen T. Hunter, "Azerbaijan: search for industry and new partners." In *Nations & Politics in the Soviet Successor States,* edited by Ian Bremmer and Ray Taras. (Cambridge: Cambridge University Press, 1993): 237.

identities were even maintained among those in leadership positions, leading to apparently contradictory declarations: "I am a Muslim and a Communist."[28]

Being the second largest religion within the Soviet territory, Islam guided a significant portion of the Soviet population (one Soviet citizen in five).[29] The traditionally Islamic societies of Central Asia, including Azerbaijan in the Southern Caucasus, appeared as though they cooperated with the socialist modernization project. Because Muslim resistance seemed absent (when compared to the religious and nationalist youth movements in republics like Armenia and Lithuania), scholars have tended to look at the nature of Islamic beliefs and practices, as well as at the configuration of cultural and national identity that preceded the socialist project. Islam is not structured around a clerical hierarchy, as its members are to have a direct experience with God. Thus, it was possible for Muslims to compromise with Soviet leaders by relegating religious experiences to individual experience in exchange for social modernization in the region. According to Froese, "This led to no theological crisis for most Muslims, who held inner spirituality as the core element of Islam. In return, Central Asia was modernized, and many Muslims moved into positions of political power."[30]

And, unlike the republics in which Christian beliefs prevailed, the predominantly Islamic republics were purely a Soviet creation. The carving of the region into separate republics did not represent how people living there understood their own identities. In fact, Bennigsen points out that Muslims in the Soviet Union had no prior understanding of "nation" in the sense of a modern nation-state. Thus, the nature of Islamic religion and the absence of nationhood marked distinctly different experiences from the republics Christianity largely influenced.

Officially, the Soviet state created four Spiritual Administrations (the Ufa muftiat, the Tashkent muftiat, the Buynaksk muftiat, and the Baku Directorate) that were designed to monitor Muslim communities. In the mid-1970s, it was estimated that 400–500 mosques continued to function, and approximately 5,000 mullahs (compared to 50,000 before 1917) served a population of 40 million.[31] Publicly, Muslim participation in Islamic rituals (such as attending Friday prayer at the mosques) was not great, yet Muslim festivals (such as Aid al-Fitr) experienced massive participation across the different regions. In the near absence of official clerics, Islamic practices became more informal, as Muslims sought ways to affirm their faith while avoiding the attention of Soviet authority. Evasion from Soviet detection was accomplished through a variety of ways: assigning unofficial mullahs, erecting unofficial mosques, designating tombs of mythical saints as holy places (circumventing the Soviet ban on *hadj*), and continuing a "Muslim way of life."[32]

The resilience of Muslim ways of life did not go undetected by Soviet authorities who noted that intellectuals and youth were "contaminated with 'religious prejudice.'"[33] Even during the relative calm following Khruschev's aggressive antireligious campaign, efforts were intensified and refined throughout Muslim societies.[34] The intensified efforts could be associated in part with the conflict in Afghanistan. With the conflict arose concerns that the West was infiltrating Muslim societies in an effort "to propagate religious sentiments and mystical dogmas," which ultimately undermined Soviet modernization.[35] Over the first six months of 1980 in Tajikistan, more than "4,000 lectures on atheism were held, as well as dozens of 'practical-scientific conferences and question-and-answer evenings,' lecture series and film lectures."[36] Secularization campaigns targeted women, using various means. Of the more popular methods of atheist indoctrination of women, education programs were deemed rather effective. These programs strove to keep girls in school and to enlist them in Komsomol girls' brigades, which trained them in leadership and feminine skills (like dressmaking). Other programs sought to educate housewives on child-rearing techniques, household economics, and health. Seeking to modernize girls' and women's attitudes (and mirroring contemporary endeavors to modernize Muslim women), these methods were hoped to eventually rid these societies of Muslim family practices, such as the tradition of paying bride price.[37] These observations, detailing the sustained and intensified efforts to strip Muslim ways of life, suggest that Muslims in no way conformed to atheism, but rather were adept in preserving private practices and keeping them just beyond the reach of Soviet regulation.

In Table 3.2, data from 1900 and 1970 show a steady growth of self-identifying atheists in the different regions of the Soviet Union. Yet, historical accounts in these distinct regions reveal state-imposed atheism was not fully internalized or accepted. Thus, the benefits of *publicly* identifying as atheist to accrue social rewards of the time while still maintaining religious identities *privately* to preserve one's culture could very well have been common across the USSR. This helps qualify those treatments of the Soviet campaign as being totalizing and absolute, allowing the possibility that people in the Soviet Union were able to think (if only privately) outside the box of Soviet propaganda.

POST-SOVIET ATHEISM AND RELIGIOSITY

Glasnost's introduction in the 1980s under Gorbachev, and the eventual collapse of the Soviet Union, brought about an environment in which religious membership and beliefs could be expressed. At the same time, economic changes arising out of systemic stagnation starting in the 1970s, and eventually through perestroika in the mid-1980s, led to considerable psychological and material insecurity for populations in several of the member countries of the USSR. Yegor Gaidar, in a recent

Table 3.2
**Growth of self-identifying atheists and nonreligious in USSR,
1900–1970**

	% Atheist*		% Nonreligious	
Baltic	1900	1970	1900	1970
Estonia	0.1	23.3	0.2	30.0
Latvia	0.0	16.6	0.1	31.0
Lithuania	0.0	10.0	0.1	19.2
Central Asia				
Kazakhstan	0.0	22.9	0.0	31.4
Kyrgyzstan	0.0	23.6	0.1	29.0
Tajikistan	0.0	14.3	0.2	19.4
Turkmenistan	0.0	14.6	0.1	20.3
Uzbekistan	0.0	16.9	0.0	25.1
Eastern Europe & Eurasia				
Belarus	0.1	15.5	0.3	24.4
Moldova	0.1	22.3	0.2	29.7
Russian Federation	0.1	23.4	0.2	28.1
Ukraine	0.0	15.9	0.2	22.3
Southern Caucasus				
Armenia	0.0	23.0	0.1	38.4
Azerbaijan	0.0	14.5	0.0	19.3
Georgia	0.0	16.5	0.0	36.3

*Data derived from Barrett, David B., George T. Kurian, and Todd M. Johnson, eds. *World Christian Encyclopedia: A comparative survey of churches and religions in the modern world, second edition [Volume 1, The World by Countries: Religionists, Churches, Ministries]*. New York: Oxford University Press, 2001.

lecture delivered to the American Enterprise Institute, pointed to the lower prices of oil and declining output of grain during the 1980s as key factors that led to Soviet economic crisis. Following the Saudis' liberalization of oil prices on September 13, 1985, the Soviet Union annually lost $20 billion in its oil trade.[38] The dramatic reduction in trade revenues and the decline in grain production inevitably led to rising scarcity of consumer goods. By 1990 a food rationing system was in place, which required that the Soviet consumer carry around *talony* (coupons) for the purchase of basics, like butter, sugar, eggs, and salt. By the winter of 1990–91, bread was sometimes unavailable for purchase. The faltering economy meant the prospects for the Soviet Union and the everyday person living there were grim.

By the end of the 1980s, the relaxed monitoring of religious life, coupled with greater material insecurity, created an environment in which religion could be openly explored, and it offered a space for psychological comfort. Data from Barrett et al. estimating the number of atheists and nonreligious from 1900 to mid-2000 indicate a marked decline in the number of atheist and nonreligious in most of the fifteen Soviet republics examined here. Table 3.3 lists by country the estimated proportion of atheists and nonreligious in mid-1990 and mid-2000. The right-hand columns depict the percentage change in atheist and nonreligious populations for mid-1990 and mid-2000 compared with 1970 and 1990, respectively. Examining numbers from the year 1990 is valuable in that it marks the beginning of the entire Soviet Union's collapse and a decade of even greater social and economic insecurity. Over the course of the decade following collapse, the proportion of atheists and nonreligious was relatively stable.

The sharp increase in the number of people claiming to believe in God was initially interpreted as a religious revival in the former Soviet Union. In fact, as the numbers of believers increased by the early 1990s, progressive laws on freedom of conscience and religion were introduced throughout the former Soviet Union. As the 1990s progressed, though, more restrictive amendments were introduced that either favored national churches or stifled free flows of religious (and nonreligious) thought. Moreover, macro-level data found that even though the numbers of believers seemed to grow over the previous 30 years, the behaviors of self-identified believers have been fraught with contradictions. Thus, the exact number atheists and nonreligious is not clear, and the exact nature of religious practice in the former Soviet Union confusing. The varying legal treatments of religious freedom and the eclectic nature of religious practice in the former Soviet Union are described below.

Legal Treatment of Religious Freedom in the Former Soviet Union

All of the former Soviet republics adopted constitutions and laws in the early 1990s (1990–1994) guaranteeing freedom of conscience and the separation of church and state. These early-established laws have been left fairly intact in the Baltic societies, especially in Estonia. Ukraine has also consistently protected rights to religious freedom and on April 22, 2005, the Soviet-legacy State Committee for Religious Affairs (SCRA) was abolished through presidential decree. Religious pluralism in Ukraine exists perhaps as a result of the ongoing competition between the three different Orthodox churches and the Ukrainian Greek-Catholic Church to gain status as the National Ukrainian Church.[39] Furthermore, Catherine Wanner's work on evangelism in

Table 3.3
Changes in percentage of atheist and nonreligious in former USSR, 1970–2000

	Atheist				Nonreligious			
	Mid-1990		Mid-2000		Mid-1990		Mid-2000	
	Percent pop.	Percent of 1970	Percent pop.	Percent of 1990	Percent	Percent of 1970	Percent	Percent of 1990
Baltic								
Estonia	12.7	−45.7	10.9	−14.2	27.1	−9.7	25.1	−7.4
Latvia	7.4	−55.4	6.0	−18.9	28.4	−8.4	26.0	−8.4
Lithuania	1.5	−85.0	1.1	−26.7	13.0	−32.3	10.9	−16.1
Central Asia								
Kazakhstan	12.0	−47.6	10.9	−9.2	32.3	+ 2.9	29.3	−9.3
Kyrgyzstan	9.6	−59.3	6.3	−34.4	24.2	−16.5	21.6	−10.7
Tajikistan	3.8	−73.4	1.9	−50.0	13.2	−32.0	12.0	−9.1
Turkmenistan	2.5	−82.9	1.4	−44.0	11.3	−44.3	9.0	−20.4
Uzbekistan	4.9	−71.0	3.5	−28.6	19.0	−24.3	18.1	−4.7
Eastern Europe & Eurasia								
Belarus	7.4	−52.3	4.9	−34.8	24.6	+ 0.8	24.0	−2.4
Moldova	8.9	−60.1	4.2	−52.8	22.2	−25.3	20.4	−8.1
Russian Federation	6.1	−73.9	5.2	−14.7	28.8	+ 2.5	27.5	−4.5
Ukraine	4.9	−69.2	4.0	−18.4	12.4	−44.4	10.9	−12.1
Southern Caucasus								
Armenia	10.1	−56.1	4.9	−51.0	17.9	−53.4	8.4	−53.1
Azerbaijan	0.8	−94.5	0.5	−37.0	12.4	−35.7	10.8	−12.9
Georgia	4.4	−73.0	2.7	−38.6	17.2	−52.6	15.3	−11.0

*Data derived from Barrett, David B., George T. Kurian, and Todd M. Johnson, eds. *World Christian encyclopedia: A comparative survey of churches and religions in the modern world, second edition [Volume 1, The World by Countries: Religionists, Churches, Ministries]*. New York: Oxford Univer-

Ukraine leads her to say religious pluralism is institutionalized in the country and thus will continue to thrive.[40]

The experiences with religious openness in the Baltic countries and Ukraine are not shared throughout the former Soviet Union. In fact, a trend toward increased state restrictions and criminalization of religious activity has prevailed in a large number of post-Soviet societies toward the latter part of the 1990s and into the new millennium. Former Soviet republics use different mechanisms through the laws on freedom of conscience and religion to restrict religious activities. Countries adopt laws that favor specific religions over others and bestow them with special functions. Georgia, for example, granted a consultative role to the Georgian Orthodox Church with its government in 2002. Later, in April 2005, the government established laws forbidding religious indoctrination in schools. Yet, observers claim that a large number of schools start classes with Orthodox prayers.[41] Another way laws serve to privilege certain religions over others is through establishing distinctions between religious "organizations" and less formal "groups." This language is utilized in Belarus' legal amendments in 2002, which also limited the scope of registered religions' activities, limiting them to specific towns or districts in which registration occurred.[42]

Establishing strict eligibility requirements to register with the state also legally enforces religious restrictions. At least three mechanisms are used to do this. One way is through increasing the number of congregants necessary to qualify as a religious organization or group. In Armenia, in 1997, an amendment raised the membership requirements from 50 to 200. Russia, on the other hand, used a second mechanism in its 1997 amendment, which required that religious groups prove their existence in the territory of Russia for no less than 15 years preceding registration. Marshall notes, though, that this potentially onerous requirement has been loosely enforced thus far.[43] The third mechanism, and most frequent, is that the process religious groups must follow to register with the state is made incredibly burdensome and bureaucratic. Difficult processes of registration are documented throughout Central Asia and in Azerbaijan. Kazakhstan, in fact, requests highly personal information for all congregational members (such as age, family status, and ethnicity). Thus, even if it is possible for religions to be legally active in different post-Soviet societies, processes are established in the laws that limit and control religious groups nonetheless.

Central Asia and Azerbaijan have taken greater measures than the other former Soviet republics to regulate religious activities. Turkmenistan and Uzbekistan, considered to have among the most authoritarian and repressive post-Soviet governments, not only make registration onerous for religious groups, but have also criminalized all groups who are not registered. Uzbekistan's National Security Service (NSS), the country's secret service, is one of the state agencies charged with supervising all religious organizations. Criminal charges against unregistered religions have, in fact, intensified over 2005 to 2006.[44] Besides criminalization, governments directly control religious organizations' activities, even those religions considered traditional to the society. For instance, religious law in Tajikistan requires state approval for each elected Muslim cleric. It seems that, unlike predominately Christian post-Soviet societies, restrictions on Muslim societies are intended to regulate all religions without serving the interests of any single one.

Religiosity in the Former Soviet Union

The initial trend in which the number of atheists and nonreligious declined throughout the Soviet Union during its collapse has been examined to understand the effects of the antireligious campaign. In his analysis of results from the 1991 and 1998 International Social Survey Program (ISSP), Greeley finds that older and younger generations in Russia and the former Soviet Union have greater religious tendencies than middle-age generations who were fully immersed within the system of state imposed atheism.[45] Such patterns in religious beliefs across different generations support positions that claim religious participation will rise as state regulation of religion diminishes. Older generations in post-Soviet societies will have lived in historical contexts in which they experienced periods of religious freedom in their youth. Younger generations (especially after the 1960s) will have experienced lax regulations and growing opportunities to critique religious regulation. Although Greeley believes these findings show that a religious revival took place by the early 1990s, his findings also support the possibility that those whose entire lives were spent within the Soviet system internalized atheism. In this respect, it is possible to say the atheist program experienced some success.

It is difficult to directly measure whether a religious resurgence has taken place in the former Soviet Union, because it is unlikely valid measures of religious activity exist from the Soviet era. After all, it was in the state's interest to underestimate the number of believers among its citizens, and citizens were likely reluctant to indentify with religiosity. Thus, even if there were some confidence in the contemporary measures of religiosity, any direct measure of whether atheism or religiosity has risen or fallen over time is not possible.[46] Measuring religiosity is also difficult, because there also remain questions around the meanings post-Soviet people attach to claiming they believe in God. Macro-level data are not direct measures of individuals' relationships between their beliefs and actions. It is possible to test the number of believers against their practices to determine the number of truly religious in a society. However, if these comparisons offer any insights, they serve to raise doubts that a religious resurgence has taken

Table 3.4
Percentage who believe in God and regularly attend church

	Believe in God? (%)	Attend Church once/month or more? (%)
Armenia*	86	30
Azerbaijan*	98	14
Georgia*	93	27
Belarus	83	15
Russian Federation	70	9
Ukraine	80	17
Estonia	51	11
Latvia	80	15
Lithuania	87	31
Kyrgyzstan	95	24

*1995 wave of the European Values Survey and the World Values Survey. Data for all other countries were collected in the 2000 wave of the European Values Survey and the World Values Survey. Source: Halman et al. *Changing Values and Beliefs in 85 Countries: Trends from the Values Surveys from 1981 to 2004.* Leiden and Boston: Brill, 2008.

place. Patterns between belief and practice are contradictory. Among the contradictions regularly observed is the dramatic divergence between self-reported belief in God and attendance of religious services. A small number of believers attends religious services regularly (see Table 3.4).

As mentioned earlier, this could lead us to believe the rates of religiosity in the former Soviet Union are overstated. Bishop Alfeyev of the Russian Orthodox Church describes from his own experiences how these contradictions play out:

> To be baptized, to be Orthodox has become a fashion. . . . I remember asking one teenager who came, together with her mother, to be baptized: "Do you believe in God?" "No," was her answer. "Why then do you want to be baptized?" I asked. "Well, everybody gets baptized nowadays," she said.

Although the encounter he describes doesn't fit the statistical trends illustrated in Table 3.4, it demonstrates how beliefs and actions are not necessarily consistent. Eastern European scholars argue that Bishop Alfeyev's story is not so strange, if taking into account the historically and culturally unique case of Soviet-led modernization. Individuals in post-Soviet societies may seek to reject communism (through baptism), yet still question if they believe in God. Likewise, they may feel devoted to God, but not express it in church attendance. In fact, scholars like Tomka contend that this latter scenario only looks contradictory from Western perspectives that rely on the use of ideal types and their own culturally-specific understandings of religious expression.[47] According to this argument, Western frameworks are ill-equipped to accurately explain the dynamic nature of belief (and nonbelief) in the former Soviet Union.

In a comparative analysis of Croatia, Hungary, Poland, and Slovenia, Zrinscak contends that the religious dynamics observed in post-communist European countries are related to at least three factors: the effects of political conflict between the communist system and the old social order, the form of social change arising after the Second World War in these countries, and the distinctions that exist between the countries. Moreover, in considering each one of these factors it is clear that generational effects would contribute to fluctuations in beliefs and practices within and between post-communist countries. For instance, the countries that were Soviet republics before World War II, when compared to central European countries like Hungary and Poland, will comprise more generational cohorts exposed to the antireligious campaigns (coercive and socialization tactics). Cohorts born in the 1920s in Russia will have a different experience with religious expression than those of the same generation born in Hungary. What is similar across the different societies of the former USSR is a relative loosening of political regulation that began in the 1960s and beyond. Zrinscak points out that individuals born in this period and later will have a significantly different experience with the communist order than those born in earlier periods. Growing up with only atheism, Larissa Titarenko explains, individuals have no conception of how their own values and practices can either be consistent or inconsistent with religious beliefs. Being fully socialized in a system in which the state allowed no religious education, individuals have no boundaries defining how they show their belief in God, especially in specifically "Catholic" or "Orthodox" ways. In fact, post-Soviet societies still do not structurally support religious education. The history of state-imposed atheism has meant religiosity in the former Soviet Union tends to be eclectic. A professed Orthodox believer can read tarot cards and horoscopes without sensing any contradiction (a pattern of behavior not unfamiliar to devout Christians living in the United States).[48]

Similar behavior is observed in Melissa Caldwell's ethnographic study of a small Protestant congregation in Moscow, the Christian Church of Moscow (CCM). She describes visiting Aleksandra Petrovna, a 75-year-old Russian pensioner who identified herself as a devout Christian believer with a strong family heritage in Russian Orthodoxy.[49] During her visit, Caldwell noted how Aleksandra Petrovna used referrals from a newspaper called *Tainaya vlast'* (*Secret Power*) that included articles and advertisements covering a diverse range of alternative religions (such as homeopathic medicine and Afro-Brazilian magic). Besides finding it peculiar that a devout Orthodox would rely on this paper as a resource for self-help, she also found the paper included articles discussing the "mysteries and healing powers of Orthodoxy."[50] This was ironic, especially because the Russian Orthodox Church was making a concerted effort to discredit these sorts of religions. For Caldwell, Aleksandra Petrovna's ability to be Orthodox while borrowing from alternative religions, and the association of Orthodox religion with supernatural power, are part of the same process. She explains

> Weberian paradigms emphasise the interconnections and interpenetrations of religion and economics, but maintain that the two remain distinct. In Russia, however, the two realms "religion" and "economics" have become fused, while "spirituality" has become separated from "religion." Ultimately, the implications of this commercialization of religion mean that by disentangling personal professions of spirituality from the institutional structures and rituals of religion, Muscovites have reinforced the distinction between belief and practice so that irreligious spirituality and aspiritual religiosity are both possible.

Drawing on material explanations for religious behavior, Caldwell argues this process is part of Muscovites' strategies to resolve the financial and emotional insecurity part and parcel with post-Soviet life in Russia.

Caldwell's research highlights social conditions that are often overlooked in the literature on religion in the former Soviet Union. Churches play an important role in providing charity, free services, and food to poorer strata in post-Soviet societies. This is an especially important function given conditions in which these societies have witnessed the steady deterioration of state-funded services and programs. For example, Caldwell observes one of her informants attending several different churches, as this informant relies on each one for the free food and resources provided. In Ukraine, religious organizations have become a key source for welfare and charity.[51] My own observations from ethnographic research in central Ukraine indicate that church membership is a strategic choice for some families. In an interview with a couple parenting five children, the husband explained how he joined a church in the hopes of being relocated to California with his family. According to him, he had friends who took advantage of their church membership in this way and now lived very comfortably in a big house in California.[52] Catherine Wanner, as well, describes how American missionaries from the Southern Baptist Church "offer free English language classes, sometimes medical care, and often biblical instruction to members or potential members of the church" at a Baptist Church in Ukraine.[53] Thus, although individuals may be devout in their beliefs in God, they may also be swayed by the practical benefits to church membership. The combination of culturally and historically specific experiences, as well as the material conditions people live in from day-to-day, are among the important factors shaping peoples' relationship to religion.

ATHEISTS IN THE FORMER SOVIET UNION

Although most studies of the former Soviet Union concentrate their energy on the increased numbers of self-identified believers in God, it remains impressive that the number of atheists in these societies remain as high as they are. To put the numbers in perspective,[54] the proportion of atheists in all of the countries of the former Soviet Union still surpass the proportion recorded in the United States (documented as 0.4 percent of the population in 2000). Taking account of the nonreligious, only Armenia records fewer (8.4 percent) than the United States (9 percent). Data suggest a large number of people identify strongly with atheism, or at least remain skeptical of religion, despite the absence of state-organized efforts to coerce people into this position.

The relatively large number of atheists and nonreligious in these societies is also significant if one considers there is little to be gained in being atheist in post-Soviet societies or in remaining unsure of God's existence. As mentioned earlier, religious organizations are among the main ways people access charity, free goods, and services in post-Soviet societies. Atheist organizations are not structured to serve in this way. And, perhaps for this reason, few atheist organizations appear to exist in the former Soviet Union. When conducting an Internet search (which, admittedly, is not a thorough account of atheist organizations), only one atheist organization, the Liberty of Conscience Institute, appears to be active in Russia, and another, Atheism in Ukraine, exists in Ukraine. Of the two, the Liberty of Conscience Institute appears most organized and is associated with the larger organization, the International Humanist and Ethical Union. On its Web site the organization notes that it is interested in advancing human rights and the full realization of the freedom of conscience:

> This issue [the constitutional right to freedom of expression and its legal form, freedom of conscience] is largely underdeveloped in Russia, both from scientific viewpoint as well as in the realm of constitutional principles. Hence, Russian legal system in this sphere is exclusively devoted to regulating the activities of religious entities and their monitoring. . . . [L]egislation, which should be directed at facilitating rights to freedom of expression, is substituted by "particular religious" legislation that is aimed at monitoring the activities of religious entities. This meets the demands of certain power structures and the religious bureaucracy, but not the society in general.[55]

The organization is not a relic of Soviet scientific atheism, for it is not interested in erasing religious influence from society and replacing it with scientific explanations. Rather, it seeks to advance freedom of conscience and reduce the role of the state in regulating religious activity. According to their mission statement, the organization seeks to establish a "system of legal guarantees for freedom of conscience on the regional, national and international levels."[56] In this endeavor, it serves as a watchdog for human rights. It has organized publicity campaigns against constitutional amendments that sought to favor the Russian Orthodox Church and has also sought to make the Russian Orthodox Church more transparent about its investments in the tobacco, banking, and petroleum industries.[57] Such activities show how atheism is no longer a state-supported belief system, and these watchdog activities are likely to keep atheism's relationship with the state distant.

The Liberty of Conscience Institute's activities demonstrate that atheists, who once were associated with state repression, now potentially serve as a progressive force in post-Soviet societies. In fact, cross-national research finds a correlation between secularization and higher quality of life factors. Countries with the highest rates of organic atheism rank high in human development (including life expectancy, adult literacy, and per capita income).[58] The correlation between atheism and human development is not as clear in post-Soviet societies, mostly as a result of their history with state-imposed atheism and an unsustainable modernization program. However, these societies were structured within a system that led people to expect a great degree of state responsibility in securing the basic necessities for its citizens. Because of this, the tyrannical qualities so frequently documented in Soviet and post-Soviet literature, did not simply lead to a passive society. Not usually highlighted in research is that progressive elements are present in social values in post-Soviet societies. Among the more significant findings from the World Values Survey[59] is that in 1995, more than 60 percent of respondents (78 percent in Belarus, 76 percent in Estonia, 62 percent in Latvia, 63 percent in Lithuania, 79 percent in the Russian Federation, and 66 percent in Ukraine) said they had a great deal of confidence in organizations for environmental protection. The same year, 54 percent of U.S. respondents and 63 percent of Norway's respondents expressed a great deal of confidence in organizations for environmental protection. When asked about their confidence in the women's movement, more than 60 percent of WVS respondents from Estonia (63 percent), the Russian Federation (70 percent), and Ukraine (62 percent) said they had a great deal of confidence in the movement.[60] Fifty-three percent of U.S. respondents and 43 percent of Norway's respondents expressed a great deal of confidence in the women's movement. In this respect, people in some post-Soviet societies have identified with rather progressive and positive perspectives at rates that even surpassed those in societies considered models for reform.

CONCLUSION

This chapter describes the shared history of state-imposed atheism in the republics within the USSR and the campaign's inconsistencies. It has examined how the laws on freedom of religion and consciousness have been treated across the former Soviet Union, as well as the dynamic nature of belief in God and religious practice since the system's collapse. It illustrates how the visionaries of the revolution, and then more specifically of the antireligious campaign, had difficulty reconciling the differences between their ideals (especially their hopes that people would embrace these ideals without resistance) and the everyday realities. People throughout the territory of the USSR were vastly different culturally. Any efforts to standardize them only heightened peoples' sense of desiring a unique identity. Because religion was part of the tightly woven fabric of one's experience and daily way of life and because some national religions were active in promoting these ideals for independence, the Soviet state was constantly forced to either assert its antireligious efforts or to temporarily retreat. The antireligious campaign's seemingly clumsy and erratic application seemed highly unsuccessful, as by mid-1990 a vast number of people throughout the republics claimed to believe in God. For onlookers, this sharp rise in believers demonstrated the resilience of religion and that the former USSR was in the midst of a religious resurgence. However, what was also apparent was that this belief did not directly lead to the typical indicators of religious participation. Rather, the unique experience of being raised in a state-imposed atheist society (each having its own cultural-historical experience) seems to have led to eclectic expressions of religiosity. This chapter concludes by pointing out that the campaign to build atheism in the Soviet Union was not necessarily a complete failure. The number of atheists and nonreligious is still quite large relative to most other societies in the world. There is also some indication the atheism that has remained intact is not a relic of Soviet scientific atheism, but one which seeks to build a post-Soviet society on the principles of freedom of consciousness valuing human rights.

NOTES

1. Paul Froese, "Forced Secularization in Soviet Russia: Why an Atheistic Monopoly Failed." *Journal for the Scientific Study of Religion* 43, no. 1 (2004): 35.

2. Eurasia essentially refers to the Russian Federation in this chapter. Embedded in the use of this term is a sense of the cultural richness included in the Federation's geographic space.

3. Bishop Hilarion Alfeyev, "Atheism And Orthodoxy in Modern Russia," http://en.hilarion.orthodoxia.org/, p. 1 (accessed June 10, 2008).

4. Paul Froese, "Forced Secularization in Soviet Russia: Why an Atheistic Monopoly Failed." *Journal for the Scientific Study of Religion* 43, no. 1 (2004): 37; Daniel Peris, *Storming the Heavens: The Soviet League of the Militant Godless* (Ithaca: Cornell University Press, 1998), 22; Bishop Hilarion Alfeyev, "Atheism and Orthodoxy in Modern Russia," http://en.hilarion.orthodoxia.org/ (accessed June 10, 2008): 4.

5. Bishop Hilarion Alfeyev, "Atheism and Orthodoxy in Modern Russia," http://en.hilarion.orthodoxia.org/ (accessed June 10, 2008): 1.

6. Daniel Peris, *Storming the Heavens: The Soviet League of the Militant Godless.* (Ithaca: Cornell University Press, 1998), 22.

7. Alexandre Bennigsen, and S. Enders Wimbush. *Muslims of the Soviet Empire: A Guide.* (Bloomington and Indianapolis: Indiana University Press, 1986), 11.

8. Daniel Peris, *Storming the Heavens: The Soviet League of the Militant Godless.* (Ithaca: Cornell University Press, 1998), 26.

9. Ibid.

10. Boiter, Albert. "Drafting a Freedom of Conscience Law," *The Columbia Journal of Transnational Law* 28, no. 1 (1990): 158.

11. Ibid., 159.

12. F. J. M. Feldbrugge, *Encyclopedia of Soviet Law (Law in Eastern Europe).* 2nd ed. (The Hague, The Netherlands: Kluwer Law International, 1985), 107.

13. Feldbrugge cites Article 52 of the 1977 Constitution. Ibid.

14. Daniel Peris, "The 1929 Congress of the Godless," *Soviet Studies* 43, no. 4 (1991): 711–732.

15. Bohdan R. Bociurkiw and John W. Strong, eds., *Religion and Atheism in the U.S.S.R. and Eastern Europe* (Toronto and Buffalo: University of Toronto Press, 1975); Ian Bremmer and Ray Taras, eds., *Nations & Politics in the Soviet Successor States* (Cambridge: Cambridge University Press, 1993).

16. Daniel Peris, "The 1929 Congress of the Godless," *Soviet Studies* 43, no. 4 (1991): 718.

17. Ibid., 718–719. In fact, it is ironic that both camps within this debate developed arguments essentially prioritizing the changing of ideas (either through socialization, or through direct ideological coercion) over material conditions. Both appear contradictory to Marx's historical materialism.

18. Ibid., 723.

19. Alexandre Bennigsen and S. Enders Wimbush. *Muslims of the Soviet Empire: A Guide* (Bloomington and Indianapolis: Indiana University Press, 1986).

20. Karel C. Berkhoff, *Harvest of Despair: Life and Death in Ukraine Under Nazi Rule* (Cambridge: Harvard University Press, 2004).

21. Bohdan R. Bociurkiw, "Religious Dissent and the Soviet State," in *Religion and Atheism in the U.S.S.R. and Eastern Europe,* ed. Bohdan R. Bociurkiw and John W. Strong (Toronto and Buffalo: University of Toronto Press, 1975), 60.

22. Yaacov Ro'i, "The Task of Creating the New Soviet Man: 'Atheistic Propaganda' in the Soviet Muslim Areas." *Soviet Studies* 36, no. 1 (1984): 28. Ro'i cites original documentation for this can be found in *Istoriya i teoriya ateizma* [The History and Theory of Atheism]. (Moscow, 1974), 160.

23. Ibid., 58. Bociurkiw prefers to define the existence of religious organization (such as the Catholic Church in Lithuania) as evidence of dissident behavior. He reasons, "religious dissent in the USSR may be defined as an overt repudiation of the existing relationship between institutional religion and the Soviet State, involving an explicit or implicit challenge to the legitimacy of the norms and structures governing this relationship. . . . It also reflects the inevitable 'politicisation' of religious dissent in the USSR resulting from the far-reaching involvement of the political authorities in the conduct of internal affairs of all officially recognized ('registered') religious groups, including the determination of the groups' statutes and selection of their leaders."

24. Irena Borowik argues the organizational and structural traditions of the Orthodox churches made it more difficult for them to sever links with the Soviet state, and therefore they were vulnerable to co-optation. "Orthodoxy Confronting the Collapse of Communism in Post-Soviet Countries," *Social Compass* 53, no. 2 (2006): 269.

25. Pedro Ramet, *Cross and Commissar: The Politics of Religion in Eastern Europe and the USSR* (Bloomington and Indianapolis: Indiana University Press, 1987), 14.

26. Zrinscak, in fact, describes how she observed "people who were more religious [in Croatia] tended not only to be more critical of the system but also belonged to families that had undergone negative experiences of communism." Sinisa Zrinscak, "Generations and Atheism: Patterns of Response to Communist Rule Among Different Generations and Countries." *Social Compass* 51, no. 2 (2004): 221–234.

27. Hank Johnston, "Religio-Nationalist Subcultures under the Communists: Comparisons from the Baltics, Transcaucasia, and Ukraine." In *Politics and Religion in Central and Eastern Europe: Traditions and Transitions*, ed. William H. Swatos (London and Westport, CT: Praeger, 1994): 22–23.

28. Paul Froese, "'I Am an Atheist and a Muslim': Islam, Communism, and Ideological Competition." *Journal of Church and State* 47, no. 3 (2005).

29. Alexandre Bennigsen, "Islam in the Soviet Union: The Religious Factor and the Nationality Problem in the Soviet Union." In *Religion and Atheism in the U.S.S.R. and Eastern Europe*, ed. Bohdan R. Bociurkiw and John W. Strong (Toronto and Buffalo: University of Toronto Press, 1975): 91.

30. Paul Froese, *The Plot to Kill God: Findings from the Soviet Experiment in Secularization* (Berkeley and Los Angeles: University of California Press, 2008), 103.

31. Ibid., 93.

32. Ibid., 95–96.

33. Yaacov Ro'i, "The Task of Creating the New Soviet Man: 'Atheistic Propaganda' in the Soviet Muslim Areas." *Soviet Studies* 36, no. 1 (1984): 27.

34. Ibid., 27–28.

35. Ibid., 32. Original quote found in an editorial piece in *Pravda Vostoka* [*The Truth of the East*], October 23, 1981.

36. Ibid., 30.

37. Ibid., 32.

38. Yegor Gaidar, "The Soviet Collapse: Grain and Oil." *American Enterprise Institute for Public Policy Research*, 2007. Washington, D.C.: American Enterprise Institute. www.aei.org (accessed August 15, 2008), 4–5.

39. Paul A. Marshall, *Religious Freedom in the World* (Lanham, MD: The Rowman & Littlefield Group, 2008), 411. The three Orthodox churches include Ukrainian Autocephalous Church, Ukrainian Orthodox Church Moscow Patriarchate, and Ukrainian Orthodox Church Kiev Patriarchate.

40. Catherine Wanner, "Advocating New Moralities: Conversion to Evangelicalism in Ukraine." *Religion, State & Society* 31, no. 3 (2003): 285. Catherine Wanner. *Communities of the Converted: Ukrainians and Global Evangelism* (Ithaca: Cornell University Press), 246–247.

41. Paul A. Marshall, *Religious Freedom in the World*, 180.

42. Ibid., 91.

43. Ibid., 344.

44. Ibid., 420.

45. Andrew M. Greeley, *Religion in Europe at the End of the Second Millennium* (New Brunswick, NJ: Transaction Publishers), 2003; Andrew M. Greeley. "A Religious Revival in Russia?" *Journal for the Scientific Study of Religion* 33, no. 3 (1994): 253–272.

46. Using the World Values Survey results over the 1990s, Norris and Inglehart compare generations in their study of secularism in the former Soviet Union as one solution to this deficiency in the data. Their statistical models suggest that secularism is still growing in post-Soviet societies, finding a linear relationship between age and secular beliefs. The results of their work contradict the hypotheses associated with religious markets theory. Pippa Norris and Ronald Inglehart, *Sacred and Secular: Religion and Politics Worldwide* (Cambridge: Cambridge University Press), 2004.

47. Miklós Tomka, "Is Conventional Sociology of Religion Able to Deal with Differences between Eastern and Western European Developments?" *Social Compass* 53, no. 2 (2006): 251–265.

48. Larissa Titarenko, "On the Shifting Nature of Religion during the Ongoing Post-Communist Transformation in Russia, Belarus and Ukraine," *Social Compass* 55, no. 2 (2008): 244. Interestingly, these seemingly inconsistent behaviors are even observed in the United States. In his fieldwork in Butte, Montana, John Mihelich has found that many Butte Catholics would have their fortunes told. Many themselves learned different ways to tell fortunes, such as the art of reading tea leaves. John Mihelich, "Fortune in Butte" Interview data from field research in Butte, Montana. Unpublished.

49. Melissa L. Caldwell, "A New Role for Religion in Russia's New Consumer Age: The Case of Moscow." *Religion, State & Society* 33, no. 1 (2005): 25.

50. Ibid., 29.

51. Ibid. Also, Alex Vinikov, "Freedom of Religion and Faith-Based Philanthropy in Ukraine," Seal: on-line resource for social economy and law professionals working at European level. http://www.efc.be/cgi-bin/articlepublisher.pl?filename=AV-SE-06-03-2.html (accessed June 10, 2008).

52. Leontina Hormel, "Family with Five Children Interview: November 27, 2002." Field research notes in Komsomolsk, Ukraine. Unpublished.

53. Catherine Wanner. *Communities of the Converted: Ukrainians and Global Evangelism* (Ithaca: Cornell University Press), 181.

54. Data derived from David B. Barrett, George T. Kurian, and Todd M. Johnson, *World Christian Encyclopedia: A Comparative Survey of Churches and*

Religions in the Modern World, 2nd ed., Vol. 1, The World by Countries: Religionists, Churches, Ministries (New York: Oxford University Press, 2001).

55. Liberty of Conscience Institute Web page. "About." http://www.atheism.ru/lci/about/?lang=eng (accessed June 10, 2008).

56. Ibid.

57. Ibid. and "Religion in Russia is Big Business—Russian Orthodox Church Investments in Tobacco, Banking and Petroleum." American Humanist Association and the Gale Group. *The Humanist* 57, no. 5 (1997): 47.

58. Phil Zuckerman, "Atheism: Contemporary Rates and Patterns." In *The Cambridge Companion to Atheism*, ed. Michael Martin (Cambridge UK: Cambridge University Press, 2005), 58.

59. Loek Halman et al. *Changing Values and Beliefs in 85 Countries: Trends from the Values Surveys from 1981 to 2004* (Leiden and Boston: Brill, 2008), 186.

60. Ibid., 187.

REFERENCES

Agadjanian, Alexander, "Revising Pandora's Gifts: Religious and National Identity in the Post-Soviet Societal Fabric" *Europe-Asia Studies* 53, no.3 (2001): 473–488.

Alfeyev, Bishop Hilarion. "Atheism And Orthodoxy in Modern Russia." http://en.hilarion.orthodoxia.org/ (accessed June 10, 2008).

Atheism in Ukraine Web site. http://www.uath.org/ (accessed June 10, 2008).

Atkin, Muriel. "Tajikistan: Ancient Heritage, New Politics." In *Nations and Politics in the Soviet Successor States*, edited by Ian Bremmer and Ray Taras, 225–260. Cambridge: Cambridge University Press, 1993.

Barrett, David B., George T. Kurian, and Todd M. Johnson. *World Christian Encyclopedia: A comparative survey of churches and religions in the modern world*, 2nd ed. vol. 1, *The World by Countries: Religionists, Churches, Ministries*. New York: Oxford University Press, 2001.

BBC News On-line, International version. "Nigeria leads in religious belief" (26 February 2004) http://news.bbc.co.uk/2/hi/programmes/wtwtgod/3490490.stm (accessed June 11, 2008).

Bennigsen, Alexandre. "Islam in the Soviet Union: The Religious Factor and the Nationality Problem in the Soviet Union" In *Religion and Atheism in the U.S.S.R. and Eastern Europe*, edited by Bohdan R. Bociurkiw and John W. Strong, 91–100. Toronto and Buffalo: University of Toronto Press, 1975.

Bennigsen, Alexandre, and S. Enders Wimbush. *Muslims of the Soviet Empire: A Guide*. Bloomington and Indianapolis: Indiana University Press, 1986.

Berkhoff, Karel C. *Harvest of Despair: Life and Death in Ukraine Under Nazi Rule*. Toronto: University of Toronto Press, 2004.

Bociurkiw, Bohdan R., and John W. Strong, eds. *Religion and Atheism in the U.S.S.R. and Eastern Europe*. Toronto and Buffalo: University of Toronto Press, 1975.

Boiter, Albert. "Drafting a Freedom of Conscience Law," *The Columbia Journal of Transnational Law* 28, no. 1 (1990): 157–188.

Borowik, Irena. "Orthodoxy Confronting the Collapse of Communism in Post-Soviet Countries," *Social Compass* 53, no. 2 (2006): 267–278.

————. "Between Orthodoxy and Eclecticism: On the Religious Transformation of Russia, Belarus and Ukraine," *Social Compass* 49, no. 4 (2002): 497–508.

————. "Religion in Postcommunist Countries: A Comparative Study of Religiousness in Byelorussia, Ukraine, Lithuania, Russia and Poland." In *Politics and Religion in Central and Eastern Europe: Traditions and Transitions*, edited by William H. Swatos, 17–35. London and Westport, CT: Praeger, 1994.

Bremmer, Ian, and Ray Taras, eds. *Nations & Politics in the Soviet Successor States*. Cambridge: Cambridge University Press, 1993.

Bruce, Steve. "The Supply-Side Model of Religion: The Nordic and Baltic States," *Journal of the Scientific Study of Religion* 39, no. 1 (2000): 32–46.

Caldwell, Melissa L. "A New Role for Religion in Russia's New Consumer Age: The Case of Moscow." *Religion, State & Society* 33, no. 1 (2005): 19–34.

CIA World Factbook Web site. https://www.cia.gov/library/publications/the-world-factbook/ (accessed July 23, 2008).

Dudwick, Nora. "Armenia: The Nation Awakens." In *Nations and Politics in the Soviet Successor States*, edited by Ian Bremmer and Ray Taras, 261–287. Cambridge: Cambridge University Press, 1993.

Feldbrugge, F. J. M. *Encyclopedia of Soviet Law (Law in Eastern Europe). 2nd ed.* Kluwer Law International, 1985.

Froese, Paul. *The Plot to Kill God: Findings from the Soviet Experiment in Secularization*. Berkeley and Los Angeles: University of California Press, 2008.

————. "'I Am an Atheist and a Muslim': Islam, Communism, and Ideological Competition." *Journal of Church and State* 47, no. 3 (2005): 473–502.

————. "Forced Secularization in Soviet Russia: Why an Atheistic Monopoly Failed." *Journal for the Scientific Study of Religion* 43, no. 1 (2004): 35–50.

————. "After Atheism: An Analysis of Religious Monopolies in the Post-Communist World." *Sociology of Religion* 65, no. 1 (2004): 57–75.

Froese, Paul, and Steven Pfaff. "Replete and Desolate Markets: Poland, East Germany, and the New Religious Paradigm." *Social Forces* 80, no. 2 (2001): 481–507.

Gaidar, Yegor. "The Soviet Collapse: Grain and Oil." *American Enterprise Institute for Public Policy Research*, 2007. Washington, D.C.: American Enterprise Institute, 1–8. www.aei.org (accessed August 15, 2008).

Gleason, Gregory. "Uzbekistan: From Statehood to Nationhood?" In *Nations and Politics in the Soviet Successor States*, edited by Ian Bremmer and Ray Taras, 225–260. Cambridge: Cambridge University Press, 1993.

Haghayeghi, Mehrdad. "Central Asia and Azerbaijan." In *Modernization, Democracy, and Islam*, edited by Shireen T. Hunter and Huma Malik, 293–309. Westport, CT, and London: Praeger, 2005.

Halman, Loek, Ronald Inglehart, Jaime Díez-Medrano, Ruud Luijkx, Alejandro Moreno, and Miguel Basáñez. *Changing Values and Beliefs in 85 Countries: Trends from the Values Surveys from 1981 to 2004*. Leiden and Boston: Brill Publishers, 2008.

Halsall, Anna, and Bert Roebben. *Religious Education* 101, no. 4 (2006): 443–452.

Hann, Chris. "Problems with the (De)privatization of Religion." *Anthropology Today* 16, no. 6 (2000): 14–20.

Hormel, Leontina. "Family with Five Children Interview Transcript: November 27, 2002." Field research in Komsomolsk, Ukraine. Unpublished.

The Humanist. "Religion in Russia is Big Business—Russian Orthodox Church Investments in Tobacco, Banking and Petroleum." American Humanist Association and the Gale Group. 57, no. 5 (1997): 47.

Hunter, Shireen T. "Introduction." In *Modernization, Democracy, and Islam,* edited by Shireen T. Hunter and Huma Malik, 1–18. Westport, CT, and London: Praeger, 2005.

———. "Azerbaijan: Search for Industry and New Partners." In *Nations and Politics in the Soviet Successor States,* edited by Ian Bremmer and Ray Taras, 225–260. Cambridge: Cambridge University Press, 1993.

International Humanist and Ethical Union Web site. http://www.iheu.org/ (accessed June 10, 2008).

Johnston, Hank. "Religio-Nationalist Subcultures under the Communists: Comparisons from the Baltics, Transcaucasia, and Ukraine." In *Politics and Religion in Central and Eastern Europe: Traditions and Transitions,* edited by William H. Swatos, 17–35. London and Westport, CT: Praeger, 1994.

Liberty of Conscience Institute Web page. "About." http://www.atheism.ru/ lci/about/?lang=eng (accessed June 10, 2008).

Loya, Joseph A. "Religion Classes in State Institutions in Post-Soviet Russia." *Religion in Eastern Europe* 26, no. 1 (2006): 52–66.

Lüchau, Peter. "Report on Surveys of Religion in Europe and the United States." University of Copenhagen: Research Priority Area Religion in the 21st Century, 2004.

Luehrmann, Sonja. "Recycling Cultural Construction: Desecularisation in Post-soviet Mari El." *Religion, State & Society* 33, no. 1 (2005): 35–56.

Marsh, Christopher, and Paul Froese. "The State of Freedom in Russia: A Regional Analysis of Freedom of Religion, Media and Markets." *Religion, State, and Society* 32, no. 2 (2004): 137–149.

Marshall, Paul A. *Religious Freedom in the World.* Lanham, MD: The Rowman & Littlefield Group, 2008.

Matossian, Mary Allerton Kilbourne. *The Impact of Soviet Policies in Armenia.* Leiden, Netherlands: E. J. Brill, 1962.

Mihelich, John. "Fortune in Butte." Interview data from field research in Butte, Montana. Unpublished.

Norris, Pippa, and Ronald Inglehart. *Sacred and Secular: Religion and Politics Worldwide.* Cambridge: Cambridge University Press, 2004.

Olcott, Martha Brill. "Kazakhstan: A Republic of Minorities." In *Nations and Politics in the Soviet Successor States,* edited by Ian Bremmer and Ray Taras, 225–260. Cambridge: Cambridge University Press.

Peris, Daniel. *Storming the Heavens: The Soviet League of the Militant Godless.* Ithaca: Cornell University Press, 1998.

———. "The 1929 Congress of the Godless." *Soviet Studies* 43, no. 4 (1991): 711–732.

Ramet, Pedro. *Cross and Commissar: The Politics of Religion in Eastern Europe and the USSR.* Bloomington and Indianapolis: Indiana University Press, 1987.

Ro'i, Yaacov. "The Task of Creating the New Soviet Man: 'Atheistic Propaganda' in the Soviet Muslim Areas." *Soviet Studies* 36, no. 1 (1984): 26–44.

Titarenko, Larissa. "On the Shifting Nature of Religion during the Ongoing Post-Communist Transformation in Russia, Belarus and Ukraine." *Social Compass* 55, no. 2 (2008): 237–254.

————. "Gender Attitudes Towards Religion in Six Post-Soviet States," in *European Values at the Turn of the Millennium*, edited by Wilhelmus Antonius Arts and Loek Halman, 363–383. Danvers, MA: Brill, 2004.

Tomka, M. "Is Conventional Sociology of Religion Able to Deal with Differences between Eastern and Western European Developments?" *Social Compass* 53, no. 2 (2006): 251–265.

Vinikov, Alexander. "Freedom of Religion and Faith-Based Philanthropy in Ukraine." *Seal On-line Resource.* European Foundation Centre, 2003. http://www.efc.be/cgi-bin/articlepublisher.pl?filename=AV-SE-06-03-2.html (accessed June 10, 2008).

Wanner, Catherine. "Advocating New Moralities: Conversion to Evangelicism in Ukraine." *Religion, State, & Society* 31, no. 3 (2003): 273–287.

World Values Surveys, 1981–2004 Online Data Bank. http://www.jdsurvey.net/ (accessed December 18, 2007).

Wuthnow, Robert, ed. *Encyclopedia of Politics and Religion.* 2nd ed., Vols. 1 and 2. Washington, D.C.: CQ Press, 2007.

Zrinscak, Sinisa. "Generations and Atheism: Patterns of Response to Communist Rule among Different Generations and Countries." *Social Compass,* 51, no. 2 (2004): 221–234.

Zuckerman, Phil. "Atheism: Contemporary Rates and Patterns." In *The Cambridge Companion to Atheism,* edited by Michael Martin, 47–65. Cambridge UK: Cambridge University Press, 2005.

Chapter 4

Atheism and Secularity in Ghana

Kwasi Yirenkyi
Baffour K. Takyi

Amid the spread of secular institutions throughout Africa, there is widespread evidence to suggest that religion shows no sign of disappearing or diminishing in the lives of the people. Indeed, as some scholars have pointed out, many Africans of today—irrespective of where they live (in the urban or rural hinterlands) still draw on their knowledge of African traditional cosmologies to their lived experiences (see, e.g., Meyer 2004; Ellis and Haar 1998). Idowu also notes that by nature, Africans are "a people who in all things are religious" (1967, 11; 1973). This observation has also been echoed by other researchers such as Opoku (1978), Mbiti (1991), Ray (2000), and Yirenkyi (1999). Most recently Jenkins (2003) has also reported that in the case of worldwide Christianity which seems to be on the decline in the West (northern hemisphere), this is not the case with respect to the southern hemisphere, especially Africa where there has been a resurgence of the Christian faith. This view is also shared by Barrett and John (2001, 383) who have reported that the African church is the fastest growing in the world (see also Kiliaini 2001, 358).[1]

In Ghana, the growth of Christianity and its influence in the lives of the people is quite instructive, since this nation was the first place in sub-Saharan Africa where Europeans arrived and traded, first in gold and later in slaves. The spread of Christianity throughout the country has something to do with the work of Christian missionaries and their activities during pre-colonial and colonial periods, particularly with the establishment of schools, and the creation of African elite in the course of time (Agbeti 1986). Not surprisingly, the areas where the Christian faith became dominant included areas such as the Colony that came under direct European rule. In the case of Ghana, this appears to be the southern regions, even though in some parts of the North especially in the Dagare areas such as Nandom, Wa, and other places where Catholic missionary activities were very prominent. Although the great mass movement toward Christianity stopped, Christian faith kept playing an important role in Nandom (van der Geest 2004).

Not only is Ghana a highly religious country, several studies have also documented that religion has become a potent social force in both public and private life.[2] Pobee (1991), Kudadjie and Aboagye-Mensah (1991), Ninsin and Drah (1987, 1991), and Yirenkyi (1999; 2000) have examined the role of the Christian churches in the recent democratization process in the country. Other scholars have also examined how religion is influencing the behavior of Ghanaians, including for example, contraceptive use (Addai 1999), HIV/AIDS behavior (Takyi 2003), education (Takyi and Addai 2002), maternal child health behavior (Gyimah, Takyi, and Tenkorang 2006), and fertility of couples (Gyimah, Takyi, and Tenkorang 2008).

Even though the single largest bloc of religious adherents in Ghana is Christian,[3] some scholars have pointed to the changing religious landscape in the country, with the traditional African Independent Churches loosing a significant number of their members to other denominations.[4] Both Nukunya (1992) and Assimeng (1986) have suggested that the growing popularity of these "new" Christian groups reflect the growing disenchantment of the people with the monotony of the mainline churches, and the fact that the new denominations often use "healing" and "salvation" in their preaching, something that appeal to the needs of an impoverished population who have been dissatisfied with their socioeconomic situation since the 1970s. Thus while the mainline Protestant churches are relatively stable, although members switch from churches within the Protestant denominations, the Catholic Church in particular has lost about 2 percent of its members—despite being still the church with most members.

Admittedly most Ghanaians consider themselves religious and Christians; this generalization also masks the realities of the African religious landscape which is somewhat fluid and includes some people who consider themselves as nonreligious, or atheists.[5] Writing about the religious landscape in Ghana, Pobee (1991) notes that while the religious context of Ghana for the most part consists of a combination of various Christian denominations, Islam, and indigenous religious practices rooted in chieftaincy and family institutions, there are also some Ghanaians who claim to be atheists, secular humanists, or agnostics.

Despite the fact that some Ghanaians self-report as unaffiliated with any religious persuasion in the country, it is unfortunate that we know very little about this group of Ghanaians. This knowledge gap has something to do with the fact that most of the existing studies on African religions focus on the foreign-originated ones (Christianity and Islam), and to some extent indigenous African belief systems, or what some scholars refer to as African Traditional Religions (ATRs). Another possible reason may have to do with the fact that in a highly religious society such as Ghana, unaffiliated people may be stigmatized, hence may be less likely to be visible as Christians and their Muslim counterparts. It is thus not surprising that a review of the existing literature on religion suggests that very little has been written about this population and it has been virtually ignored in the discourse of religions in Africa. This is not exactly the case with some parts of Europe and North America where there is an increasing interest and a growing literature on atheism.[6]

Our main objective in this chapter then is to fill some of the gaps in our knowledge about the African atheists or secular humanists in Ghana, one of the most religious nations in West Africa. We are also interested in exploring the magnitude or size of the atheist community in that country. Our central questions in this chapter deal with Ghanaians who self-identify as atheists or non-believers. We pose some of the following questions: How many atheists or secular people are there in Ghana today? Have rates of atheism/secularism increased or decreased in recent decades? Who are these Ghanaians who identify as atheist? Are atheists most likely to come from a certain segment of society or class? Is atheism discouraged by the government, if at all? Are there atheists or secular organizations in Ghana? Do these organizations or movements, if any, play a role in the political arena? Do atheists face any challenges in the country today?

IDENTIFYING ATHEISTS: SOME DEFINITIONAL AND OTHER CHALLENGES

Who is an atheist? One of the key issues confronting the scholar of African religions deals with definitions and the identification of the atheists' population. The terms *"atheism"* and *"secular humanism"* in the context of Ghana, and perhaps other African countries, are difficult to define since they are understood differently by different people. Given this limitation or constraint, we define an atheist loosely in this paper as a person who "does not believe in the existence of God" or "one who claims no religious affiliation." In the discussion, we will broaden the term to include secular humanists and freethinkers.

In Ghana, there are those who do not claim any identification with any religion and do not believe in God. They call themselves atheists or agnostics. There are also those who claim to be Christians but reject a belief in God and describe themselves as atheists. These individuals may or may not be active in any church communities. For example, some of our survey respondents in 2008 did not find any inconsistencies in claiming to be Christians and at the same time stating that they do not believe in the existence of the Judeo-Christian God. However, there are other traditional Christians who challenge the self-identification by these Christians who claim to be atheists. According to these critics, how can one call himself/herself a Christian without believing in Christ, as God incarnate, "the ground of salvation"? While some Ghanaians debate these definitions about who is a Christian and who is not, others both in the country and other societies do not find the term *atheist* and the claim to be a Christian objectionable. Along these discussions Ghanaians are not unique. For example, in the United States, some Unitarian-Universalists self-identify as Christians but do not believe in God.

Another challenge faced by Ghanaian atheists has to do with other peoples' attitudes toward them. For example, during the field survey, any time we introduced ourselves to people including university professors and students and told them about the purpose of our research, we were frequently informed that Ghanaians are generally reluctant to identify themselves as atheists for fear of being ridiculed or stigmatized by others. Those who called attention to this attitude always added that atheists or secular humanists may not be physically attacked if they identify themselves as atheists but may be criticized or ridiculed by the community. In explaining this attitude, the people who talked to us stated that since the overwhelming majority of Ghanaians are Christians, the messages from some of the pulpits of these churches indicate an urgency to convert non-Christians and that would include atheists. Therefore, they pointed out that the appeals or the attacks are not specifically aimed at atheists but at people who have not accepted Christianity as the only true way by which people are saved. In sum, the Christians are concerned about their salvation. Whatever interpretation is given to these attitudes from theists, specifically Christians, there is no doubt that atheists are very concerned about the protection of their freedom of expression, the protection of their democratic rights as citizens, and their ability to make their own choices. We also learned that the government has no stance on this issue and does not interfere or harass atheists, or any religious groups for that matter. They all agree that there are constitutional protections for all religions in the nation. On the whole, Ghanaians generally believe that they have freedom to worship. Therefore any harassment, subtle or not, becomes a matter of concern for those who see themselves as victims, especially in a very democratic society like Ghana.

There is another view that claims that the whole idea of atheism is foreign to Africans leading to the accusation that Ghanaian atheists have been influenced by western culture. What these Christian critics have ignored in their argument or fail to notice is that Christianity itself is a foreign religion, influenced heavily by the same western culture. In response Christians counter this criticism by arguing that though it is an imported religion Christianity was established in some North and East African countries including Egypt, Algeria, Tunisia, Libya, Morocco, Sudan, and Ethiopia during the first centuries of the Christian era. In effect Christianity was established in Africa long before it went to some European countries. Therefore the longevity has made it a familiar or close to an indigenous religion in parts of Africa despite the fact that its influence disappeared or waned in some of these areas.

The extent to which this perceived stigma, real or imagined, affects atheists' freedom of expression is not known or easy to measure. What is clear in our study, however, is that it poses a challenge for social researchers because it affects the openness needed between the researcher and the atheist. For example, in our study when asked: *"How do you describe yourself?"* we provided four answers for respondents to choose from. They were requested to circle all the answers that apply. Some simply ignored or skipped the question and did not identify themselves. Some wrote not applicable, and some described themselves as Christians but do not believe in the existence of God. We attempt to explain these responses by saying that some of these respondents probably did not understand the meaning of the question or that they were afraid to identify themselves. However, we believe it is the latter because the trained research assistants insisted that they explained the key terms to the respondents.

METHODS

Despite the limitations we have alluded to earlier for the scholar studying atheism in Ghana, we have drawn on a limited set of data to provide some insights into the atheists or secular humanist community in that country. For this study, we relied on data from two main sources. The first data comes from a survey conducted in Ghana in July and August 2008 among a segment of Ghanaians including respondents from the University of Ghana, Legon, some areas in Accra, Takoradi, and also Keta and surrounding areas.[7] With the help of trained research assistants from the University of Ghana, those selected for the study were interviewed on a host of questions dealing with religion and atheism in Ghana. Of those interviewed (n = 96), nearly half (49.5 percent) were between the ages of 18 and 29, another 24 percent were between 30 and 40 years old. Two out of every three people surveyed was male (68.8 percent). In addition, about 60 percent of our respondents had some formal education beyond the primary level. This includes those who said they had a secondary (high-school) education, had attended a training college, or similar higher institutions such as a Technical school or university. There were also professionals such as pharmacists, medical officers and managers, a soldier and a police officer and a farmer. Over-all, slightly more than two-thirds of our sample were urban residents (68.8 percent).

Because the first data set is limited in many ways (for example, it was not broadly representative of Ghanaians and was a small sample size), we decided to use a second data set that is nationally representa-tive and has some information on religion in Ghana—albeit the ques-tions did not ask about atheism. This data set is the Ghana Demographic and Health Survey (GDHS) which have been conducted since the mid-1980s. So far, four separate surveys have been conducted as part of the GDHS—1988, 1993, 1998, and 2003. These cross-sectional surveys (GDHS) were designed to provide policy makers with the most up-to-date information on demographic and health processes in Ghana. The sample employed a two-stage cluster sampling method using enu-meration areas (EAs) as the sampling frame in identifying the women who were interviewed. In all, about 150 EAs were used to identify households from the various ecological zones, and rural and urban localities. From these households, women aged 15–49 were surveyed. Since the 1990s, men aged 15–59 have also been surveyed under the auspices of the DHS. To better represent the population, the sample was weighted using a weighting factor developed by DHS.

In addition to the demographic and health items—the main focus of the DHS surveys, the GDHS also collected detailed information on the respondents' socio-demographic characteristics, including for example, their age, education, place of residence, and religious affiliation. Reli-gious affiliation was ascertained by asking the respondents the following question: "What religion do you belong to?" Responses to this question were used to construct a measure of religious affiliation or involvement that had the following values: Catholics, Protestants, other Christians, Muslims, traditionalists, and those who reported no religion. It is the responses on religion that we use for our analysis. Since we are inter-ested in the nonreligious group, we created a new variable which was coded as "1" if the respondents said they were not affiliated with any religious traditions in Ghana and "0" for all others.[8] Because comparable data that allow us to track changes over time are available only for the women sample, the analysis we report here is restricted to women.[9]

FINDINGS

Results from our interviews, which involved both fixed-choice responses and narrative accounts, provide some information about the atheist community in Ghana. Since we were interested in getting infor-mation about the atheist community, one of our questions asked them to tell us how they describe themselves. The most cited definitions by our respondents were: "no belief in the existence of God," "having

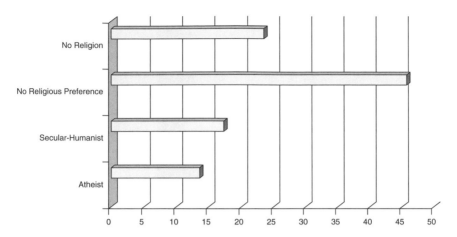

Figure 4.1. Religious Beliefs and Self-Description of Study Respondents

no religion/no belief in any religion," and "not religious." Indeed Figure 4.1 shows that 14 percent of those interviewed identify themselves as atheists, 17 percent secular humanists, and the remainder indicating that they have no religious preferences or no religious affiliation. These observations are not surprising as it should be pointed out that some Unitarian-Universalists claim to be Christians and atheists at the same time because they do not believe in God. Thus, most of the definitions given by our respondents seem to fit perfectly what we expected about atheism in Ghana.

On how long they have been atheists, the majority of our respondents said "for a long time" or what others indicated "many years." On the reasons given for becoming atheists, several of the people responded as follows: "disappointed with Christianity." Others indicated they had no time for religion, or were disenchanted with the clergy, or following family traditions.

On the question of the size of the atheist community, when asked *"In your estimation, how many atheists or secularists do you think are in Ghana today?"* The answers ranged from a few hundreds to some thousands, and others estimated about 1 percent (out of a population of twenty million). Twenty of the respondents said they had no idea or were not sure. The rest gave varying answers from "a few people" to "many." Another twenty-eight respondents did not answer that question, making us to believe the veracity of their responses to this question. Indeed we suggest that the lack of knowledge on the part of these respondents makes it more difficult to have any realistic assessment of the size of atheists in Ghana. Thus, the actual size of atheist population in Ghana is open to a wide interpretation. We asked whether they think the rate of atheism/secularism in Ghana has increased or

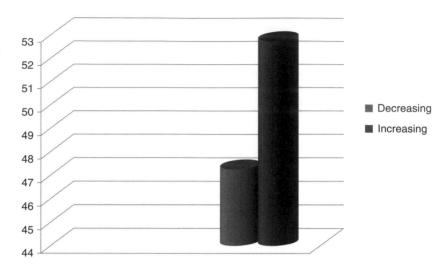

Figure 4.2. Is Atheism increasing or decreasing in Ghana?

decreased in recent years, half of the respondents (50 percent) said that based on their knowledge, they believe atheism is on the rise rather than decline in Ghana (Figure 4.2).

On the question of why is it so difficult to obtain this information, the first reason cited by our informants was the stigma previously discussed that is attached to atheists, secular humanists, and freethinkers simply because they do not believe in the existence of the Judeo-Christian God. For those who claim a belief in other gods such as practitioners of African Traditional Religions, their critics, especially Christians perceive the traditional gods as idols and not gods and hope that one day these traditionalists would convert and accept Christ as their savior. Others had noticed or experienced some verbal criticisms from the pulpits or from other religious leaders or organizations, or individuals against atheists and secular humanists.

According to the respondents, some of whom were University of Ghana students, there are no known atheist or secular-humanist associations on their campus or the other state-owned university campuses. It is also not likely that they are at the other state universities. A number of the private universities are owned by churches and are not likely places for these organizations though most of their students have no affiliation with these universities they attend. Indeed, when asked whether they knew of any organizations in the country that cater specifically to the interests of atheists, most of them (90 percent) responded in the negative. Among the reasons cited for the absence of an organization devoted to unaffiliated people in Ghana was the idea that since most people do not want others to know of their private

Table 4.1
Knowledge and views on atheism, 2008 Ghana atheists survey

	%	n
Know of any atheists		
No	56.4	53
Yes	43.6	41
Is rate of athesim increasing or decreasing		
Decreasing	47.3	43
Increasing	52.7	48
Know of secularist organizations in Ghana		
No	90.3	84
Yes	9.7	9
Class background of atheists in Ghana		
No	92.1	82
Yes	7.9	7
Are atheists discriminated against in Ghana		
No	61.3	57
Yes	38.7	36
Are atheists stigmatized in Ghana		
No	21.5	20
Yes	78.5	73
Total	100.0	96

*Because of the exclusion of missing cases, the sample size may not add up to 96 in some cases.

lives, there is no need to associate with such organizations that may expose them to the public. If atheists are reluctant to make their stands open it means the stigma is intimidating them and therefore do not want to expose themselves to ridicule. We probed such an observation by inquiring about discrimination and stigmatization of nonreligious believers in Ghana. While about 39 percent of the participants said they were discriminated against, most of them said they face some form of stigmatization in the country (see Table 4.1).

Overall, the findings from our survey suggest an absence of any reliable information about the size of the atheist community in Ghana. We compensated for these data limitations by analyzing responses given by a representative sample of women on their religious identity to provide some rough estimates of this population. In the four surveys that have been conducted in Ghana as part of the Demographic and Health

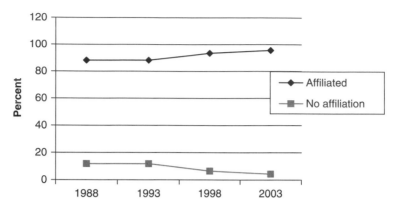

Figure 4.3. Changes in the the affiliated and unaffliated population in Ghana, 1988–2003

Surveys, the respondents were asked to indicate their religious affiliation. Those who did not identify with any of the religious groups were classified as unaffiliated or nonreligious (Figure 4.3). It is the latter group that we use as proxy variable to identify what we believe may be the atheist population in the country.[10]

Contrary to what the survey respondents indicated, our analysis of data from the 1988, 1993, 1998, and 2003 Ghana Demographic and Health Surveys indicate that the proportion of Ghanaians who identify themselves as nonreligious has actually been declining.[11] From a high of 12 percent in the late 1980s, by 2003 the nonreligious population in Ghana had declined to about 4 percent, an eight percentage point difference or change between the two time periods. Interestingly enough, as the population of nonreligious Ghanaians declines, so do we see a corresponding increase in the respondents who belong to some religious communities. Such a finding is consistent with recent reports about the growing religiosity of Ghanaians (see Gallup International 2002).

In Table 4.2 we examined the characteristics of the Ghanaian women surveyed as part of the DHS by their religious affiliation. We do this to provide some insights into the background of the affiliated and the unaffiliated in Ghana. In 1988, 4,488 women were surveyed, of whom 3,957 said they were affiliated with some religious organization and 531 said they were not. Among the affiliated women (n = 3,957) 20.9 percent had never been married. In contrast, only 11.5 percent of the unaffiliated or nonreligious women (n = 531) had never been married. However there were more currently married women among the unaffiliated (78.95 percent) than the affiliated (69.2 percent) group. In terms of education, the percentage of religious women who had some education was higher (63.9 percent) than those reported among the nonreligious women (32.6 percent). Even though more than half (55 percent)

Table 4.2
Marital status, education, and ethnic identity of religious and non-religious Ghanaians, GDHS, 1988–2003

	1988 Affiliated	1988 No Affiliation	1993 Affiliated	1993 No Affiliation	1998 Affiliated	1998 No Affiliation	2003 Affiliated	2003 No Affiliation
Marital Status								
Never married	20.9	11.5	21.2	6.9	24.3	14.1	29.3	9.6
Currently married	69.2	78.9	68.3	84.9	64.0	74.4	61.5	80.4
Formerly married	9.9	9.6	10.5	8.2	11.7	11.5	9.2	10.0
Education								
None	36.0	67.4	30.8	66.5	26.8	63.3	26.1	74.7
Elem	55.6	31.5	57.8	31.8	18.0	18.2	20.1	16.5
HS	7.3	1.1	9.6	1.5	52.8	18.5	51.0	8.8
PostHS	1.0		1.8	0.2	2.4		2.7	
Ethnicity								
Akan	55.3	36.2	52.5	28.8	54.8	37.6	51.8	27.1
Ga&Adg	9.2	6.2	8.6	3.5	8.4	6.4	8.4	4.0
Ewe	15.7	17.9	13.7	23.4	15.6	19.1	12.9	18.3
Mole&Dag	9.2	24.3	13.7	29.7	6.7	8.6	12.4	21.9
Others	10.6	15.4	11.5	4.5	14.5	28.3	14.6	28.7
Urban Residence								
No	64.3	79.1	59.2	85.3	62.9	81.8	50.1	82.8
Yes	35.7	20.9	40.8	14.7	37.1	18.2	49.9	17.2
N	3957	531	4024	538	4529	314	5441	250

of all Akans report some affiliation, among the unaffiliated also, they represent slightly more than a third of the population (36.2 percent). This pattern is to be expected as Akans account for nearly half of the population in Ghana. The other groups with a sizable proportion of unaffiliated women are Mole Dagbanis (24 percent) and Ewes (18 percent). It is clear for all four survey years those rural women are more likely to be unaffiliated compared to their urban folks. For the most part, the pattern reported for the 1988 sample is similar to that of the women surveyed in the subsequent years.

ATHEISM AND THE CHANGING CULTURAL CONTEXT

Ghana is generally characterized as a traditional society because the majority of the population is engaged in agricultural production. One may be right in describing it as a nation on the road of modernization, though it has not yet arrived. It is rapidly becoming a modern society as many people move into the cities, resulting in a breakdown of the traditional family and other social structures. Modern technology is bridging some of the gaps between traditional and urban culture. For example, millions of Ghanaians in rural and urban areas alike have cell phones, televisions, and other modern amenities. They are learning to manipulate modern technology. Obviously, this is only one factor in modernization. In addition, there have been changes in the relationship of religion to the modern society, often referred to as secularization. In many ways secularization is having an impact on the Ghanaian society. The concept of secularization, originally developed by Max Weber, has many meanings. For example, Weber's meaning refers to a society or a social system that appears to be less dependent on religious legitimation (1951, 1952, 1958b, 1963; see also Martin 1969, 1978). Paul Ricoeur describes it as "the emancipation of most human activities from the influence of ecclesiastical institutions" (see Stewart and Bien 1974, cited in Monk et al. 2003, 287). The term may also imply a "greater institutional differentiation and a more rational, utilitarian, and empiricist outlook on life and on decision making by individuals and groups" (Roberts 2004, 306; see also Berger 1967, 1979). These definitions demonstrate how difficult it is to define the term because of its many meanings.

We now turn briefly to the reasons that led some of our respondents to become atheists. Toward that goal we posed a general question: what are the reasons or factors which led you to atheism? We wanted to know if any aspects of modernization or secularization have contributed to the factors that led our respondents to become atheists. One of the initial assumptions was that our respondents would include in their descriptions aspects of secularization or modernization as some of the major factors that have shaped their lives in the cities where they pursued especially their education and professional life. Most likely many became atheists in the urban areas where they live. The survey had actually indicated that majority of the respondents live in urban areas.

On the one hand, the Ghanaian religious arena indicates a sense in which religion has lost some of its influence on the larger society. For example, in the traditional past chiefs had tremendous power and influence over their people and in the traditional religious arena they were the symbols of religious authority. Although chiefs continue to play constructive roles in their traditional areas, they no longer assert the same powerful religio-cultural and political influence on their people. Church organizations played similar powerful roles within their church structures. However, today values of the larger society that are reflected in the Ghanaian Constitution and in other areas of Ghanaian life are not necessarily religious values. Politicians are not elected based on any religious criteria. However, one may not be able to separate religious moral values from political and other values that help shape the society as a whole.

There are many social scientists who are still involved in the secularization debate. For example, Swatos rightly points out that since the "1980s the concept of secularization has become a contested discussion among scholars who debate its predictive and descriptive accuracy and continued relevance in the postmodern world" (2006).

Following the secularization debate and its impact on religion, Berger has noted that "the world today, with some exceptions is as furiously religious as it ever was, and in some places more so than ever" (1992, 2; cited in Roberts 2006, 310). One thing that is clear in Ghana and many parts of Africa is that secularization has not shown any evidence of the decline of religions. We also do not see any evidence that secularization has any specific effect on the growth or decline of atheism in the country. Future research in this area is needed to fill the knowledge gap. Our study shares a similar conclusion with Roberts, who states that the movement toward a purely secular outlook is not an inevitable process that spells a substantial and long-term decline of religion. He further points out that rational theorists argue that secularization does not mean a decline of religion, but it may entail a reformation of traditional religions and the spawning of new religious movements (2006, 313). There is no doubt that some of the Catholic and Protestant churches are in decline, but numerous Pentecostal or Charismatic churches have sprung up, especially since the 1980s, in urban and rural areas in Ghana. Among them are mega-churches that Ghana had never before seen.

CONCLUSIONS

Our focus in this study is to fill in some knowledge gaps about African atheists, secular humanists, and freethinkers in Ghana. There is no doubt that atheism has established some roots in Ghana. To a large majority of Ghanaians, the society promotes the freedom of all religions. However, although the majority of the respondents believe that Ghana enjoys freedom of religion, some of the respondents as well as some scholars who did not participate in the survey believe that there is some stigma attached to atheists in Ghana. They all believe that there is no reason to believe that atheists will be physically harmed because of who they are. In an interview when we posed the question: How can this be addressed, the key word from a number of them is *education*. Many of them also believe that with a stable democratic political system and increasing freedom of speech in the society, atheists like most other groups may enjoy the privileges granted by the constitution. They look forward to unhindered freedom to form free associations without any stigma attached to their beliefs. One hopes that effective education will promote affirmation of religious diversity in the nation.

This study has achieved a limited goal. For example, we still know little about atheists in Ghana. There is not sufficient evidence to indicate that atheism is growing or declining in Ghana. It is our hope that any future study of atheism in the country will include an examination of these issues. At least for now, unlike the United States where some of the old laws still exist in some states that prevent nontheists from holding office (Cimino and Smith 2007, 407), Ghana has no laws targeted against atheists or freethinkers as a whole.

NOTES

1. The growth is not reported among Christians only because there have been widespread reports from the region about the growing influence of Islam as well.

2. More than 96 percent of the population surveyed in a 2000 Gallup International poll considered themselves as religious (Gallup International 2000).

3. Christians in Ghana run the gamut of the various denominations, ranging from mainline Protestants, Evangelicals, Catholics, African Independent Churches, and Assemblies of God to Seventh Day Adventists.

4. Indeed besides the mainline Christian denominations (i.e., old established churches) such as Protestants and Catholics, growth has risen in the population of "other Christians" or denominations. The latter include a collection of groups that include African syncretic, and faith-healing organizations, as well as charismatic and Pentecostal Churches, whose growth has been phenomenal (Yirenkyi 1999; Gifford 1998).

5. We consider these people as Ghanaians who do not believe in God and do not consider themselves religious.

6. The literature includes some of the following best-selling books: Richard Dawkins, *The God Delusion*; Sam Harris, *The End of Faith* and *Letter to a Christian Nation*; Christopher Hitchens, *God Is Not Great: How Religion Poisons Everything.*

7. These people were not randomly selected and ranged in age between the ages of 18 and 70.

8. We acknowledge the limitations in our using these unaffiliated women as provided by the recoded GDHS files as proxy indicator for atheists.

9. Data on men were collected in the 1993 survey, but it was limited to only a select sample of men whose wives were interviewed. Since then, detailed information about Ghanaian men has been collected, but given our interest in looking at trends, these data are not included in our analysis. Moreover, existing studies also indicate that African women tend to be more religious than their male counterparts, so we suspect that this restriction would in no way affect the basic results of our study.

10. We acknowledge the potential limitations arising from our use of this group of people to identify atheists, but given that there was a category for all those who claim a belief in African traditional religions, we sincerely believe that the unaffiliated ones are probably secularist.

11. This is true if we think the "nonreligious group" members are the same as those who self-identified as atheists in the 2008 survey.

REFERENCES

Aboagye, M. R. 1994. *Mission and democracy in Africa: The role of the Church.* Accra, Ghana: Asempa Press.

Agbeti, Kofi J. 1986. *West African church history: Christian missions and church foundations: 1482–1919* Leiden: E. J. Brill.

Assimeng, M. 1986. *Saints and social structures.* Tema: Ghana Publishing.

Barrett, B. David, and M. Todd Johns. 2001. *World Christian trends, AD 30 2200.* Pasadena, CA: William Carey Library.

Bediako, K. 1995. *Christianity in Africa: Renewal of a non-Western religion.* Edinburgh: Edinburgh University Press.

Berger, Peter. 1967. *The sacred canopy.* Garden City, NY: Doubleday.

Berlinski, David. 2008. *The Devil's delusion: Atheism and its scientific pretensions.* New York: Crown Forum.

Christian History Institute. 2006. The explosion of Christianity in Africa: An unprecedented spread of faith. *Glimpses Bulletin* 151.

Cream, Thomas. 2007. *God is no delusion: A refutation of Richard Dawkins.* San Francisco: Ignatius Press.

Dawkins, Richard. 2006. *The God delusion.* New York: Houghton Mifflin.

Der, B. G. 2001. Christian missions and the expansion of Western education in Northern Ghana, 1906–1975. In *Regionalism and public policy in Northern Ghana, ed.* Y. Saaka, 107–38. New York: Peter Lang Publishing.

Ellis, Stephen, and G. Haar. 1998. Religion and politics in sub-Saharan Africa. *Journal of Modern African Studies* 36:175–201.

Flew, Anthony, and Roy Abraham Varghese. 2007. *There is no God: How the world's most notorious atheist changed his mind.* New York: Harper.

Ghana Statistical Service (GSS) and Macro International (MI). 1999. Ghana Demographic and Health Survey Country Report. Accra and Washington, D.C.

Gifford, P. 1994a. Some recent developments in African Christianity. *African Affairs* 93:513–534.

———— 1994b. Ghana's charismatic churches. *Journal of Religion in Africa* 24: 241–265.

————. 1995. *The Christian churches and the democratization of Africa.* New York: E. J. Brill.

————. 1998. *African Christianity. Its public role.* London: C. Hurst & Co.

Gyimah, S. O., Baffour K. Takyi, and Eric Yeboah Tenkorang. 2008. Denominational affiliation and fertility behavior in an African context: An examination of couple data from Ghana. *Journal of Biosocial Science* 40:445–458.

———, B. K. Takyi, and K. Addai. 2006. Challenges to the reproductive-health needs of African women: On religion and maternal health utilization in Ghana. *Social Science & Medicine* 62:2930–2944.

Haught, John F. 2008. *God and the new atheism: A critical response to Dawkins, Harris, and Hitchens.* Louisville: Westminster John Knox Press.

Hahn, Scott, and Benjamin Wiker. 2008. *Answering the new atheism: Dismantling Dawkin's case against God.* Steubenville, OH: Emmaus Road Publishing.

Harris, Sam. 2007. An Athiest Manifesto. New York: Knopf. http://www. truthdig.com/dig/item/200512_an_atheist_manifesto/ (accessed August 31, 2009).

Hedges, Chris. 2008. *I don't believe in atheists.* New York: Free Press.

Hemeyer, Julia. 2006. *Religion in America.* 5th ed. Upper Sadler River, NJ: Pearson Prentice-Hall.

———. 2006. Freedom from Religion Foundation. www.ffrf.org.

Hitchens, Christopher. 2007. *God is not great: How religion poisons everything.* New York: Twelve Books, Hachette Book Group.

———. 2007. *The portable atheist: Essential reading for the nonbeliever.* Cambridge, MA: Da Capo Press.

Idowu, E. B. 1967. Orita. *Ibadon Journal of Religious Studies* 1 (1).

———. 1973. *African Traditional religion: A definition.* London: SCM Press.

Jakobson, Janet R, and Ann Pellegrini. 2008. *Secularisms.* Durham: Duke University Press.

Kiliani, Method. 2001. Ecumenism in a multi-religious context. Ecumenical Review 53 (1): 358+.

Mbiti, John. 1991. *Introduction to African religions.* 2nd rev. ed. Johannesburg, South Africa: Heinemann International.

Meyer, Birgit. 2004. Christianity in Africa: From African independent to pente-costal-charismatic churches. *Annual Review of Anthropology* 33:447–474.

Monk, Robert C., Walter C. Hofheints, Kenneth T. Lawrence, Joseph D. Stamey, Burt Affleck, and Tetsunao Yamamori. 2003. *Exploring religious meaning.* 6th ed. Upper Saddle River, NJ: Prentice Hall.

Ninsin, K. A, and F. K. Drah. 1991. *Ghana's transition to constitutional rule.* Accra, Ghana: Universities Press.

Opoku, Kofi, A. 1978. *West African traditional religion.* Accra: FEP International Private Limited.

Philip, Jenkins. 2003. *The next Christendom: The coming of global Christianity.* New York: Oxford University Press.

Pobee, J. S. 1991. *Religion and politics in Ghana.* Accra, Ghana: Asempa Publishers.

Ray, Benjamin C. 2000. *African religions: Symbol, ritual, and community.* 2nd ed. Upper Saddle River, NJ: Prentice Hall.

Roberts, Keith. 2006. *Religion in sociological perspective.* 4th ed. Belmont, CA Wadsworth.

Smart, Ninian. 1995. Worldviews: Crosscultural explorations of human beliefs. 2nd ed. Englewood Cliffs, NJ: Prentice Hall.

Swatos, William H, Jr., and Daniel V. A. Olson. 2006. *The secularization debate.* Totowa, NJ: Rowman & Littlefield.

Takyi, B. K. 2003. Religion and women's health in Ghana: Insight into HIV/ AIDS preventive and protective behavior. *Social Science & Medicine* 56:1221–1234.

Takyi, Baffour K, and Isaac Addai. 2002. Religious affiliation and women's educational attainment and empowerment in a developing society. *Sociology of Religion* 63:177–193.

Van der Geest, K. 2004. We are managing! Vulnerability and responses to climate variability and change among rural households in northwest Ghana. Master's Thesis, Faculty of Social and Behavioural Sciences, University of Amsterdam.

Weber, M. 1958a. *The Protestant ethic and the spirit of capitalism.* Translated by Talcott Parsons. New York: Scribner. Originally Published in 1904–1905.

Yirenkyi, K. 1999. *Research in the social scientific study of religion.* Vol. 10, 171– 189. Stamford, CT: JAI Press.

———. 2000. The role of Christian churches in national politics: Reflections from laity and clergy in Ghana. *Sociology of Religion* 61 (3) 325–338.

Chapter 5

The Triumph of Indifference: Irreligion in British Society

Samuel Bagg
David Voas

In December of 2007, the leader of Britain's Liberal Democratic Party told a reporter that he did not believe in God. It caused a minor stir in the papers, but nothing came of it. In fact, it was quickly forgotten; far more notable that month was Tony Blair's long-awaited conversion to Catholicism. Hardly anyone was surprised or upset that Nick Clegg, the leader of Britain's third-largest party, was an atheist: the only curiosity was his choice to make that public. Faith of any kind tends to be treated as a private matter in Britain, so the public declarations of both Clegg and Blair were regarded as "unusual."[1] While a British politician's secular political beliefs must of course be considered by his constituents, his religious convictions are typically kept quiet; they could only distract from the important political issues. To a Briton, this all makes perfect sense: religion, or the lack of it, is simply irrelevant to policy-making. In fact, its recent prominence, exemplified by Blair's public faith, is widely seen as an infringement of some kind on the natural British system.

Of course, this system is not universal across the developed world, and one of Britain's closest cultural kin—the United States—provides a particularly striking contrast. Faith in America is fiercely public, and the lack of it a shameful deficiency. One can only imagine the scandal that would ensue if a major party leader or presidential candidate in the United States were to make a similar admission: it would be political suicide. According to a recent study, atheists are the most despised minority in the country, consistently ranking lower than blacks, Muslims, and homosexuals on a number of different measures.[2] Britain, on the other hand, is far more tolerant of unbelief. Atheists, for the most part, are normal citizens. Like some religious fundamentalists, they can be perceived as "too extreme" if they act outside of a certain framework, but so long as they don't proselytize too aggressively or seriously advocate the abolition of religion from all spheres of life, their private rejection of religion is of no consequence.

A BRIEF HISTORY OF AVOWED ATHEISM IN BRITAIN

In the history of the world, the status of atheists in modern Britain is unique. Indeed, even in Britain religious attitudes were not always so permissive. Historian David Berman writes about the repressive stance that seventeenth- and eighteenth-century British authorities took toward atheism, whereby religious authors denied that rational, convinced atheists could even exist. The 1771 entry on "Atheism" from the *Encyclopedia Britannica* reads "It is justly questioned whether any man seriously adopted such a [nontheistic] principle. These pretensions, therefore, must be founded on pride or affectation." According to Berman, this was part of an effort to delegitimize the agendas of atheism's proponents and discourage its acceptance among the Christian population. Whether or not the repression was a conscious process on the part of *Britannica's* authors and the many others who made similar statements, Berman argues convincingly that such proclamations at least had that effect.[3] Even the intellectual elite were not spared: Hobbes and Hume were both heavily criticized for atheistic sentiments in their writings, and as late as 1811 Percy Shelley was expelled from Oxford for authoring an atheistic pamphlet.[4]

Starting in the mid-nineteenth century, though, atheism—once unique to eccentric intellectuals—became associated with radical politics and the working class uprisings of that period. The Church was essential to the power structure that reformers like Robert Owen, George Jacob Holyoake, and Charles Bradlaugh sought to overcome.[5] Their popularity across all classes helped to lend legitimacy to their beliefs. Bradlaugh, the most "thorough" of the three in his atheism, drew enormous crowds to his speeches against the church and even served in Parliament after a long and much-publicized battle over the oath of allegiance. Initially, he was not allowed to take his seat because it involved swearing to "Almighty God," and his word as an atheist could not be trusted. However, he was finally allowed to serve after winning several reelections and worked to legalize an alternative to the oath. Bradlaugh founded the National Secular Society (NSS) in 1866 as local secular societies flourished all across Britain.[6]

The atheistic overtones of many of these reform movements were largely a reaction to the religious revival of the Victorian era, however, and when the revival began to lose momentum, so did the movement for "secularism," as Holyoake had named it. As passionate religion fell out of fashion, so too did fervent denial of it. Secular societies declined in number and membership, and the movement gradually died down.[7] Though public intellectuals like Bertrand Russell, A. J. Ayer, and Chapham Cohen kept on denying God in their writing and speeches, atheism as a movement lay dormant in Britain for decades.[8] But the stage had been set, and atheistic opinions had lodged themselves in the British mind: as the twentieth century progressed, British opinion on the subject evolved slowly and without fanfare toward acceptance of atheism as a legitimate ideology.

By the time atheism resurfaced as one line of attack on the establishment during the social revolution of the 1960s, it had been integrated within a rationalistic moral philosophy and life stance dubbed "humanism." One effect of this reframing trick was that the atheistic viewpoint no longer appeared as a simple rejection of God or Christianity—and in fact, many Christian moral tenets are mimicked in humanist ethics. When the Anglican Church fought against the women's and gay rights movements, though, they were harshly rebuked on nonreligious moral grounds. The British Humanist Association (BHA), the second of the two major secular activist groups, was born during this revival of radical politics.[9]

The BHA, amalgamated from several different preexisting groups in 1963, is quite different in character from the NSS, which was founded in an era with relatively few secular people. As a result, the main goal of the NSS was tearing down the privileges afforded to religion; as noted above, this is still its major stated objective.[10] It is often seen as more categorically antireligious than the BHA, which was founded when far more people were ready to reject the reigning religious paradigms and so could afford to be more conciliatory in its stance against religion. The BHA merely had to voice the concerns of the many who already supported their positions, rather than convince a religious supermajority that it shouldn't mix religion with politics.

Both organizations survive to this day, but as a result of the conditions under which they were formed, the NSS focuses more on the protection of the secular from the abuse of the religious and the radical separation of church and state, whereas the BHA seeks to provide concrete alternatives to religion, in the form of the humanist moral system and replacement ceremonies, such as weddings, funerals, and baby-namings. To put it a different way, the NSS is abolitionist toward religion—they would get rid of it entirely—whereas the BHA is substitutionist: they would replace it with something that has a similar function but different content. The memberships of both groups have fluctuated in sync with the prominence of religion in public discourse, but even at their heights, both could claim only a miniscule following compared to that of the churches. Like many lobbying groups, however, they have a larger national presence and far more political influence than their memberships would suggest.[11]

In 1965, a survey question asked respondents whether they would vote for a prime minister who was otherwise qualified and represented their preferred party, but who did not believe in God. Fifty-eight percent of British voters answered that they would.[12] This may seem low at first, but it shows a stark contrast with the United States, where the parallel figure at the time was below 20 percent;[13] today, the United States still polls with less than 50 percent of the voting public expressing confidence in an atheist candidate.[14] By contrast, Britain's Parliamentary Humanist Group—with members across both houses and all major parties—counts over 80 openly atheistic members of Parliament among its ranks.[15] Additionally, it is commonly accepted that certain Labour leaders have been atheists, though they never made a point to publicize their views.[16] One commentator has written, rather aptly, that

> if one considers that, in 1842, George Jacob Holyoake was jailed for professing atheism, but that 160 years later, in 2002, British atheism's most pressing concern was its ongoing exclusion from Radio 4's *Thought for the Day* (allegedly a breach of human rights!), it becomes clear quite how much acceptance and toleration it has gained in such a relatively short time.[17]

Indeed, since the revival of the 1960s and 1970s, the radicalism associated with atheism has all but disappeared.

Instead, the British pride themselves on their self-proclaimed "moderation," tending to view both fundamentalist religion and "militant" or crusading atheism with skepticism, but being quite tolerant of anything in between. Britons have become more "secular" in their everyday lives (churchgoing, membership, and Sunday School enrollments have all been in decline for over a century) but this doesn't necessarily mean an increased prominence for atheism. On the contrary, being "secular" often means simply not caring enough about religion either to defend *or* deny it, so active atheism as a phenomenon is most often a feature of particularly religious societies. Even the "New Atheists" who have appeared in the past decade—Hitchens, Dawkins, and the rest—fit this trend: first, they have all appeared since 9/11 as religion has become increasingly important to global society; and second, they are largely based in America—even the British among them have frequently directed their gaze across the pond.

In the Victorian era, with conservative evangelical churches attracting huge crowds,[18] there was a reaction that culminated in the founding of the NSS. In an era when the Church was campaigning hard against an onslaught of social reforms, the BHA pushed back. And in an era when fundamentalist Islam is the newest perceived threat to Western culture, the New Atheists are among those who have answered the call to fight the negative impact of religion. But for most of the time, between these surges in religious fervor, British unbelief doesn't have a particularly fearsome enemy in the Anglican Church. In a society where earnest religion is often not taken seriously and where a religious prime minister worries about being considered a "nutter,"[19] the motivation for atheists to fight against the status quo is hardly compelling. When the twin pillars of the monarchy and the Established Church, once the foundation of British society, have become little more than decorative artifacts in the eyes of most citizens, atheists have little to worry about.

Nevertheless, the British character is also deeply reverent; a distinctly Burkean pathos is still present behind the "consumer society" that characterizes modern-day Britain. The fact that the Monarchy and the Established Church still exist at all speaks volumes about the quintessentially British respect for authority and tradition, especially in light of the abolition of both institutions in many of its European neighbors. After all, the current status of religion is only noticeably poor because of its former prominence. It is still by far the most widely attended voluntary activity,[20] and more than 70 percent of British people still identify, however weakly, as Christian.[21] Though church attendance is very low in comparison to former totals, there is a widespread feeling that religion—and in particular the Church of England—is a good thing to have around. Many parents strive to send their children to "faith" schools, where the injection of religion into the daily routine is supposed to encourage a more obedient and successful "ethos."[22] A prayer before the opening of the houses of Parliament, the presence of bishops in the House of Lords, and the Queen's role as the head of the church are all taken for granted by a majority of Britons; though a few certainly question all three of these practices, the tide shows no signs of turning against them.

In light of this conflicted attitude, Liberal Democratic leader Nick Clegg was left in an awkward position as he both asserted his unbelief and attempted to cast his position as neither extreme nor anti-Christian. "I have enormous respect for religious people," he quickly explained, and followed that by pledging to raise his children as Christians with the help of his Catholic wife. To top it off, he maintained that though he was not an "active" believer, he had an "open heart and an open mind" about the subject of religion.[23] Clegg's situation was not unlike that of the British people, muddling through a confusing, mismatched set of beliefs and rarely practicing and yet unwilling to give up the sense of Christian-ness that has been central to the formation of British identity and culture.

SOCIAL SCIENTIFIC APPROACHES

In common usage, the term "atheism" denotes a conscious, active disbelief in God. By its roots, however, it means "a" + "theos": living "without" or "away from" God. Though we've just laid out a history of distinctly avowed atheism, the truth is that in modern Britain, there are many ways to live without God. Most obvious are the "out-and-out" atheists just described, who are the always visible but also among the smallest groups of the irreligious. But the biggest difference between people, even just regarding their religious behavior, is not their answer to the question of God. Even for many British believers, the role that "God" plays is next to nothing. Some who consider themselves Christians may use this nominal category as an ethnic label rather than a religious one.[24] There are others for whom God has never been a serious factor, and as a result, the very terminology of theism and atheism might not be familiar to them. It is not just the avowed atheists, but all of these people—and anyone in British society who can be fairly called irreligious—that we wish to describe in this chapter.

Traditionally, there are three metrics that social scientists use to measure religiosity: belief, behavior (or practice), and belonging (or affiliation). One might say that people are "perfectly" religious if their beliefs are strong and faithful to a tradition, if they practice in some way on a regular basis, and if their religious affiliation is central to their identity. Thus, we might measure irreligion by the absence of these characteristics and paint the irreligious ideal as disbelieving, nonpracticing, and unaffiliated. However, describing only those people who fit either model would leave most Britons unaccounted for. That is, there are plenty of "Anglicans" whose beliefs could hardly be called orthodox, confirmed theists who never pray or attend church, and nonbelievers who go to the occasional service and identify as Christians. Even Richard Dawkins, probably the most famous living atheist, has called himself a "cultural Christian."[25] Classifying such people as either religious or irreligious can be dangerous, because it ignores the complexities inherent in religious identification.

Each metric in itself is quite complex: we must attempt to gauge not just whether beliefs, practices, and affiliations exist, but also whether their existence is significant to the individuals and faith traditions involved. Belief in supernatural entities, for example, is extremely high, but belief in and understanding of the Trinity is drastically lower. Clearly, the latter belief is a more significant identifier of religiosity than the former. Measurement of behavior is also notoriously difficult, as self-reported church-going is often more than twice as high as observed attendance.

Finally, tracking belonging (that is, the number of people who identify as religious) might appear to be simpler than estimating belief and practice, but it turns out that differences in the way the question is asked can cause significant variation in levels of self-identification. When a tick-box in the context of ethnicity and nationality, for instance, prompts people to self-identify as "Church of England" or "Christian," the numbers for affiliation tend to be far higher than when the relevant question is open-ended. In the 2007 British Social Attitudes survey, which asks respondents if they consider themselves as "belonging to a particular religion" in the context of a wide-ranging review of beliefs and attitudes, fully 46 percent gave no religious identification. By contrast, less than 20 percent answered "none" in a Gallup survey asking, among other census-type questions, "What is your religions denomination?" The only possible explanation is that the Christian affiliation of at least a quarter of the population is so tenuous that it hinges on the wording and context of the question.[26]

THE STATE OF BRITISH SECULARITY

Given these complications, we should begin our analysis with the least complex categories: those who are definitely religious and those who are definitely not. In a recent article titled "The Rise and Fall of Fuzzy Fidelity in Europe,"[27] David Voas uses data from the European Social Survey to define these groups. He classifies someone as "actively religious" if she claims to attend services at least monthly and rates herself as above average on a scale measuring religiosity and "privately religious" if she does not attend church regularly but rates herself similarly highly on scales measuring both religiosity and the "importance of religion" to her life. This way, we find about a quarter of Britons to be religious in some reasonably traditional way: 15 percent actively so and another 10 percent privately. More significant than the mere presence of some religious adherence in these people is the resemblance of their religiosity to established traditions and its importance to their lives.

Is the rest of society irreligious, then? Not quite. To be so unambiguously, by our measures, would require the respondent to attend church and/or pray only at major holidays or less and to rate herself very low on both the religiosity and "importance of religion" scales. On this basis about another quarter of Britons qualify as irreligious.

We are left with half of the British population unaccounted for. This percentage may be called the "woolly middle,"[28] and it exemplifies the ambivalent British attitude toward religion. These numbers are confirmed by the 2008 British Social Attitudes survey suggesting that 17 percent definitely believe in God and another 37 percent either disbelieved God's existence or thought His existence was impossible to make judgments about. Forty-five percent were in the middle somewhere, believing in God only some of the time, having doubts about that belief, or believing only in an impersonal higher power of some kind. Yet another survey found that 18 percent felt that they were "practicing members of an organized religion," another 49 percent were "nonpracticing members of an organized religion" or "spiritual but not religious," and finally another 26 percent were "not religious."[29] Certainly there is some religious or spiritual impulse in this woolly middle, but the ambiguity surrounding it gives the social scientist reason to doubt its significance.

One theory about such fuzzy fidelity explains that dwindling practice and membership in the church over the years is associated with declining willingness to participate in all voluntary organizations,[30] and that sweeping claims about the decline of religion overstate their case. In this view, those with fuzzy fidelity are still Christians in most of the relevant ways. It makes intuitive sense: if one obvious sign of a supposed religious decline can be explained as a result not of detachment from religion itself but simply as one more instance of a pervasive social phenomenon, then perhaps religion is not suffering the drastic fall that is frequently ascribed to it.

However, this thesis depends on the assumption that practice is the only declining variable—or that it is at least declining faster than the others—and this is simply not the case. Belief in God has declined as well, but more notably, those who still hold some sort of fuzzy fidelity hold a different *kind* of belief than the traditionally religious. It is a belief that often does not require them to go to church or pray with any consistency. It is a belief that leaves them unsure of their affiliation to the church. And it is a belief that often rejects major tenets of Christianity, replacing them with some combination of naturalism, alternative spirituality and indifference.

Another explanation of fuzzy fidelity comes from observers like Paul Heelas, Linda Woodhead, and Colin Campbell, who take this tendency toward alternative spiritualities as a sign of the "easternization of the West" or "the spiritual revolution," to use the titles of books by those authors.[31] A decline in traditional adherence accompanied by resilient belief in the supernatural is explained with reference to the increase in Eastern practices like Yoga and meditation. This view is also an alternative to traditional secularization narratives: Heelas et al. theorize that some people are merely switching from one religious tradition to another, rather than abandoning religion entirely. Even they concede, however, that the rise in alternative spirituality is not enough to offset the decline in traditional religiosity.

The most powerful explanation of the woolly middle phenomenon is perhaps the most intuitive: Britons who make up this section of society are between the religious and the irreligious temporally as well as descriptively. In other words, the people who are now in the middle have generally come from parents who are more religious than they are and have children who will be, on average, less so. In this way, fuzzy fidelity is merely a stepping stone between religion and irreligion in an increasingly secular society.

This simplified narrative still misses something about the enormous size of the middle and the persistence of certain characteristics within it; for example, both nominal Christianity and a belief in some sort of God are maintained by almost everyone in this category. And while the woolly middle is somewhere between the religious and the irreligious in terms of religiosity, they tend to have less education and lower incomes than both their religious *and* their irreligious compatriots.[32] This suggests that there is something about higher levels of education and income that lead people to a more definitive stance on religion (be it pious or atheistic) and casts doubt on naive versions of the secularization thesis predicting that higher education and income necessarily lead to greater secularity. Instead, it seems, there is something distinctive about this middle ground, the historical narrative that has led Britain to its creation and the direction it is likely to take in the future.

THEORIZING RELIGIOUS DECLINE

Colin Campbell defines irreligion as a response to the dominant religious culture of a society; thus, irreligion is as varied as its inverse. In any case, the irreligious response generally takes the form either of indifference or hostility to that dominant culture. In societies that are particularly religious, the reaction of hostility is most frequent because when religion is an important cultural force, it must be reckoned with in one way or another. This is the reaction of most of the avowed atheists discussed above, so we'll pause for a moment to examine how it occurs.

Broadly, there are two avenues through which people reach their hostility toward religion: the intellectual and the moral. The product of intellectual rejection is the stereotypical atheist of modernity: the thinker who is no longer satisfied with traditional justifications for God's existence. However, it is likely that moral rejection is far more common, at least in times of swelling irreligion. In the typical moral rejection, an individual begins to realize that her own intuitions contradict the morality enforced by the dominant church and starts to question the truth of religion based on the inadequacy of its moral system. These people may not identify as atheists, but they are certainly irreligious in that they have rejected the dominant religious tradition of their culture. As we've established, when there is a surge in atheism, it is usually because of a reaction to particular actions taken by the church, and so it is likely that a moral rejection is the primary instigator of hostility during such periods.

However, a hostile reaction often fades in the face of changing religious doctrines and norms: indifference is a far more sustainable variety of irreligion. Thus, the story of British secularization is less about the reaction of hostility than that of indifference, and it is the decreasing importance of religion to daily life that has defined the last century of British religious life.

Religious change before the modern era is of an entirely different character than what we see today; even the climate of the early nineteenth century is too dissimilar to serve as a useful comparison. The late Victorian period was the first time that irreligion became a concrete option, when questions like "Do you believe in God?" began to make sense intellectually and when being burned at the stake wasn't the automatic reward for an answer in the negative. It was then that the mechanisms shaping religious decline today began to crystallize.

The most comprehensive data on this era of religious fervor, which is usually said to last from 1850 to 1880, come from the Horace Mann church census of 1851. It can be taken to represent levels throughout that 30-year period, and interestingly enough, it recorded that only about half of Britain's population was attending church in any given week. This is not to say that the other half of Britain was irreligious, just that the religion of the working classes was "dormant and un-influential and peculiar in character," much like the fuzzy fidelity of today.[33] Most of the middle and upper classes attended church, but for the poorer working classes, food, clothing and shelter were too much of a priority to allow time for churchgoing.[34] Thus, "the sense of reli-gious decline after about 1880 was a reflection of the weakening of middle-class churchgoing" rather than a fall from the complete partici-pation of the entire population.[35] Of course, the working class repre-sented most of the population of Britain during this era, and so many of them were also participants in the religious revival that dominated British culture. But there were many who did not, and so the situation of some segments of the Victorian working class—indifferent but still nominally attached—prefigures the situation of the entire population since. Though the distractions of secular culture faced by all Britons nowadays—football, shopping, and sleeping in—are rather different than the "distractions" faced by the working poor in the nineteenth century, the comparison is nonetheless instructive.

Several historical explanations for the decline of British religion in the twentieth century have been provided by recent historical and sociological writing. A particularly influential theory is articulated by social historian Callum Brown, who views the 1960s and early 1970s as a period of revolutionary change in the religious composition of the nation, unmatched by any movement either before or since. Brown suggests that this was the crucial period for secularization in Britain and even dates 1963 as the single most important year.[36] He makes his case by citing the change in public discourse that occurred during that time period, and the sharper declines in certain measures of religiosity that began to appear only after this revolution.

The rapid change in discourse that he notes is real, and cultural norms of the type Brown describes can certainly change measured lev-els of religiosity, but we must examine how this change fits in with the framework we have already outlined. When we use our broader meas-ures from above, it seems that the decline in religiosity is far more gradual than he suggests, without a discontinuity during the 1960s. A more likely explanation of the phenomenon Brown describes is that the revolutionary changes in discourse were the tremors of a society coming to terms with tectonic shifts in the religiosity of its population, shifts that had previously gone unnoticed but had been occurring for generations. Again, this doesn't invalidate Brown's analysis, it merely places it within a larger context.

THE CRUCIAL STORY: GENERATIONAL CHANGE

If we are tracking the religiosity of a population not by evaluating cultural norms, but instead using the three specific dimensions of religiosity articulated in the previous section, we can see two ways in which such variables could rise or decline: change over time within individuals and gaps in transmission between generations. Many factors, in turn, could cause such differences, but any change in religiosity, such as the one posited by Brown, must register in one or the other of these metrics.

Consider one of the most startling figures about British religion: the steady and constant increase in religiosity with age. This could either be the result of "age effects," that is, an increase in religiosity within individuals over time, or "generational effects," a decline in the religiosity of each successive generation, suggesting transmission failure. The relative importance of each effect can be easily determined: if the religiosity of people born around the same time rises as that cohort ages, then we can conclude that age effects are more important. However, if religiosity remains constant as that cohort ages, then we have good evidence that the overall change is mostly due to generational effects, because on average, individuals *within* a birth cohort maintain the same levels of measured religiosity. The data show conclusively that the latter is true: generational effects dominate. Each generation retains its average levels of religiosity, but each successive generation is less religious than the one before. The data on parent-child religious relationships from a different survey also exhibit this pattern, showing that religious parents in Britain have an approximately 50 percent chance of transmitting their affiliation, belief, and practice on to their children, giving religion a "half-life" of one generation.

So why is the transmission of religion so difficult in Britain? The answer is suggested by the two measured variables that tend to be lowest of all and thus can be said to be leading indicators for decline: attendance in church and the importance of religion to daily life. While Christian identification and belief in some sort of God remain high for most of the woolly middle, both of these other measures are almost universally quite low. This phenomenon may be an example of "behavioral drift," which refers to the way that religious practice can erode irrespective of changes in belief or affiliation.[37] People may stop going to church so often, but they will still identify with the religion of their birth and often believe in the same God. Religious practice is more immediate and has more competition than either belief or affiliation; regular practice demands time and energy, while maintaining belief and affiliation requires very little of either. In fact, a decision to change beliefs or affiliation would probably take far more time and energy than simply not thinking about them.[38]

When parents have drifted away from regular church attendance and pray less in the home, their children will not take on the same beliefs or affiliations as the parents did during their own childhoods. If the children do take on some form of religiosity, it will tend to be of a more confused variety. With less formal religious instruction and a reduced emphasis on the importance of religious observance in their formative years, most children of drifting parents will carry this confused or reduced religiosity with them for the rest of their lives. An ounce of behavioral drift on the part of a generation of parents will lead to a pound of secularity in their children.

This narrative of behavioral drift leading to gaps in intergenerational transmission explains the "how" of religious change, but not necessarily the "why." As we've noted, such religious change is not universal, so why did it happen in Britain, in the twentieth century and not before, and not in some other similar countries? In order for behavioral drift away from religion to occur, a number of conditions must converge. Most obviously, religious attendance must not be a compulsory activity. Secular alternatives must also be available to satisfy at least some of the other functions fulfilled by the church, especially during the crucial Sunday morning time slot. But most importantly, the religious environment has to be such that nonattendance is socially acceptable. In nineteenth century Britain, the first two assumptions came to fruition, but they also did in the United States at roughly the same time, and the United States has not experienced such rapid drift. A major reason the United Kingdom has diverged in the twentieth century from the United States, then, is the substantial difference in the social acceptability of irreligion.

ACCEPTANCE FOR THE SECULAR

This, then, is the $64,000 question: what led to social approval for irreligion in Britain, particularly for the middle and upper classes who were generally more frequent attenders? In what way was the religious environment different from that of the United States, which had a similar cultural inheritance and which modernized at a similar pace? The most obvious difference is the established Anglican Church in England, and although its presence cannot account for everything, its influence is definitely a salient difference.

With this in mind, many have advocated a "supply-side" or "markets" theory, whereby the demand for religion is constant across all human societies, but the multitude of suppliers in America compete for that demand and effectively channel it. The monopoly supplier in Britain, on the other hand, is supposed to be relatively static and unresponsive, so that it is less successful on the whole.[39] Norris and Inglehart have demonstrated with evidence from the World Values Survey, however, that this explanation falls flat when used to explain examples other than the United States; in general, there is little to no correlation between religious diversity and strength of participation, even within Western societies.[40] It is more likely that the phenomenon has to do with the specific character of the relationship each country has with religiosity, a relationship that is broader in both cases than a simple market/monopoly dichotomy would suggest.

In the United States, liberty has always been seen as a fundamentally religious concept. In the Puritan conception, for instance, liberty simply *was* the freedom to choose God.[41] As Tocqueville put it, "Americans so completely confuse Christianity and freedom in their minds that it is almost impossible to have them conceive of the one without the other."[42] As a consequence of the deeply felt freedom of religious choice and the responsibility that went with that choice, religious beliefs were often a major part of the individual identity of Americans. In Britain, by contrast, there was a default in the established church. In many ways, a religious presence was taken for granted, so there was no need to socially enforce it. The story is similar for identity: if one didn't choose a religious identity, then by default one was considered an Anglican. There were plenty of breakaway denominations in the United Kingdom, but they were almost universally more conservative or doctrinally strict than the Anglican Church, which was comparatively impotent in enforcing adherence because of its insistence on tolerance and broad national appeal.[43] The default choice was also the least dogmatic choice, and so those who tended to be religiously inspired gravitated toward the doctrinally strict churches such as Methodism, Catholicism, or even Quakerism. Those less interested in religion were free to have their mind on other things, because their decision was already made for them.

Though we have seen similar patterns in most places where established churches have interacted with postindustrial society, there is plenty in the British situation that is unique to the Anglican Church itself. In some countries, where the dominant church was severe, oppressive, or intolerant, there has been deep disgust with the church. The French Revolution was the prime example of such revulsion. At the opposite end of the spectrum, there was the United States, where religion was seen as a companion to political freedom, rather than as an oppressive force. In the middle there was the Anglican Church, established but quite liberal and tolerant, at least since the nineteenth century. William Wolf writes in "The Spirit of Anglicanism" that

> At its best it is the spirit of liberality, of comprehensiveness [i.e., tolera-tion of differing viewpoints], of reasonableness, and of restraint. It stresses the historically given rather than the theoretical, the moral rather than the highly speculative. The spirit of Anglicanism appeals to the con-science and to the individual as responsible for working out his or her own salvation.[44]

The Anglican Church took on its present form after the Elizabethan settle-ment, which was adopted primarily with a practical purpose; to persuade people to stop killing each other after years of religious war. As a result, it became the "church of reconciliation" between four distinct camps: the Anglo-Catholics, the evangelical Protestants, and the liberal advocates both of pure reason and of empiricism.[45] The Church emphasizes histori-cal ties and national identity over theoretical attachments, and individual conscience over enforcement of dogma. In essence, Anglicanism is extreme only in its breadth. Thus, the only defectors were those who were so dogmatic that they could not accept its wealth of opinion.[46]

The Anglican Church was ripe for the behavioral drift that began in the latter nineteenth century. When secular alternatives began to present themselves, many Britons had no doctrinal allegiances pulling them back. Neither was their nonattendance threatening to their identity or social sta-tus, as they could still convincingly call themselves Anglicans in the broadest sense. The default option was chosen widely, as defaults often are, but with very little fervor. The Americans, forced to choose, would commit strongly to a tradition, but the British, not made to think twice about their religious choices, passively accepted the benign, tolerant national default, and moved on with the rest of their lives. To drift away from church for an American within a denomination was to withdraw from the community and to remove a central fact of one's identity. Laps-ing from practice, for an Anglican in Britain, was a much less dramatic affair, as he could keep both his identity and his community intact.

TRANSFORMING BELIEFS

Behavioral drift away from church attendance is the initial impetus for change in this model, but soon afterward it is followed by a decrease in religious belief and affiliation. Among the other conditions that facilitate a decline in belief is the presence of public atheists as examples for the general population. While we've established that secularity in Britain often triumphs not through conscious decision-making but through the slow evolution of behavior patterns and failure of intergenerational transmission, there must be a few trendsetters in atheism if a decline in belief is to accompany and reinforce the behavioral drift. It doesn't mean that every one of their followers will then become atheistic, just that the extreme position must be publicly taken in order to legitimize the moderate ones. In a process that Voas has earlier termed "diffusion," the traits of a few visible figures may be copied by many others, and even if the original character and meaning of the trait is lost in the process, the copies still stand on their own. For example, cultural diffusion occurs when celebrities stop wearing fur because it represents cruelty to animals, and people on the street stop wearing it because it is now unfashionable.

In America, the only public atheist that anyone is likely to remember is Madalyn Murray O'Hair, a revolutionary communist who tried to defect to the USSR but was rejected at the border. Britain, however, has a long tradition of upstanding public atheists, many of whom were alluded to in the first section. People began to announce their atheism relatively early on, with Holyoake and Bradlaugh especially becoming household names. The "Bradlaugh Affair" in Parliament was a constant feature in newspapers throughout the 1880s, and though the slant was not usually glowing with praise for the agitator, neither was it universally negative.

Bradlaugh had struck a chord with many in the British working class who resented the quintessentially upper-class Anglican Church.[47] For them, it was often not the default choice that it was for most Britons, because as they moved in droves to sprawling cities, both the churches and the secularists had burgeoning new markets to exploit, much like those in America. But the iconoclasm of Bradlaugh made a lot more sense in Britain—with its established Church and violent religious history—than it did in America, where religion had always been linked with freedom and tolerance. Thus, the more radical among the working classes during this period of upheaval took on an antireligious stance when given the opportunity. Although some certainly turned to more conservative religions with a populist flavor, many in the working class turned to socialism—and through it, secularism—as an ideology.

From here on, a clear-cut case of cultural diffusion can be demonstrated. Though a figure like Bradlaugh may have adopted his crusade against the church as a Spinozist philosophical rejection of theism, his followers did so for reasons that most likely had nothing to do with their stance on metaphysics. More importantly, for the larger audience that Bradlaugh did not directly influence, the popularity of anti-Christian viewpoints may have lent such a worldview a kind of credibility it had previously lacked. Bradlaugh and his followers seared the image of the respectable, hard-working atheist into the consciousness of a generation and provided a feasible alternative to traditional Christian belief for all Britons. For those who drifted behaviorally from religious practice after the religious high-water mark of the 1880s, the legacy of the "Victorian infidels"[48] was crucial in opening the doors to widespread de-Christianization of belief.

Though the radical politics associated with it went into hibernation, the tradition of public atheism continued: Bertrand Russell, despite being a member of the aristocracy, was particularly outspoken, and authors such as George Bernard Shaw and H. G. Wells were also known atheists. There was a strong concern in the NSS with representing secular opinions in the popular press, and the Rationalist Press Association, founded in 1895, circulated antireligious pamphlets and cheap reprints of secularist literature among the general population. Although it is unlikely that specific letters to the editor or copies of Hume changed a significant number of minds, their constant presence in the cultural consciousness facilitated the gradual abandonment of religious beliefs, which had been made possible on a wider scale by the drift away from regular practice and thus from the reinforcement of doctrine that churchgoing would have provided.

It is important to pause here and note a few things about the narrative we have drawn so far. First, each "stage" is really an ongoing process that is coextensive in time with every other stage; and second, the trajectory of events is neither definitive nor inevitable. Behavioral drift has occurred throughout history and still occurs for many today, and there are plenty of people for whom it will never happen. For some individuals, an abandonment of belief will lead to a reduction in practice rather than vice versa. In trying to draw together the most frequent trends and paint the broadest picture possible, we will necessarily fail to capture every individual story. Especially with religion, there are as many narratives of change as there are people in the world, so we can attempt to describe only the most general trends. However, we can still say that *overall*, a reduction in practice precedes a decline in belief, and in the majority of cases, both will precede a decline in identification with a religion.[49]

THE FALLING APPEAL OF CHRISTIAN AFFILIATION IN A MODERN CHRISTIAN NATION

With practice in free-fall and beliefs on the decline, nominal affiliation with Christianity often seemed resilient. For example, while actual church attendance reached a peak somewhere in the latter half of the nineteenth century, baptism rates in the Church of England remained fairly constant, sometimes even rising, until the 1930s.[50] Even if individuals did not go to church or believe in the God of their fathers, they still considered religion a positive force, and for the most part, they saw no reason to dissociate themselves from it. The radical unbelief of Bradlaugh had been diffused into passive, "practical atheism," whereby religion or the lack of it mattered very little to people. But few reasons had yet been presented that would convince normal British citizens to reject God outright.

This is where the revolutionary social change posited by Brown comes in. Although the 1960s did not see drastic shifts in any of the variables used to measure religiosity, it did trigger cultural confrontation and brought social attitudes up to date with the demographic realities of a Britain that was far less religious than when those attitudes were formed. For the first time since Bradlaugh's day, people began to seriously challenge the widespread assumption that religion, on the whole, was a force for good, and because of demographic changes, the religious climate this time was far more open to such public challenges. This was the era of legal battles over restrictions on birth control, homosexuality, and divorce, the onset of religious satire on public television, and the hyper-sexual, drug-laden "summer of love," all of which the Church vehemently opposed.[51] The second major wave of irreligious movements began, and the BHA was founded amidst this fervor.

The movements eventually lost energy, but many of the changes stuck. No longer was it generally assumed that the Church of England had the answer to moral questions; rather, it was now often assumed to have the wrong one. Its role morphed from definitive moral arbiter to one voice among many. Even if it was (and is) still privileged, it is certainly not the only voice that is taken seriously by the British people. This change allowed people to openly flout the moral authority of the Church, loosening the last tether that kept them to the foundation of Christian affiliation. The loss of the moral superiority of the Church allowed people, finally, to drift away from identification with Christianity. Before this point, whatever an individual's particular beliefs or practices were, his Christian affiliation signified to others that he was a moral person and that he respected the Western traditions of law and liberty. While being Christian still means that to many people, an alternative was provided at this point that many have chosen to take ever since: affiliating with no religion at all.

CONCLUSIONS

Britain has a thorny relationship with religion, and its relatively long history of atheists plays no small part in that. Interestingly, the times of greatest prominence for atheism have tended to coincide with the periods of greatest religiosity, and for this reason, the late Victorian era is often seen as the golden age of British atheism. Even the latest revival of interest in atheism can be attributed largely to the recently elevated prominence of religion in the news. This small and largely Ameri-centric trend aside, though, modern Britain is neither particularly religious nor overtly irreligious, but secular:[52] neither religion nor irreligion plays a large role in daily life. The religious tend to be fairly quiet about their beliefs, as do the atheists. Most of the country is somewhere between active religiosity and total irreligion, but their ability to hold these fuzzy beliefs exists in large part because they are rarely used or challenged. Religion is simply not very often on the British mind—whether God exists or not, He plays very little role in the lives of most people. And yet, despite the lack of daily interference, Christianity has not disappeared from the backdrop of society, with a majority of Britons holding to belief in some sort of God and identification as some sort of Christian however doubtfully or occasionally.

The process by which Britain came to this complex secularity is the subject of much debate. There is still much left unanswered by this chapter, but the broad narrative outlined here can give us some clues and hypotheses for future research. Demographically, the religious decline seems to be a result of failed transmission of religious identity from parents to children, which is in turn caused by a decrease in the prominence of religious activities in childhood. Parents may not have stopped attending and may still identify with the beliefs and denomination of their childhood, but they are unwilling or unable to make their children follow in their religious footsteps. The prominence and respectability of atheists in the public sphere, a secularizing culture, and the extreme tolerance of the Anglican Church all contribute to the generation gap. If maturing adults have less reinforcement from home, see plenty of attractive secular alternatives to religious beliefs and practices, and have few social incentives to remain regular participants, they will be less likely to become religious adults.

Affiliation may be slower to change than either beliefs or practices, because the alternatives are less attractive—"none" is not a particularly appealing or salient identity. However, even this is changing, as atheism has been gaining more and more respectability, both contributing to and benefiting from the increasing secularity of society at large. Even if people are not turning in mass numbers to atheism, a populace that cares less about religion in general will care less when certain of its members reject it, as long as they do so without making too much of a fuss. Of course, this process has been far from conscious. It was not the long-awaited triumph of rational thought over religious orthodoxy that many expected: many atheists still hold other supernatural beliefs. Neither was there suddenly any decision made that atheism was respectable. Instead, increasing acceptance has been the result of slow shifts in behavior patterns and the gradual realignment of attitudes to match those new behaviors.

There is no sign of these trends reversing in the future, but this does not mean that atheism will become universal or even a majority position. On the contrary: in a society where religion is unimportant, the opinions of people about religion tend to be far less definite, and this is the climate in which fuzzy fidelity has thrived. Indeed, it has taken a return to prominence of religion, in the form of both political and pietistic Islam, to force a reevaluation of that fuzzy fidelity by atheists and religious conservatives alike. We don't yet know how these new circumstances will affect the religious composition of the country, but we can only guess that the British will counter the revival of religion in public life in the way that they have done since the Victorian era. Attitudes will continue to shift away from religious orthodoxy, though not necessarily toward anything else concrete, as Britain comes to terms with its unconventional secularity.

NOTES

1. "Nick Clegg says: I don't believe in God," *The Times*, Dec. 19, 2007: "His admission is nonetheless unusual for a British political leader, most of whom have tended to try to avoid upsetting believers and non-believers alike by referring to or hinting at their faith before saying religion is a private matter."

2. Penny Edgell, Joseph Gerteis, and Douglas Hartmann, (2006) "Atheists as 'Other': Moral Boundaries and Cultural Membership in American Society," *American Sociological Review* 71 (2): 211–234.

3. David Berman, *A History of Atheism in Britain* (Kent, UK: Routledge, 1988); particularly "The Repression of Atheism," p. 1–47. The Britannica entry is quoted in this chapter, on page 1.

4. Ibid., 64, 101, and 134.

5. Colin Campbell, *Towards a Sociology of Irreligion* (London: Macmillan, 1971), 46–57.

6. Ibid., 50.

7. Ibid., 50.

8. Ibid., 57–83.

9. Callum Brown, *Religion and Society in Twentieth-Century Britain* (Harlow, UK: Pearson Education, 2006), especially "The Sixties Revolution, 1960–1973," 224–270.

10. http://www.secularism.org.uk/generalprinciples.html (accessed August 31, 2009).

11. Colin Campbell, *Towards a Sociology of Irreligion*, 91–96. http://www.humanism.org.uk; personal conversations with Terry Sanderson, president of NSS and Andrew Copson of the BHA.

12. George H. Gallup, ed., *The Gallup International Public Opinion Polls: Great Britain 1937–75: Volume Two 1965–1975* (New York: Random House, 1976), 829.

13. Penny Edgell et al. "Atheists as 'Other': Moral Boundaries and Cultural Membership in American Society," 215.

14. Ibid.

15. Stephen Bullivant, "Sociological Perspectives," draft chapter from "The Salvation of Atheists: The Catholic Engagement with Atheism," doctoral work in progress, University of Oxford, 2008, 22.

16. "Nick Clegg is a believer . . . in families, not God," *The Times*, Dec. 20, 2007: "Neil Kinnock, Michael Foot, and Hugh Gaitskell were the last political leaders to admit to being non-believers."

17. Stephen Bullivant, "Sociological Perspectives," 23.

18. Edward Royle, *Modern Britain: A Social History* (London, UK: Arnold Publishers, 1997), 316–330.

19. "Blair Feared Faith 'Nutter' Label," *BBC News*, Nov. 25, 2007.

20. Grace Davie, "Praying Alone? Church-going in Britain and the Putnam Thesis: A Reply to Steve Bruce," *Journal of Contemporary Religion* 17, no. 3 (2002): 329–335.

21. See 2001 Census of Population; 72 percent in England and Wales and 65 percent of those in Scotland are categorized as Christian.

22. Though the reasons for their popularity are, admittedly, more complex.

23. "Nick Clegg says . . ."

24. Abby Day, "Researching Belief without Asking Religious Questions," in *Fieldwork in Religion* 4, no. 1 (2009).

25. "Dawkins: I'm a cultural Christian." *BBC News*, Dec. 10, 2007.

26. David Voas, "Surveys of Behaviour, Beliefs and Affiliation," in *Handbook of the Sociology of Religion*, ed. J. Beckford and N. J. Demerath (Thousand Oaks, CA: Sage, 2007), 128–150.

27. David Voas, "The Rise and Fall of Fuzzy Fidelity in Europe," *European Sociological Review* 25, no. 2 (2009): 155-68. The argument in this section is developed more fully in this "Fuzzy Fidelity" article.

28. Robert Piggott, personal conversation.

29. Ipsos-MORI poll; details to be confirmed. (2003) http://www.ipsos-mori.com/researchpublications/researcharchive/poll.aspx?oItemId=773 (accessed August 31, 2009).

30. Much of this draws on R. D. Putnam, *Bowling Alone: The Collapse and Revival of American Community* (New York: Simon and Schuster, 2000); applications of the idea to Britain include Grace Davie, "Praying Alone? Church-going in Britain and the Putnam Thesis: A Reply to Steve Bruce," 329–335.

31. Colin Campbell, *Easternization of the West*. (London: Paradigm Publishers, 2007); Paul Heelas, and Linda Woodhead *The Spiritual Revolution* (Oxford: Blackwell Publishing, 2005).

32. Though the average difference is relatively small, the data show strongly that the effect exists.

33. Edward Royle, *Modern Britain: A Social History*, 337, quoting *Manchester Domestic Missionary*, 1848.

34. Ibid., 335, quoting Thomas Frost.

35. Ibid., 337.

36. Callum Brown, *Religion and Society in Twentieth-Century Britain*, 224.

37. David Voas, "The Continuing Secular Transition," in *The Role of Religion in Modern Societies*, ed. D. Pollack and D. V. A. Olson (London: Routledge, 2007), 25–48.

38. This intragenerational change would not manifest itself in the BSA statistics we used to show the primacy of generational effects over age effects, because the self-conception of those parents has not changed very much; thus, the fact that the religiosity of each cohort appears to hold steady is unsurprising.

39. Among those who have advocated this approach are Roger Finke, Rodney Stark, Laurence Iannaccone, William Bainbridge, and R. Stephen Warner.

40. Pippa Norris and Ronald Inglehart, *Sacred and Secular: Religion and Politics Worldwide* (New York: Cambridge University Press, 2004), 95–106.

41. See John Schaar, "Political Thought of John Winthrop," *Political Theory* 19, no. 4 (1991): 493–518.

42. Alexis de Tocqueville, *Democracy in America*, trans. H. C. Mansfield and D. Winthrop (Chicago: University of Chicago Press, 2000).

43. Edward Royle, *Modern Britain: A Social History*, 316–326.

44. William J. Wolf, "Anglicanism and its Spirit," in *The Spirit of Anglicanism*, ed. William J. Wolf (Wilton, CT: Morehouse-Barlow, 1981), 186.

45. Ibid., 178.

46. A conversation with Tim Jenkins contributed a great deal to this analysis.

47. Edward Royle, *Modern Britain: A Social History*, 330.

48. Edward Royle, *Victorian Infidels* (Manchester, UK: Manchester University Press, 1974).

49. Robin Gill, *Churchgoing and Christian Ethics* (Cambridge: Cambridge University Press, 1999), chapter 3. See also David Voas and Alasdair Crockett, "Religion in Britain: Neither believing nor belonging," *Sociology* 39, no. 1 (2005): 11–28.

50. David Voas, "Intermarriage and the demography of secularisation," *British Journal of Sociology* 54, no. 1 (2003): 83–108.

51. Callum Brown, *Religion and Society in Twentieth-Century Britain*, 224–70.

52. Here, we mean "secular" in the sense to follow, not in the sense of French laïcité or American secular government.

Chapter 6

Atheism and Secularity in the Arab World

Jack David Eller

Most of the public and many experts would no doubt agree with the assessment of Ernest Gellner, the eminent scholar of anthropology and history, that "I think it is fair to say that no secularization has taken place in the world of Islam: that the hold of Islam over its believers is as strong, and in some ways stronger, now than it was 100 years ago. Somehow or other Islam is secularization-resistant." (p. 2)[1] Especially in a time of war, it is not surprising that the more extreme and polarizing, if not literally distancing and exoticizing, images of "the enemy" would prevail, drowning out the voices of moderation and complexity in the din (a particularly ironic term, since *din*—pronounced "deen"—is the Arabic term for faith or religion). Certainly the loudest voices in the contemporary Islamic world are the nonsecularists and the antisecularists. However, the claim that there is no secularization is Islam would be very surprising to Fu'ad Zakariyya, Husain Ahmad Amin, Muhammad Nur Farahat, and Farag 'Ali Fuda, for instance, whom Alexander Flores calls the four main spokesmen of "outspoken secularism" in Egypt today (p. 28)[2] or to earlier secularists such as Taha Husayn, Ya'qub Sarruf, Faris Nimr, Nicola Haddad, Salama Musa, and Lewis Awad, not to mention the influential Ali Abd al-Raziq; or to parties and organizations such as *Jam'iyyat al-Nida' al-Jadid* (New Appeal Society), *Jam'iyyat al-Tanwir* (Enlightenment Society), *Hizb 'Almani* (Secular Party, with its slogan "Religion belongs to God, the homeland belongs to us all"), and *Tayyar al-'Almani* (Movement for Secularism); or to secular regimes and governments including Nasser's and Mubarak's Egypt, Bourguiba's Tunisia, even Hussein's Iraq, and of course Ataturk's Turkey.

Clearly then, while secularism may not be the dominant force in Islamic societies—and then again, in a certain sense, it may be, as we will examine below—it is a real force. The assumption or conclusion that secularism does not exist at all in those contexts, or that it is a small insignificant factor, or that it is in retreat, is a product of a variety of factors including unfamiliarity with the realities on the ground, exaggerated attention to the "resurgent" religionists, and the conventional "Orientalism" that views non-Western societies as irreconcilably different from and inferior to the West. But it appears that the problem may go deeper, to a profound misunderstanding of what secularism is, what Islam is, and for that matter what religion in general is. We will have the occasion, and the obligation, to consider all of these issues below.

In this chapter, we will be focusing on the "Arab world," but that calls upon us to determine what precisely to what the "Arab world" refers. Simplistically, the Arab world (*al-'alam al-'arabi*) consists of those places where Arabs live. But what is an Arab? Albert Hourani, the great historian of Arab societies, writes

> Most Arabs, if asked to define what they meant by "the Arab nation," would begin by saying that it included all those who spoke the Arabic language. But this would only be the first step, and it would carry them no more than one step farther to say it included all who claimed a link with the nomadic tribes of Arabia, whether by descent, by affiliation, or by appropriation (through the medium of language and literature) of their ideal of human excellence and standards of beauty. A full definition would include also a reference to a historic process: to a certain episode of history in which Arabs played a leading part, which was important not only for them but for the whole world, and in virtue of which indeed they could claim to have been *something* in human history.[3]

Thus, "Arab" does not specify any particular race or country or even, necessarily, religion; there were Arabs before there was Islam. "Arab" is not a synonym for "Muslim." Many—in fact, the vast majority—of the world's Muslims are not Arabs: of the 1.4 billion Muslims, less than three hundred million are to be found in the traditionally "Arab" countries, which include Saudi Arabia and the Gulf states, Iraq, Syria, Jordan, Lebanon, and the strip of North Africa (known as the Maghreb in Islam) that contains Egypt, Sudan, Libya, Tunisia, Algeria, and Morocco. The Arab world does not contain major Islamic states and regions such as Iran or Turkey, Pakistan and Afghanistan and Central Asia, northern India, Bangladesh, Saharan and sub-Saharan Africa, and of course Malaysia and Indonesia, the latter of which is far and away the most populous Muslim-majority country.

Nor are all Arabs Muslims: between 8 and 12 percent of Arabs are Christians, particularly in Lebanon and Egypt, and Arabs can theoretically belong to any religion. Finally, not all people living within the "Arab world" are Arabs, nor are all Arabs resident in the "Arab world." Kurds constitute an important minority in Iraq (15–20 percent) and Syria (5–10 percent). Berbers occupy much of Morocco (35 percent) and Algeria (20 percent). Significant numbers of non-Arabs live in the Gulf states, if only as temporary laborers, including Persians, Indians, Baluchs, and Filipinos. A mere 39 percent of Sudanese are Arab. Meanwhile, many Arabs find themselves outside the conventional "Arab world" in such states as Israel, Chad, Turkey, Iran, and Mali, not to mention Europe and the United States.

The complex and contested nature of Arab identity suggest that few generalizations can be made about this constituency; "Arab" is not any one concrete thing. Neither is "Islam" any one concrete thing: there are multiple doctrinal schools, historical interpretations, and local versions of Islam. That is to say, there is serious—although often invisible to the West—internal controversy and debate over what exactly Islam is, what it was in the past, what it should be in the future, and, perhaps most critically, how it should relate to "the West," to "modernity," and to "secularism." It only seems obvious, then, that secularism would not be any one concrete thing either; this is true in Christian and other societies, so there is no reason why it should be untrue in Islamic ones. Some Arab people have embraced secularism thoroughly, others rant against it in absolute terms, and others have found a way— or at least proposed that there is a way—to integrate it with religion. As we will discuss below, some like Abdullahi Ahmed An-Na'im plead that one can only be a true Muslim in a secular state.[4] The possibility of such an opinion indicates that the familiar notion of secularism as religion-less or even antireligion is inadequate. In a word, we will find in this chapter that secularism takes on its own local meaning in *al-'alam al-'arabi*—or at least that it will as they work out their own local version of Arab modernism and Arab secularism.

THE LANGUAGE OF SECULARISM AND RELIGION IN THE ARAB WORLD

To begin to situate the Arab Islamic experience of secularism in its required context, we must consider how religion and its secular alternative are conceived and expressed specifically in the Arabic language. We cannot assume that either religion or secularism is understood and practiced in the same way in *al-'alam al-'arabi* as it is in the Western-Christian world.

As we have already discovered, *din* is the Arabic word for "religion" or "faith" or "belief." The particular *din* of Islam originates from the Qur'an, the scripture that was revealed to Muhammad during the more than twenty years of his prophecy (Muhammad is regarded as a *rasul* or messenger). The Qur'an represents the final and authoritative word of the one god, Allah. A *muslim* is one who submits to the will of Allah, *Islam* is the religion or *din* of submission to Allah, and *salam* or peace is the experience of submission to Allah (all three of which words derive from the same Arabic root, *slm*).

Islam sees itself as absolute and conclusive monotheism, without the mysterious doctrines of incarnation and trinity. Essential to Islamic monotheism is the concept of *tawhid* or oneness/unity: there is one god, Allah, and none other like him. Accordingly, the two most fundamental errors that a human being can make are polytheism and atheism. *Shirk* is the Arabic term for polytheism or idolatry, believing in or worshipping any god besides Allah (which is tantamount to atheism, because no such gods exist). In the time before Muhammad's revelations, most humans were idolaters or murky monotheists, living in ignorance of the one true god—a condition known in Arabic as *jahiliyyah* or the era of religious ignorance (*jahl* means "ignorance").

Kufr more particularly signifies disbelief or infidelity, which can take two forms: *kufr-i jahli* or disbelief from lack of knowledge or understanding of Allah and *kufr-i juhudi* or disbelief from rejection of the truth of Allah. The latter is clearly worse. A person denies or rejects the truth of the *tawhid* of Allah, who refuses to submit to Allah's will, is a *kafir*, an unbeliever or infidel. Typically, a *kafir* is a person who has never accepted the authority of Islam; for the backslider, the apostate, the term *murtadd* is reserved, and as in many religions, this is the worst position that a human can occupy. *Takfir* is the act of denouncing a person or group as an infidel or fallen Muslim.

Two of the key issues in Islam are religious leadership or authority and the relationship between religion and politics or power. On the first issue, there have evolved a variety of spiritual and/or textual specialists in different times and places. The general term *'alim* or *'alam* designates "one who knows" or "one with knowledge," *'ilm* referring widely to knowledge (more recently, "science") and narrowly to religious knowledge. Collectively these leaders or teachers are called *ulama* or *ulema*. Another common term is *imam*, literally "leader" (which holds special significance for Shi'ite Muslims). *Ayatullah* or *ayatollah* is a specifically Shi'ite title for a religious scholar/leader, literally a "sign" (*ayah*) of Allah. By whatever name, the *ulama* used their learning and wisdom to guide the community of believers, the *umma*. However—and this is crucially important—Islam has never had a formal professional clergy or priesthood comparable to that in Christianity, particularly but not exclusively Catholicism. There was and is no "church" in Islam, and any discussion of the role of religion in society must keep this difference in mind.

This takes us naturally to the issue of "church and state," or more generally the problem of religious authority and "political" or "governmental" authority. In Arabic, *al-hukm* can mean government or governance, although it also refers to legal rulings or jurisprudence arising from the Qur'an or the "traditions/customs" (the *sunna*) based on the precedents set by Muhammad during his lifetime, many of which are recorded in the *Hadith*, a book second in importance only to the Qur'an. The revelations to the prophet and the sayings and doings of the prophet provide models or examples for subsequent, including modern, political rulings and constitute a code or law, the *shari'a*.

Whether or not Muhammad or his successors were ever "political" figures is a debate that we will take up in the next section and is a debate conducted in the contemporary Arab world. At any rate, the term *caliph* or *khalifah* evolved to specify a "successor" to the authority of Muhammad (political, spiritual, or both); for some sects of Islam, the *khalifah* was to belong to the prophet's family line. *Sharif* is a title reserved for descendants of Muhammad through his daughter Fatima and his son-in-law Ali.

For many Muslims at least, Islam is more than "religion" in the modern Western sense of the term; in a traditional formulation, Islam is *din wa dawla*, "religion and state," and *din wa dunya*, "religion and world." As suggested above, the scriptures and models of the founding era of religion came to be used in the way that case law is used in the West. In practice, then, Islam provided the basis and substance for *fiqh* or jurisprudence, upon which an authority (*faqih*, plural *fuqaha*) would rule on cases in his own time. While sometimes criticized, especially by nineteenth- and twentieth-century modernizers as a form of *taqlid* or blind imitation of the past, Islam actually has always struggled for *ijma* or consensus but allowed for *ikhtilaf* or difference of opinion. Diverging interpretations, and diverging schools of interpretation, grew from the shared texts and traditions, warranted by the Islamic concept of *ijtihad* or independent reasoning from precedent. Some sections of the Qur'an or actions of Muhammad seem clear and definitive enough and considered *nass* or "proof texts"; others, though, are less clear or immediately relevant and become the subject of practices like *qiyas* or reasoning by analogy—which inevitably leads to varying conclusions.

Undeniably, then, Islam from its earliest days has been diverse and evolving, containing many opinions on virtually all subjects. It seems certain, then, that the *din* should encompass ideas and attitudes that are even questionable by or contrary to—indeed, heretical to—common standards. One such attitude is secularism, a term that was not known to the medieval Islamic (or for that matter Christian) world but that had its counterpart even then (as we will demonstrate below). Since sustained contact with the West began in the late eighteenth century, the word *al-'alamaniyyah* was coined as an Arabic equivalent for secularism, derived from *'alam* for "world." Another word that is sometimes used for secularism is *al-'ilmaniyyah*, which is commonly believed to derive from *'ilm* for "knowledge" or "science" but is apparently simply an alternate pronunciation of the previous term, *al-'alamaniyyah*. A few writers and activists have proposed the word *al-dunyawiyyah* from the root *dunya* or "physical world" as opposed to heaven or spiritual world, and readers may encounter that term in the literature. Indisputably, in much Arabic and Islamic thinking, *al-'alamaniyyah* is a negative thing, akin to atheism (many call it outright *kufr*), as is questioning authority and precedent or introducing "innovation" (*bid'ah*).

SECULARISM IN PRE-MODERN ISLAM

While the term "secularism" is new to the Arab world, it is a point of some contention whether or not the experience is. In one sense, we have just seen the nature of the problem: was Islam *originally* both "religion" and "politics," which in interpretive practice means, were Muhammad and/or his immediate and subsequent successors both temporal and spiritual authorities, otherworldly guides and worldly governors? In another sense, the problem goes much deeper than the "separation of church and state": do the—distinctly Western-Christian—concepts of "church," "state," and their "separation" apply in Arabic religion at all? Therefore, is the sacred/secular division relevant in Islam? For example, as Parvez Manzoor has opined, unlike the Christian church or the Buddhist *sangha*, Islam "did not have any sacerdotal institutions, any churches, and hence was spared the sacred-secular dichotomy of the West" which was a cultural-historical consequence of the "institutionalization" of religion (p. 90).[5] On the one hand, perhaps Islam never distinguished political power from spiritual power; on the other hand, perhaps it always did. And finally, at the most profound level, we may find that the very idea of "religion" in distinction to "the world" or "society" is at best a foreign one and at worst a false one—also a product of Western-Christian experience but neither entirely universal nor entirely useful.

The Arab tradition that Islam is *din wa dawla*, "religion and state" flows from the widely understood career of its founder, Muhammad. According to this tradition, Muhammad was not only a prophet but a jurist, virtually a mayor, of the city of Medina and then of Mecca and the growing "Arab-Islamic empire." In the legitimating function of religion, this paradigm of prophet-politician would establish Islam as religion–politics and its leadership as spiritual–temporal or otherworldly–this worldly. There are two ways that this phenomenon might work. In the stronger case, the religious leaders would be *one and the same as* the political leaders; for instance, the *khalifah* or the *ulama* individually or collectively would wield actual governmental authority, or the political/military leadership would be spiritually or divinely authorized. Such was the assertion of the medieval scholar al-Mawardi

(991–1031), who regarded the caliphate "as being a necessity derived from the divine law rather than from reason."[6] No doubt many a ruler and pretender to the throne advanced the same argument. This is, understandably, the "prevailing view among Islamists," "that classical Islamic society does not distinguish between the religious and political aspects of communal life. The Caliphate was both the religious and the political leadership of the community of Muslims, whose individual believers and subjects belonged to a polity defined by religious allegiance" (p. 363)[7].

In the weaker case, the spiritual and the temporal authorities would be distinct but connected, establishing a joint temporospiritual system, as in the account of Abu-Rabi':

> . . . the state has never been disconnected from religion. The traditional ulama class legitimized the state with the leverage it had with the masses. Historically, "official Islam" enjoyed the protection and patronage of the ruling elite in Muslim society. . . . The ulama, especially in the Sunni world, have more or less stood with the status quo by refusing to support opposition to existing political authority.[8]

Ibn Taymiyya (1263–1328), writing in the midst of the Mamluk period, concurred, insisting that "good government depended on an alliance between *amirs*, political and military leaders, and the *ulama*, interpreters of the law."[9] The great Ibn Khaldun (1332–1406) himself held that the caliphate and the crown "existed side by side," even if he was in favor of the politicizing of religion.[10]

However, an energetic and convincing position is that political and religious power were not only differentiated but separate and even as often as not at odds with each other. Muhammad Sa'id al-Ashmawi in 1987 wrote that "God wanted Islam to be a religion, but men have turned it into politics" (p. 92–93)[11]. (Notice, though, that this type of secularism is hardly antagonistic to religion.) Muhammed Talbi in his 1992 book *'Iyal Allah, afkar jadida fi alaqat al-Muslim bi-nafsi-hi wa-l-akharin* (*The Family of God: New Reflections on the Muslim's Relationship with Himself and Others*), goes yet further, positing that

> the Islamic *umma* never was a political unit. It was always founded on spiritual unity, the unity of witness and adoration. Its unity was never political. On the political level there have constantly been conflicts and wars, right from the moment of the "great sedition" (*al-fitna l-kubra*) to the present day.[12]

One of the most influential criticisms of the political nature of early Islam came from Ali Abd al-Raziq, a key secularist figure of the early twentieth century. In his 1925 work *al-Islam wa Usul al-Hukm* he asserted that Muhammad never even created or governed a "state" at all; asked to summarize his book, he said:

> Islam did not determine a specific regime, nor did it impose on the Muslims a particular system according to the requirements of which they must be governed; rather it has allowed freedom to organize the state in accordance with the intellectual, social, and economic conditions in which we are found, taking into consideration our social development and the requirements of our times.[13]

In his analysis, then, Muslim politics is necessarily "secular" in the original sense of the term—"of the current age/time"—because it is not given by religion and only exists in adjustment to contemporary social conditions.

After studying the first centuries of the Muslim era, Lapidus concludes that indeed religion and politics were typically separate:

> In fact, religious and political life developed distinct spheres of experience, with independent values, leaders, and organizations. From the middle of the tenth century effective control of the Arab–Muslim empire had passed into the hands of generals, administrators, governors, and local provincial lords; the Caliphs had lost all effective political power. Governments in Islamic lands were henceforth secular regimes—Sultanates—in theory authorized by the Caliphs, but actually legitimized by the need for public order. Henceforth, Muslim states were fully differentiated political bodies without any intrinsic religious character, though they were officially loyal to Islam and committed to its defense.[14]

As time passed and Arab/Islamic society grew and evolved, "this initial differentiation of religious and communal institutions from the political institution of the Caliphate grew more profound and more clearly defined. In later centuries . . . the Caliph lost his de facto political power to secular military and administrative regimes, albeit to regimes nominally loyal to Islam."[15]

Ibn Warraq, in a stinging attack on Islam, goes further, to discuss a serious, even if minority and unpopular, current of "rationalism" or "freethought," sometimes verging on atheism, in medieval Islam. He holds up, for example, the Mu'tazilites as a movement influenced by Greek philosophy and committed to reason (*'aql*). Reason in their view even constrained or compelled Allah (when they still believed in him): their doctrine of human rationality and "self-determination leads to the rejection of the notion of God's arbitrary rule; divine omnipotence is limited by the requirements of justice."[16] Ahmed bin Habit rode his rationalism into virtually disbelief. Others, still faithful, subjected the Qur'an, the traditions of Muhammad, and the doctrines of Islam to critical inquiry.

Various other kinds of *zindiq* (heresy, more specifically "dualism") cropped up in Islam as well. Ibn al-Muqaffa questioned aspects of the *din*, while Ibn Abi-l-Awja went so far as to assert the eternity of the natural world and to deny the existence of a supernatural creator.[17] Warraq lists a large number of other philosophers and freethinkers in Arab history, many of whom were persecuted or executed, including Salih Abd al-Quddus, Hammad Ajrad, Aban bin Abd al-Humayd bin Lahiq al-Raqqasi, Qays bin Zubayr, Abu'l Atahiya, Abu Tammam, Ibn al-Rawandi, and of course the infamous Abu 'L-ala Ahmad bin Abdallah al-Ma'arri, who wrote scathing verses in the eleventh century calling religion a "fable invented by the ancients" and "noxious weeds"[18] and asserting the superiority of reason over prophecy and belief.

Certainly, then, the premodern Arab world did not lack its "secularists" or rationalists, even if the society was not kind and tolerant toward them. However, the more profound issue, raised at the outset of this section, is whether the sacred/secular dichotomy applies to Islam at all, if to any religion. Plenty of Muslim observers have commented on the Western-Christian basis of the very concept of "secular," founded on an unacceptable dualism of "world" versus "spirit" and a fundamental desacralization or even denigration of the "world." To begin, Bernard Lewis reminds us that, unlike in the early centuries of Christianity, which left an indelible mark on that religion, in Islam:

> political authority was not a human evil, not even a lesser or a necessary evil; it was a divine good. The body politic and the sovereign powers within it are ordained by God himself, to promote his faith and to maintain and extend his law. The Muslim, like the Christian, sees God as involved in human affairs and as subjecting his people to a variety of tests. But for the Muslim, God's main concern is to help rather than to test his people, in particular to help them achieve victory and paramountcy in this world.[19]

In other words, while Islam undeniably has spiritual aspirations and otherworldly interests (like heaven), it is also a very thisworldly religion—which may sound like a contradiction to many readers but is not.

An-Na'im, for instance, posits that from the Muslim point of view, "Islam provides a comprehensive model for individual and communal life, in the public as well as the private domain."[20] It is more than "private belief" as religion has come to be seen since the Enlightenment in the West—more than "private" and more than "belief." It is, as we noted above, law and tradition and precedent and model and paradigm. It touches, potentially and depending on the particular *ijtihad* employed, every aspect of human life, society, and the world. As Lewis writes in another place,

> The idea that any group of persons, any kind of activities, any part of human life is in any sense outside the scope of religious law and

jurisdiction is alien to Muslim thought. There is, for example, no distinction between canon law and civil law, between the law of the church and
the law of the state, crucial in Christian history. There is only a single
law, the shari'a, accepted by Muslims as of divine origin and regulating
all aspects of human life: civil, commercial, criminal, constitutional, as
well as matters more specifically concerned with religion in the limited,
Christian sense of that word.[21]

Of course he overstates his case, since *shari'a* law is not the only law in
all Arab and Muslim societies, but it has the capacity—and in more
than a few situations the intent—to be the one and only law.

While this view of religion as an all-encompassing worldly and
social system may confuse and offend Western readers, it is in fact not
contradictory from an Arab–Muslim perspective. More like medieval
Christianity than most observers might realize or care to accept, Islam
is an otherworldly originated and legitimated system for life in this
world; perhaps less like medieval Christianity, while its source and nature is otherworldly, its attention is very much directed here, to the
real world of human problems. Fazlur Rahman says it best:

> Although God consciousness and the conviction of the Last Day are
> powerful and persistent themes in the Qur'an, there is no doubt that
> belief in God or human accountability play a strictly functional role
> here. . . . In Qur'anic terms no real morality is possible without the regu-
> lative ideas of God and the Last Judgment. Further, their very moral
> function requires that they exist for religiomoral experience and cannot
> be mere intellectual postulates to be "believed in". . . .
> But the substantive . . . teaching of the Prophet and the Qur'an is
> undoubtedly *for action in this world*, since it provides guidance for man
> concerning his behavior on earth in relation to other men. God exists in
> the mind of the believer to regulate his behavior if he is religiomorally
> experienced, but that which is regulated is the essence of the matter.[22]

In short, traditional Islam is as much thisworldly as otherworldly—as
much "secular" as "sacred"—and it is, in Rahman's formulation, sacred
in the interests of the secular (for *maslaha*, human interest or well-being)
and otherworldly *for the benefit of* this world. To regard the "secular" as
somehow outside of or oppositional to "religion" is foreign to Islam.
That is to say, ultimately, that Islam apparently always had two of the
key criteria of "secularism"—some measure of separation of religion
from state, and a regard for and focus on the world of human existence.

ARAB SECULARISM IN THE MODERN ERA

As the modern age dawned on *al-'alam al-'arabi*, two important conditions obtained: first, it was a subordinate component of a much

larger Islamic empire dominated by non-Arabs, namely the Ottoman Turkish state; and second, it and the Ottoman state within which it was contained were coming under increasing pressure from an ascendant Western civilization, which was soon to take the form of invasion and colonization. Arab secularism must be seen in the context of these grander processes of colonialism, nationalism, globalization, and modernization in general.

The early modern circumstances of Arab religion and society depend heavily on the Turks, who found themselves on the decline by the mid-1700s—ending their assaults on Central Europe (after having long since lost the Islamic outposts in Spain) and facing defeat from their northern rival Russia. The Christian communities had already come to the attention of a rising France and Austria, which demanded the right to defend and administer those populations; because of military and financial weakness, the Ottomans were forced to submit. By 1792 Selim III recognized the necessity to modernize his army, which meant Westernizing it, and even those limited reforms were met by resistance from religious and political conservatives.

The urgent need for, and the inevitably occurrence of, change was made immanent by the French occupation of Egypt in 1798. Although it was temporary (ended by way of British assistance to the Turks), the invasion inaugurated the cultural shocks that are still felt in the Arab world—as well as the lens through which it sees much of present-day history. Interestingly, although the French landing in Egypt was part of the revolutionary movement in France, distinguished by rationalist/secularist/nationalist fervor, it was not utterly hostile to or dismissive of religion: Napoleon's proclamation to his new Egyptian subjects began with the words, "In the name of God, the Merciful, the Compassionate; there is no God but God, He has no offspring and no partner." But it went on to assert that the new administration would be "built on the basis of freedom and equality"—setting the stage for the fusing of secular culture and religion that would characterize the Arab world from then on.[23]

The defeat in Egypt and the growing encroachments of Europe had two immediate effects, both in the direction of "secularization." In Egypt Muhammad Ali was established in power after the French withdrawal, and he became the first well-known and successful modernizer in the Arab world. He opened modern Western-style schools "to produce personnel for government and administration, not to produce a person imbued with Islamo-Egyptian culture."[24] By 1860 the products of these institutions were rising to administrative positions, including Isma'il Pasha, who took over political control in 1863. Egypt would go on to become probably the center of Arab modernism and secularism, then and today, as we will explore below.

Meanwhile, at the center of the empire, Mahmed II initiated a series of reforms starting in 1826 that would come to known collectively as the *Tanzimat*. Among these moves were the disbanding of the Janissary corps (the traditional soldiery of the empire) in favor of a modern-type military, for which purposes officer-training colleges were created. Also, medical schools and programs for civil servants were established, newspapers were introduced, and governmental administration was reorganized and modernized; even Western-style clothing was adopted.

Thus, at the center of Ottoman power and in the Arab periphery (not only Egypt, but Tunisia, Syria, and Lebanon, which were also feeling the penetration of the West and responding with their own versions of reform, often for their own local reasons, as especially in the case of Tunisia), modernization was arriving in force by the mid- to late-1800s. One of the components of this modernization was secularization, or perhaps what we might better call liberalism, especially in terms of education, politics, and culture. Among its first Arab advocates was Rifa'a Badawi Rafi' al-Tahtawi (1801–1873), an Egyptian who studied in Paris for five years under the orders of Muhammad Ali, learning French and English literature. For him as for many of his contemporaries and descendants, the immediate problem was the perceived backwardness and weakness of Arab vis-à-vis the expanding West; for him as for them, the solution was to learn selectively from the West. In that sense a liberalizer or modernizer or reformer, he was far from an atheist or anti-Islamist. In fact, he represents the main trend in Arab–Islamic modernization, which is to borrow discerningly from Western civilization while often sharply criticizing some or most of that civilization, all within a distinctly Islamic idiom.

Al-Tahtawi in particular studied and admired aspects of European political theory, notably the ideas of individual freedom and democracy. In his writings such as *Manahij al-albab al-misriyya fi mabahij al-adab al-'asriyya* (loosely translated, *The Paths of Egyptian Hearts in the Joys of the Contemporary Arts*),[25] he described and praised Western democracy, but in a recognizably Islamic way. To those who resisted learning anything from the West, he wrote, "Such people are deluded; for civilizations are turns and phases. These sciences were once Islamic when we were at the apex of our civilization. Europe took them from us and developed them further. It is now our duty to learn from the just as they learned from our ancestors" (p. 18)[26]. That is, civilization—presumably even Arab–Islamic civilization—is a product of its unique moment of development, that is, a *secular* product in the original sense of the term.

While al-Tahtawi recommended the rule of law and civil freedom, he continued to accept the absolute executive power of the political authority; in this regard he was no modern democrat. However, his most revolutionary contribution was an emphasis not on religion or even on Arabism as the root of Egyptian identity but on membership in the *watan*, the country or nation. He advanced a modern concept of *wataniyyah* (nationhood) and *hubb al-watan* ("love of country/territorial patriotism") as the essence of Egyptianness—one that included Islam but also harkened back to ancient pre-Islamic Egypt as well.

Others followed more or less in al-Tahtawi's footsteps, including Khairuddin al-Tunisi and Abdel Rahman al-Kawakibi. The former in particular, in his 1867 *Aqwam al-masalik fi ma'rifat ahwal al-mamalik* (*The Road Most Straight to Know the Conditions of the State*) urged Arabs to embrace "whatever is conducive to the welfare of the Islamic community and the development of its civilization, such as the expansion of the bounds of science and learning and the preparations of the paths which lead to wealth . . . and the basis of all this is good government."[27] Al-Tunisi was not the only non-Egyptian (he was Tunisian, obviously) to join the movement; a number of Syrian/Lebanese writers also added their voices to the reform efforts, especially Christians, including Faris al-Shidyaq and Butrus al-Bustani (both Maronites).

However, the two greatest figures of the nineteenth century both operated in the Egyptian context; these were Jamal al-Din al-Afghani (1839–1897) and Muhammad 'Abduh (1849–1905). Both, but perhaps al-Afghani more than 'Abduh, embodied the contradiction of being utterly opposed to colonialism but not opposed to everything that the colonialists thought and did. Al-Afghani, of whom 'Abduh was a student and follower, harshly criticized Western science and reason for the suffering and destruction it caused, condemning it as "undiluted ignorance, sheer barbarism, and total savagery."[28] Even so, he understood the requirement that Arabs discover and master the sources of Western economic, technical, and military power, yet he demanded that this all be done in a distinctly Islamic way.

Thus, according to Badawi, "Al-Afghani wanted to reform Islam, not to modernize it."[29] Yet, reformation in this case is an ostensibly modern phenomenon: it entailed questioning not only Western practice and assumptions but medieval Muslim ones as well. It entailed, that is, "a new Ijtihad [interpretation] and the discarding of the authority of the established scholars."[30] The answers to Arab–Islamic problems were in Islam, if correctly understood—which meant that his predecessors incorrectly understood it. The primary novelty of his approach was to see Islam less as a religion than as a civilization or culture (a clearly nineteenth-century European idea): as Hourani puts it, for al-Afghani "The aim of man's acts is not the service of God alone; it is the creation of human civilization flourishing in all its parts"[31]—which is, once again, a "secular" attitude in a sense. While hardly a rationalist of the Western sort (in fact, he wrote a tract entitled *al-Radd ala'l-dhahriyyin*, meaning *The Refutation of the Materialists*) he did maintain the compatibility of science and Islam, to the point of debating the well-known Western scholar Ernst Renan on the subject. Contrary to Renan's claim that Islam was essentially incompatible with modern science (a typical "orientalist" view), al-Afghani held "that the essence of Islam was the same as that of modern rationalism" and that the Qur'an anticipated many things that Western science had only just discovered. Even more, he insisted that Islam contained the moral and personal code that "could save the secular world from that revolutionary chaos" observable in the political, social, and economic upheavals of the day.[32]

The student Muhammad 'Abduh concurred with the master that the West was "a political force to be resisted and a social ideal to be imitated," which led not to an abandonment of Islam but a reformulation of it.[33] The Arab world was surely in a state of decay and stagnation, he allowed, and many benefits could be derived from the West, but these benefits—science, limited government, and rational thought—were not only well-suited to Islam but were actually contained in the foundations of Islam (the *salafiyyah* or ways of the ancestors/forefathers). A rejuvenated and rightly-interpreted—some might say "modernized"—Islam would solve nineteenth-century Arab problems. For he recognized, in the classically secularist way, that "laws vary as the conditions of nation vary,"[34] that is, that a society and even a religion is a product of its historical moment. Western civilization could not be simply transplanted into Islamic territory, but neither was Islam a static and fixed thing. One of his greatest complaints against Islam was its habit of *taqlid* or blind imitation; drawing on the opposite tradition, *maslaha* (interest/ well-being/usefulness) and *talfiq* ("piecing together" or combining the best of multiple sources of knowledge/interpretation), he distinguished between what was permanent and obligatory in Arab–Islamic civilization and what was temporal and optional or at least modifiable.

Through such modern media as the journals *al 'Urwat al Wuthqa* (commencing in 1883) and more influentially *al Manar*, he propagated the notion that Islam was every bit as rational as European science and philosophy and that Islam could be the basis for a modern progressive Arab way of life. He went so far as to integrate the idea of evolution and the prophecy of Muhammad, as well as to support the notion of causality (which some Muslims saw and see as a denial of Allah's final authority). Islam, in his mind, was a religion of reason, of nature, and of the future, and he went so far as proposing changes to the curriculum of the leading Egyptian university, Al Azhar, to add modern natural and social sciences. This modern knowledge was essential to the wealth and happiness of the people and to the strength of the society and was therefore not un-Islamic or un-Arab—if taught in Arabic with a firm moral underpinning. Many of his changes were enacted, although he was forced to resign from the reform committee in 1905, partly due to pressure from conservatives.

Al-Afghani and 'Abduh were hardly the only figures of modernization and reform in the colonial Arab world, nor were they the most radical. Muhammad Rashid Rida contributed to and perpetuated the work of both, in a more conservative and theological vein. Farid Wajdi, in his *al-Madaniyyi wa'l-Islam* (*Islam and Civilization*), raised the laws of society and history discovered by the West to virtually the same level as the laws revealed in Islam but insisted that they were identical. "In such works," Hourani opines, "Islam was, so to speak, 'dissolved' into modern thought."[35] Lufit al-Sayyid demoted Islam still further, reaching a basically pluralistic or relativistic position that, while Islam provided the basis for Arab civilization, other religions could and did serve that function for other civilizations—and that therefore religion was in an important sense "functional" and not the only contributing factor to that function.

Among the Christian Arab modernists of that and the following generation were Shibli Shumayyil, Farah Antun, Georgie Zaidan, and Salama Musa. Shumayyil (1850–1917) in particular introduced Darwinism to the Arab world and championed the separation of religion from government; a much more thorough secularist than his predecessors, he "believed that the religion of science necessitated a declaration of war on older religions" and that "nations grew stronger as religion grew weaker."[36] Antun (1874–1922), drawing his inspiration from the classical philosopher Ibn Rushd, was such a complete secularist and separatist that Rashid Rida accused him of atheism. Musa (1887–1958) was more positively hostile not only to Islam and religion but to Eastern civilization as a whole, asserting that "society cannot advance or progress unless the role of religion in the human conscience is restricted; progress is the new religion of humanity."[37]

We have already encountered the polemical religion/state separatism of Ali Abd al-Raziq (1888–1966). Taha Hussain (1879–1973) sought to debunk early Muslim culture and literature as well as politics: beyond rejecting the divinity of the Caliphate and of the political authority of Islam, he also wrote a controversial book in 1926 called *On Pre-Islamic Poetry* in which he questioned the authenticity of certain aspects of the Qur'an and accused Muslims of forging much of so-called pre-Islamic culture. In his 1938 *The Future of Culture in Egypt* he went so far as to suggest that Egypt essentially was a part of the West and not of Islamic civilization at all.

ARAB SECULARISM FROM INDEPENDENCE TO THE PRESENT

Albert Hourani refers to the period from 1798 to 1939 as the "liberal age" in Arab–Islamic thought, and although it is certainly true that there were liberalizing agents and forces afoot, as we have just seen, it would be incorrect to assume that these were the only ones in action. Zaki Badawi suggests that four concurrent movements were in operation: the liberal/Westernizing, the secularist, the conservative, and the Islamic revivalist. All responded to the same basic social/political/

economic conditions, all grappled with the challenge not only of Western civilization but of colonialism, globalization, and modernity in general, and all referred to—and most, including the liberals and some secularists—the specific heritage of Islam, raising the question of Islamic or Arab "specificity."

If the colonial era in *al-'alam al-'arabi* had opened hesitantly with the 1798 invasion of Egypt, it was in full effect by the French conquest of Algeria (starting in 1830) and of Tunisia (starting in 1881), the British administration of Egypt (from 1882) and Sudan (from 1898), and of course the defeat of the Ottoman Empire during World War I, which brought French and British occupation to the Arab heartland. With these events, the victory of the West seemed complete, and the crisis of the East seemed acute. Interestingly if not ironically, the period from the 1880s, through the independence of the various Arab or Muslim states, until 1967 at least, may be remembered as the great age of Arab secularism. In fact, according to the analysis of Ibrahim Abu-Rabi', of the four main currents of twentieth-century Arabic thought—nationalist, liberal, Marxist/leftist, and Islamist—three might rightly be dubbed "secularist."

Secularism was one movement or dream among many until outside events once again—specifically the First World War and the break-up of the Turkish empire—brought secularism to power in Ataturk's new modern state of Turkey. As described elsewhere in this volume, Ataturk sought to modernize Turkey by eradicating the most backward and superstitious elements of religion and by putting the remainder of religion in its place within a secular society, which meant out of public/political affairs and under the authority of the state, which included after 1924 a "Department of the Affairs of Piety" to manage and administer religion secularly.

In the Arab world from Iraq to Morocco, most often postcolonial state government, including "development and administrative strategies, coercive functions, information flow, and educational systems were firmly in the group of men whose training and outlook were overwhelmingly secular" (p. xiii).[38] As John Esposito adds,

> While the separation of religion and politics was not total (as it is not in fact in many secular countries in the West), the role of Islam in state and society as a source of legitimation of rulers, states, and government institutions was greatly curtailed. . . . The central government also attempted to bring Islamic institutions (mosques, religiously endowed properties or *awqaf*, religious courts, etc.) under state control.[39] (p. 2)

This was, in the words of John Entelis, an era of optimism, coming after the flush of successful independence movements, "envisioned [as] a sustained period of 'modernization' involving expanded social opportunity, sustained economic growth, and cultural diffusion or 'Westernization'";

despite the fact that such regimes were often "blatantly authoritarian," hopes were still high and such rigid social control from the central was frequently seen as necessary if not actually beneficial (p. ix).[40]

The most conspicuous cases of secular Arab governments, usually with more or less strongly secularizing policies for their societies, were Algeria, Tunisia (especially under the rule of Habib Bourguiba from 1957 to 1987), the Ba'athist regimes as in Syria and Iraq, and of course Egypt under Nasser and his successors, Sadat and Mubarak. Tunisia may be the most overt example: after French invasion in 1881, a "Young Tunisian" movement soon began, along the lines of the "Young Turk" movement within the Ottoman Empire, that sought to reform society through "adaptation of desirable and useful Western social, economic, and political values." (p. 32).[41] It is not at all insignificant that Tunisia, like the rest of the Maghreb, was a French colony, exposed to a particularly stringent version of secularism known as *laicisme*; a product of revolutionary France, *laicisme* (related to the English word "laity") was a radical program of not only separation but suppression of religion, which, in the words of Rachid al-Ghannouchi literally "declared war against the church," and it was men who were "graduates of the French school of thought" who inherited the levers of power there (p. 97).[42]

Bourguiba sought to modernize his country in a definitely Western mold. He introduced reforms of politics and government, the media, and education. He also championed a "code of personal status" that contradicted Muslim custom and *shari'a* law in a variety of ways, including outlawing polygamy and extending women's rights in marriage, which institution was reconceived as a voluntary civil contract rather than a religious bond. His administration embraced family planning and limited *waqf* religious properties and endowments. In his later years he became a staunch opponent of militant Islamism.

Algeria has been another case of post-French secular government. By World War I there were "new voices protesting the colonial conditions," not traditionalist or Islamic ones but "city voices speaking almost exclusively in French and demanding not the world of the Qur'an, the Sunna, or of the local holy men but the world envisioned by European thinkers—Voltaire, Rousseau, Auguste Comte. . . . At first assimilationists and later liberal nationalists, these men were overwhelmingly secular in outlook" (p. 75).[43] The Algerian struggle against French occupation, starting in 1954, also "was instigated by secular militants,"[44] and the struggle eventually brought to power the Front de Liberation Nationale (FLN), which governed as an Arab socialist and revolutionary party with "a thin veneer of Islam" while it "pursued an essentially secular path of political and economic development."[45] As recounted below, in the late 1980s the FLN faced a stiff challenge from a populist Islamic party that caused it to negate the electoral victory of the Islamists—thus choosing secularism over democracy.

Ba'athism was a form of Arab nationalism that took hold predominantly in Syria and Iraq. From the word *ba'ath* for "resurrection," it was a movement arising in the 1940s from the Syrian Arab Socialist Party of Akram Howrani and the Arab Resurrection Party of Michel Aflaq; Aflaq in particular had studied in Europe and was influenced by the ideas of Herder on nationalism and Lenin on imperialism. By the 1950s the Ba'ath Party held a significant share of seats in the Syrian parliament, and in 1958 it eventually but temporarily achieved one of its pan-Arab goals by merging Syria into a "United Arab Republic" with Egypt. In 1963 political coups brought Ba'athists to power in Syria and Iraq, in the latter of which Abd-al Karim Qasim was overthrown in a purge that would subsequently lead to Saddam Hussein's reign (1979–2003).

The Ba'ath regimes, especially the Iraqi version and especially the Hussein version, highlight the tendency of "secular" Arab governments to exploit religion even if they did not practice religion and to devolve into authoritarianism or worse. In fact, many observers despair that Ba'athism was and is not so much opposed to religion as to anything that stands in the way of its absolute authority. Nevertheless, its policies do pit it against Islam in many ways and against radical political Islam in almost every way.

Morocco is a unique case of a monarchy that survived colonialism but whose postindependence "model of state-building unmistakably reflects the elements of a secular state: liberal orientation, a constitution, parliament, political pluralism, professional organizations, and a modern educational system" (pp. 167–68).[46] One of the great figures on that scene was Muhammad Ibn al-Hassan al-Wazzani (1910–1978), a "secularist" and nationalist who admired the politician Ataturk and the scholar al-Raziq. He believed in constraints on the power of the sovereign, based both in Western liberal values and his reading of Islamic history, such that caliphs and even the *ulama* have no political authority. He was thus a firm religion–state separatist and a proponent of the National Charter of Rights, a document modeled after the French *Declaration des Droits de l'Homme and du Citoyen.*

Egypt is our final but perhaps the best-known instance of a secularist administration, which has now lasted several decades through at least three rulers; as we have seen, Egypt has in fact been a center of Arab secularism for generations. Home to al-Afghani, 'Abduh, and many more secular heroes, the Egyptian revolution of 1952 "brought to power men who [were] fully alive to the need for accepting the techniques of modern industry, and living in the universe of modern political discourse," even if they were intent to put a distinctly Arab spin on them.[47] Like Ataturk whom he emulated in many ways, Jamal Abd'ul Nasir, also known as Gemal Abdel Nasser, put "national" interest and identity ahead of religious: he envisioned an Egyptian unity, and an Arab unity, and even a non-Western unity that clearly did not rest on

Islam. Along with unity he emphasized Western-style republicanism (although certainly not democracy) and industrialization, and while he aimed to advance the cause of pan-Arabism, he also had to confront the problem of Islamist opposition, particularly in the form of the Muslim Brotherhood. In fact, in 1966 Nasser had one of the most prominent leaders and theorists of the Brotherhood, Sayyid Qutb, executed, "arresting and imprisoning thousands, and driving many others underground or into exile. By the late Nasser period [his regime ended in 1971], the state had coopted the religious establishment and silenced its Islamic (and indeed any and all) opposition."[48] Anwar Sadat (ruled 1971–1981) roughly carried on the policies of Nasser while moderating somewhat toward the Islamists; this did not prevent his assassination at the hands of the *Jamaat al-Jihad* or "Society of Holy War." His successor and still president in 2009, Hosni Mubarak, initially attempted to steer a course of "political liberalization and tolerance while at the same time responding quickly and firmly to those who resorted to violence to challenge the authority of the government," including but not limited to the Islamists, but within a decade this policy gave way to more aggressive response to the challenge of both religious extremists (those who advocated the violent overthrow of the government) and moderates (those who participated within the established political and legal framework) resorting to "harassment and imprisonment" against threats Islamic and otherwise.[49]

THE LIMITS OF ARAB SECULARISM AND ITS PROSPECTS FOR THE FUTURE

As is plain to see, the promises of the Entelis' "era of optimism" were not entirely realized; indeed, he determines that the golden days of benign authoritarianism turned more malignant in the 1960s and 1970s, with the dictatorial state morphing into the *mukhabarat* or Arab police state. This was one, but by no means the only, reason why secularism began to fall from favor in many parts of *al-'alam al-'arabi*. In fact, one sure sign of a turning tide was the "conversion" of a number of previously liberal or Marxist Arab thinkers back to Islam, including Adil Hussain, Tariq al-Bishri, Muhammad Imarah, Rashid al-Ghannouchi, and Munir Shafiq. At the same time, openly Islamist, even militant and violent groups and parties, began to emerge, triumph, and—in the case of Iran—achieve power.

Again, there are many explanations for the distaste toward secularism in recent decades, not all of which have to do with secularism itself. One of the most glaring explanations is the association of secularism with the foreign and still dominant West: many thoughtful Arabs perceive it as yet more cultural imposition, a form or arm of neocolonialism. Additionally, the expectations of economic growth and prosperity were not met: scholars and the masses alike noticed that increasing "modernization" did not seem to bring wealth and economic independence but rather increasing dependence on and hegemony of the West; Arab regimes actually often appeared to be in collusion with the West (especially the Persian Gulf states, Saudi Arabia in particular), or at best unable to mount an effective response. In a word, the secular-nationalist option seemed have failed.

A number of commentators note the wider failure to develop a modern secular "civil society," which took various shapes. For one—and this complaint is echoed in from many sources—the secularizing forces in most Arab states were always a small elite group. As Abu-Rabi' puts it, the "social base" of secularist nationalist modernization was always "narrow," attracting little of the general populace of the state.[50] Even worse, he suggests that in many instances there was not only a class but a tribal or sectarian division between the ruling secular elite and the majority of the citizens. Furthermore, and partly because of this structural weakness, regimes could not and did not support the development of independent institutions of a civil society, such as trade organizations, professional groups, free political parties, and the like. Again in Abu-Rabi's formulation, leaders tried to accomplish modernization without modernism—without the cultural and social foundations upon which such values and practices are securely built.

Finally, there were political reasons—both internal and external—for the perceived retreat of secularism. One was the continuing irritant of the Israel–Palestine issue. The Arab defeat in the 1967 war was seen by many as a total indictment of the secular modernizing project. Later, the collapse of the USSR and the exhaustion of Marxism drove others away from that source of secularist thought. More than few observers claim that the West did not really want or support truly free and successful Arab democratic and secular systems; however, perhaps most directly, secularism was often associated with the bitter experience of political oppression and even violence at home. As John Voll states, "the processes of Westernization as experienced in North Africa [and most of the Arab world] in the past century lead not to democracy but to authoritarianism" (p. 14).[51] Thus, much of the resistance to secular regimes, from Iran to Algeria, was not only or mostly about the secularism but about the tyranny and repressiveness of those regimes.

We must then see the rise of Islamism in the late twentieth and early twenty-first centuries as partly a response to the failed economics and exclusionary politics of the existing Arab states. In this sense, however, this resurgent and muscular religion is in a sense an effect of secularization—and in a sense more than a bit secular itself. Bichara Khader writes that the new Islamism is not traditional religion, certainly not eternal religious truth, but rather "the product of a given space and time. You do not need to search in the Koranic texts to understand Islamism. Instead, you need to analyze and interpret the social, political, and economic realities in which it has developed. The explanation lies not in theology, but in the human sciences" (p. 58).[52] Islamism is religion, to be sure, but it is religion *in reaction* and thus is very much a creature of its particular historical and social context, of its "age," and thereby "secular" in the original sense of the term.

As Abu-Rabi' summarizes,

> The debate about religion in contemporary Arab society is more than merely theological or metaphysical controversy. It is about all things that have gone wrong in contemporary Arab society; it is, in fact, about the identity of an Arab society that fell under the impact of the humanistic/ capitalistic/post-Enlightenment West of the nineteenth century.[53]

Such Islamism has always been one of the currents in the response to the encroaching West. Thus, the "causes" of the Islamic movement are more than slightly secular: unemployment, poverty, inadequate housing, corruption, repression, cultural/political/military weakness, most recently unaffordable or simply unavailable food, and so on. One Algerian man complained that his only four options were unemployment, participation in the black market, emigration to France, or membership in the Islamic Salvation Front (FIS, the party that "successfully" challenged the ruling FLN for power, only to be denied that power by force).[54] One last time, the origins and strength of contemporary Islamic movements "are to be found primarily in the political and economic circumstances of these countries rather than in the religious and cultural traditions of their inhabitants."[55]

Reference to Islamic "movements" reminds us too that, while there is religion (among other things) in their message, there is secularity and modernism in their medium. Islamists form political parties and use all of the tools of modern technology (print, television, computers, the Internet, not to mention modern weapons) to achieve their goals. Some Islamists engage in debates with secularists and other opponents, as occurred in 1986 in Egypt between secularist Fu'ad Zakariya and Islamists Shaykh Muhammad al-Ghazali and Yusuf al-Qardawi (with converted Islamists Tariq al-Bishri and 'Adil Husayn serving as commentators—an event which was formally entitled "A Seminar [on Islam] and Secularism" (*Nadwa hawla al-Islam wa al-'ilmaniyya*).[56] Similar encounters happened in 1997, including a debate between Syrian secularist Sadiq Jalal al-'Azm and conservative Shaykh Yusif al-Qaradawi (which was broadcast on the Arab television station al-Jazira) and another between Nasir Hamid Abu Zayd and Egyptian religious thinker Muhammad 'Imara. Running arguments also take place in newspapers and journals. Some, like Khalid Muhammad Khalid, have gone so far as to endorse representative democracy, multiparty elections, and freedom of the press, as desirable and compatible forms of Islamic politics.

Ultimately, if a religious movement actually seizes power, by force or by vote, it must then govern. Although this might seem like the defeat of secularism (the closing of the space between religion and state), in an ironic manner it is a triumph for secularism, as the religious movement must now function like a government in the real world. A regime like Khomeini's in Iran or the Taliban's in Afghanistan may indeed institute the *shari'a*, but must also deliver the mail, pick up the trash, and maintain the army—all secular activities. As evidence of the contradiction implicit in the merger of religion and temporal power, in 1988, Khomeini declared that the state had the authority to rule even in opposition to Islamic law or ritual duty.

One final point to be made is that today's confident Islamism is not inevitably the end of secularism in the Arab world. Just as Islamism represents a response and challenge to secularism, so secularism reappears as a counter-response and counter-challenge—perhaps, in some cases, more confident and radical than before. In answer to the Islamist wave, Muhammad Sa'id al-'Ashmawi in 1987 published *Political Islam*, which renews the argument from al-Raziq that "Islam was from the beginning an apolitical religion concerned solely with spiritual and ethical guidance. The form Islam has subsequently taken—as 'religion and state'—for him is a deviation and a perversion of that true conception" (pp. 32–33).[57] Even most insistent voices like those of Fu'ad Zakariyya and Faraj Fawda (also known as Farag Foda) joined the chorus; Zakariyya, for instance, has called the mentality of the Islamists "medieval" and warned urgently about the need to oppose Islamism as a political force:

> Any struggle between political parties and tendencies in Egypt . . . remains a struggle between two human positions, whereas the Islamic tendency, if successful, would move this struggle to a completely different level. It would become a struggle between heaven and earth, between the party of God and the party of the devil. . . . Once the governing body comes to speak in the name of the *shari'a*, opposition turns to unbelief, any difference becomes an insolence in the face of God's law or an apostasy that has to be punished applying the appropriate *hadd* [Quranic punishment—in this case, death]. The conditions of political and social struggle will become much worse and much more difficult. I am not exaggerating if I say that the idea of the struggle itself will then be thoroughly uprooted.
>
> Therefore the interest of the left, and with it all nationalist forces, in maintaining the proper conditions for a legitimate political struggle imposes on all the duty to close ranks and stand against a tendency threatening to eradicate the principle of struggle itself.[58]

Fawda, regarded by some as more outspoken and articulate than Zakariyya, paid the ultimate price for criticizing his enemies as "obscurantists" (*zalamiyyun*) and ridiculing them publicly: he was assassinated on June

8, 1992—which act was lauded by Ma'mum al-Hudaybi, the head of the Muslim Brotherhood at the time, as the proper fate for an apostate.

While such attempts to stamp out secularism may have a chilling effect on some of its proponents, they also have the potential to push some individuals from a tolerant secularism to a confrontation one or even to outright rejection of Islam and all religion. Already these products of repressive tyrannical religion (which was itself a product of repressive tyrannical politics) have appeared, in the person of Ibn Warraq, Ayaan Hirsch Ali, and the almost two dozen subjects of Susan Crimps' and Joel Richardson's new book *Why We Left Islam*.[59] So, while secularism and even atheism may not be the driving forces in the Arab world, they are forces that have existed in some form or another from the very beginning of its Islamic phase and that appear certain to survive, reemerge, and redefine Islam and *al-'alam al-'arabi* for a future age, for a future *saeculum*.

NOTES

1. Ernest Gellner, "Islam and Marxism: Some Comparisons, " *International Affairs* 67, no. 1 (1991): 1–6.

2. Alexander Flores, "Egypt: A New Secularism?" *Middle East Report* 153 (1988):27–30.

3. Albert Hourani, *Arabic Thought in the Liberal Age, 1798–1939* (London and New York: Oxford University Press), 1.

4. Abdullahi Ahmed An-Na'im, *Islam and the Secular State: Negotiating the Future of Shari'a* (Cambridge, MA and London: Harvard University Press, 2008).

5. S. Parvez Manzoor, "Desacralizing Secularism," in *Islam and Secularism in the Middle East*, ed. Azzam Tamimi and John L. Esposito (Washington Square, NY: New York University Press, 2000), 81–96.

6. Hourani, op. cit., 10.

7. Ira M. Lapidus, "The Separation of State and Religion in the Development of Early Islamic Society," *International Journal of Middle East Studies* 6, no. 4 (1975):363–385.

8. Ibrahim M. Abu-Rabi', *Contemporary Arab Thought: Studies in Post-1967 Arab Intellectual History* (London and Sterling VA: Pluto Press), 15.

9. Hourani, op. cit., 21.

10. Ibn Khaldun, *The Muqaddima*, Vol. 3, 2nd ed., Franz Rosenthal, trans. (Princeton: Princeton University Press, 1989), 427.

11. Quoted in Maurice Boormans, "Cultural Dialogue and 'Islamic Specificity,'" in *Islam, Modernism, and the West: Cultural and Political Relations at the End of the Millennium*, ed. Gema Martin Munoz (London and New York: I. B. Tauris Publishers, 81–93), p. 92–93.

12. Quoted in ibid., 91.

13. Quoted in Leonard Binder, *Islamic Liberalism: A Critique of Development Ideologies* (Chicago and London: University of Chicago Press, 1988), 131.

14. Lapidus, op. cit., 364.

15. Ibid., 384.

16. Ibn Warraq, *Why I am Not a Muslim* (Amherst, NY: Prometheus Books, 1995), 247.

17. Ibid., 254.

18. Ibid., 283.

19. Bernard Lewis, *The Political Language of Islam* (Chicago and London: The University of Chicago Press, 1988), 25.

20. An-Na'im, op. cit., 49.

21. Bernard Lewis, *What Went Wrong?* (New York: Harper Perennial, 2002), 100.

22. Falur Rahman, *Islam and Modernity: Transformation of an Intellectual Tradition* (Chicago and London: The University of Chicago Press, 1982), 14.

23. Quoted in Hourani, op. cit., 49.

24. Rahman, op. cit., 59.

25. Hourani, op. cit., 72.

26. Quoted in Azzam Tamimi, "The Origins of Arab Secularism," in *Islam and Secularism in the Middle East*, ed. Azzam Tamimi and John L. Esposito (Washington Square, NY: New York University Press, 2001), 13–28.

27. Quoted in Hourani, op. cit., 88.

28. Quoted in M. A. Zaki Badawi, *The Reformers of Egypt* (London: Croom Helm, 1976), 23.

29. Ibid., 29.

30. Ibid., 28.

31. Hourani, op. cit., 114.

32. Ibid., 123.

33. Badawi, op. cit., 40.

34. Quoted in Hourani, op. cit., 137.

35. Ibid., 162.

36. Badawi, op. cit., 22–23.

37. Quoted in ibid., 24.

38. John Ruedy, "Introduction," in *Islamism and Secularism in North Africa*, ed. John Ruedy (New York: St. Martin's Press, 1996 [1994]), xiii–xx.

39. John Esposito, "Introduction: Islam and Secularism in the Twenty-First Century," in *Islam and Secularism in the Middle East*, ed. Azzam Tamimi and John L. Esposito (Washington Square, NY: New York University Press, 2001) 1–12.

40. John P. Entelis, "Introduction," in *Islam, Democracy, and the State in North Africa*, ed. John P. Entelis (Bloomington and Indianapolis: Indiana University Press, 1997), ix–xxv.

41. Kenneth J. Perkins, "'The Masses Look Ardently to Istanbul': Tunisia, Islam, and the Ottoman Empire, 1837–1931," in *Islamism and Secularism in North Africa*, ed. John Ruedy (New York: St. Martin's Press, 1996 [1994]), 23–36.

42. Rachid al-Ghannouchi, "Secularism in the Arab Maghreb," in *Islam and Secularism in the Middle East*, ed. Azzam Tamimi and John L. Esposito (Washington Square, NY: New York University Press, 2001), 97–123.

43. John Ruedy, "Continuities and Discontinuities in the Algerian Confrontation with Europe," in *Islamism and Secularism in North Africa*, ed. John Ruedy (New York: St. Martin's Press, 1996 [1994]), 73–85.

44. Ibid., 78.

45. John L. Esposito and John O. Voll, *Islam and Democracy* (New York and Oxford: Oxford University Press, 1996), 152.

46. Emad Eldin Shahin, "Secularism and Nationalism: The Political Discourse of 'Abd al-Salam Yassin," in John Ruedy, ed. *Islamism and Secularism in North Africa*, ed. John Ruedy (New York: St. Martin's Press, 1996 [1994]), 167–185.

47. Hourani, op. cit., 348–349.

48. Esposito and Voll, op. cit., 174.

49. Ibid., 177.

50. Abu-Rabi', op. cit., 52.

51. John O. Voll, "Sultans, Saints, and Presidents: The Islamic Community and the State in North Africa," in *Islam, Democracy, and the State in North Africa*, ed. John P. Entelis (Bloomington and Indianapolis: Indiana University Press, 1997), 1–16.

52. Bichara Khader, "The Euro-Mediterranean Partnership: A Singular Approach to a Plural Mediterranean," in *Islam, Modernism, and the West: Cultural and Political Relations at the End of the Millennium*, ed. Gema Martin Munoz (London and New York: I. B. Tauris Publishers), 47–62.

53. Abu-Rabi', op. cit., 53–54.

54. Mark Tessler, "The Origins of Popular Support for Islamic Movements: A Political Economy Analysis," in *Islam, Democracy, and the State in North Africa*, ed. John P. Entelis (Bloomington and Indianapolis: Indiana University Press, 1997), 93–126.

55. Ibid., 93.

56. Nancy E. Gallagher, "Islam v. Secularism in Cairo: An Account of the Dar al-Hikma Debate," *Middle Eastern Studies* 25, no. 2, (1989):208–215.

57. Alexander Flores, "Secularism, Integralism, and Political Islam," *Middle East Report* 183 (1993):32–38.

58. Quoted in ibid., 37.

59. Ibn Warraq, *Why I Am Not a Muslim*; Ayaan Hirsch Ali, *Infidel* (New York: Free Press, 2007); Susan Crimp and Joel Richardson, eds. *Why We Left Islam: Former Muslims Speak Out* (Los Angeles: WND Books, 2008).

Chapter 7

Atheism and Secularity in India

Innaiah Narisetti

The Republic of India, with a population of one billion, is 81.3 percent Hindu, 12 percent Muslim, 2.3 percent Christian, 1.9 percent Sikh, and less than 1 percent Buddhist. The census has no column to note the number of unbelievers or atheists. The Indian constitution is secular but the governments and general society are nonsecular. The separation of state and religion is never implemented, neither in letter nor in spirit. Secularism is interpreted as "equal respect to all religions," an interpretation that puts limitations on the development of a truly secular spirit. Every religion at some point has entered into politics, all political parties use religion as a way to catch votes, and every religion takes advantage of this situation in getting tax exemptions. This mutual understanding among the parties concerning religion does not allow secular laws to be put into practice. All religions get holidays for their festivals, which are officially declared as national holidays. Governments practice religious rituals during opening ceremonies, inaugurations, ground-breaking occasions, and so on. Elected representatives normally take an oath in the name of God, whereas very few take an oath on their conscience or the constitution.

However, the Indian constitution also envisages scientific temper as a fundamental duty; human rights are also fundamental. The first prime minister of an independent India was Jawaharlal Nehru (1889–1964). He stood for secular values and a uniform civil code that transcended religious laws. But he was also head of the ruling Congress party, which never allowed him to have his own way in implementing secularism. Among India's politicians since Nehru, atheists, rationalists, and humanists can be counted on one's fingers; most prominent are the late Mr. Ram Manohar Lohia, a socialist leader who was an ardent atheist and propagandist, and Bhimrao Ambedkar, a Buddhist leader who was also a secularist who converted some lower caste Hindus to Buddhism and fought against caste hierarchy, although without much success.

Indian public schools do have secular education; the government of India has established national-level textbook guidelines that are followed by state-level textbooks. They are by and large secular. However, private schools run by religious institutions are based on the teaching of their respective holy books, and they are inculcating the children with blind beliefs.

In the absence of secular political parties, various nongovernmental organizations are functioning at numerous levels to propagate secular values, which has proven to be an uphill task. The fact is, membership within all the secular organizations in India is negligible among the population of one billion. It would be surprising if the total membership exceeded more than half a million. Most of the organizations confine their activities to their respective states, India being a vast country with fourteen official languages and twenty-eight states. Indian secular organizations are indeed few, with limited resources and facilities.

RADICAL HUMANIST MOVEMENT

The Radical Humanist movement in India began under the leadership of Manavendra Nath Roy (1887–1955), who did pioneering work in spreading a scientific outlook among intellectuals, university professors, media persons, and scientists. M. N. Roy pleaded for the scientific study of history, since Indian history is full of myths and stories without any scientific evidence. He also advocated a scientific approach concerning politics. His Radical Humanist movement commenced its task from 1948 onward, immediately after India attained independence. M. N. Roy helped to shape a philosophical and scientific outlook to various disparate unbelief movements throughout India. He organized reorientation study camps where the scientific orientation was promoted. Roy also established Radical Humanist, Renaissance, and Rationalist organizations and elevated them to the international level, often questioning the prevailing Gandhian spiritual ideology of his day. After the death of Roy in 1955, several intellectuals and institutions carried on his spirit of scientific, rational inquiry through study camps, training classes, publications, seminars, and magazines.

INDIAN SECULAR MOVEMENT

Professor A. B. Shah (died 1982) was the founder of the Indian Secular Society. He was from Pune and lived in Mumbai, where, with the help of Hamid Dalwai, he tried to educate Muslims. He also established Satya Shodak Mandal, with the purpose of bringing Muslim youth into the mainstream of secular society. His book *Muslim Politics* provoked much discussion. Facing the wrath of many Hindus by questioning the ban on killing cows, he vigorously propagated the scientific method as a solution to several problems facing obscurantist India. His book *Scientific Method* made a rare breakthrough in Indian academia when it was prescribed as a textbook in Bangalore University when H. Narasimhaiah was the vice chancellor. Shah started several publications and magazines (*Humanist Review, New Quest,* and *The Secularist*) and educational reform campaigns for humanism and secularism. Currently, Mr. V. K. Sinha edits *The Secularist* and *New Quest* magazines from Mumbai.

Shah's scientific approach to religion and politics faced several difficulties, especially from fundamentalist Hindus and Muslims. He organized study camps, meetings, seminars, and symposia, instituting a dialogue of all sections of religious organizations. He challenged the cult gurus and fanatic Muslim mullahs, and he opened debates about holy books. He stood for human values and human rights. He tried to spread the ideas through scientific method and education. The movement took strong roots in some states of India, especially Maharastra, Andhra Pradesh, Delhi, Gujarat, Rajasthan, and Kerala.

INDIAN RATIONALIST MOVEMENT

The Rationalist Association, which started in Bombay during the 1930s, has slowly picked up momentum over the years. Abraham Solomon, Lokhandawala, M. N. Roy, M. V. Ramamurhty, R. Venkatadri, Avula Gopalakrishna Murthy, and Innaiah Narisetti have all been active participants and leaders of the movement. There currently exists a Federation of Indian Rationalist, Atheist, and Humanist organizations (FIRA), which was started by Mr. Basava Premanand, recent editor of *Indian Skeptic*. He was succeeded as president by Dr. Narendra Naik in 2007. FIRA is an umbrella organization that includes groups and committees from all over India, including the Ananthapur Rationalist Association, Andhra Pradesh, Atheist Center, Kerela Bangalore Rationalist Humanist Association, Patna. Dakshina Kannada Rationalist, Hyderabad Rationalist Forum, Tamil Nadu, and Tarksheel Society.

PERIYAR MOVEMENT

Periyar E. V. Ramasamy (1879–1973) was a great social revolutionary who opposed caste hierarchy and Hindu Brahmin domination of other castes and sought equal rights in temple priesthood. Hitherto, only members of the Brahmin caste were allowed to become priests. Periyar wanted all castes, including the downtrodden castes, to be able to officiate at marriages and perform religious ceremonies in temples. He wanted the abolition of untouchability, which was the creation of Hinduism. Periyar's vigorous and spirited role in the Vaikom Satyagraha (1924–1925) contributed in no small measure to the triumph of that first historic social struggle in the history of modern India. This paved the way for the "untouchables" to use public roads without any inhibition and for other progressive egalitarian social measures. The Self-Respect Movement, founded by Periyar in 1925, carried on a vigorous and ceaseless campaign against ridiculous and harmful superstitions, traditions, customs, and habits. He sought to dispel the ignorance of the people and make them enlightened. He exhorted them to take steps to change the institutions and values that led to meaningless divisions and unjust discrimination. He advised them to change according to the requirements of the changing times and keep pace with modern conditions. Self-respecters performed marriages without Brahmin priests (*purohits*) and without religious rites. They insisted on equality between men and women in all walks of life. They encouraged intercaste and widow marriages. Periyar also propagated the need for birth control, as far back is the 1920s. He gathered support for lawful abolition of the Devadasi (temple prostitute) system and the practice of child marriage. It was mainly due to his consistent and energetic propaganda that the policy of reservations in job opportunities in government administration was put into practice in the then Madras Province (which included Tamilnadu) in 1928.

While in prison, Periyar was elected as the leader of the South Indian Liberal Federation, popularly known as the Justice Party. As a result of Periyar's persistent efforts, the degrading practice of serving separately the Brahmins and the "others" in the restaurants in railway stations was abolished in 1941. The conservative section in the Justice Party disliked Periyar's radical social reform program, his critical view of religious literature, and the propagation of rationalist ideas. Unmindful of their opposition, he continued his forward march and gathered around him the youth and the common people. It was during 1942–1943 that Maniammai joined the movement and came to attend to the personal needs of Periyar. She was devoted to the leader and served him sincerely. They married later in 1948.

DRAVIDAR KAZHAGAM (1944–1973)

The Justice Party's provincial conference held in Salem in 1944 marked a turning point in Periyar's movement. The name of the Party was changed to Dravidar Kazhagam. The members were asked to give up their posts, positions, and titles conferred by the British rulers. They were also required to drop the caste suffix of their names. It was in this historic Salem conference that Periyar allowed Mr. K. Veeramani, the current president of Dravidar Kazhagam, to stand on the table and address the gathering. Arignar Anna introduced him to the audience as the Thiru Gnanasambandar of the Self-respect movement. (Gnanasambandar was a precocious devotee and composer of hymns in Tamil in the Saivite lore.) Followers of Periyar were looking for an opportunity to part with him. When he married Maniammai in 1948, he quit Dravidar Kazhagam, stating that Periyar had set a bad example by marrying a young woman in his old age; he was 70 and she 30. Those who parted company with Periyar formed Dravida Munnetra Kazhagam (DMK), under the leadership of C. N. Annadurai (Arignar Anna).

In 1956, the Dravidar Kazhagam undertook an agitation of burning the portrait of Lord Rama because he symbolized the preservation of *Varna dharma* (caste system). Periyar was placed under preventive arrest on this occasion. In those days, the board "Brahmins Hotel" was displayed, following the lead given by the Brahmins, to indicate that only vegetarian food was served there. Dravidar Kazhagam objected to the *Varna dharma* connotation and started an agitation symbolically in front of a hotel in Madras (Chennai) in 1957. Batches of volunteers agitated daily, and 1,010 of them courted arrest until March 1958, when it culminated in success. Dravidar Kazhagam subsequently decided to undertake further agitation, demanding an end to the practice of appointing only Brahmins as *Archakas* (priests) in Agamic temples, as a way of removing one of the root causes of Varna-Jaathi.

The United Nations Educational Scientific and Cultural Organization (UNESCO) eventually gave an award to Periyar, and the Union Education Minister Triguna Sen, in Madras (Chennai), on June 27, 1970. The citation hailed Periyar as "the Prophet of the New Age, the Socrates of South East Asia, Father of Social Reform Movement, and Arch enemy of ignorance, superstitions, meaningless customs and base manners."

Unmai, a Tamil monthly (now a fortnightly) and *Modern Rationalist*, an English monthly, were started by Periyar in 1970 and 1971, respectively, to propagate the ideals of rational humanism more extensively. The Allahabad High Court lifted proscription of the Hindi version of Periyar's book on Ramayana in 1971. In the same year the proscription of "Ravana Kavyam" proscribed by the Congress Government of the Madras State was removed. On January 12, 1971, the DMK government enacted a law giving equal opportunities to qualified persons to become the *Archakas* of Hindu Agamic temples irrespective of their birth in any Varna or Jaathi (caste). Periyar gave an inspiring clarion call for action to gain social equality and dignified way of life at Thiagaraya Nagar, Chennai on December 19, 1973. He fell ill on the next day and breathed his last on December 24, 1973.

Currently, some 200,000 families are Periyarists, self-respecters, and/or secularists, and for the first time, a rationalist-humanist university has been established as Periyar Maniammai University at Vallam, Thanjavur, Tamil Nadu. Mr. Veeramani has been elected as chancellor, and Dr. N. Ramachandran has been appointed as vice-chancellor. Both are atheists and rationalists.

THE ATHEIST CENTRE

The Atheist Centre was founded by Gora (1902–1975) and Saraswathi Gora (1912–2006) in 1940 at Mudunur Village in Krishna District, Andhra Pradesh. On the eve of Indian independence, the Atheist Centre was shifted to Vijayawada in 1947, and since then it has been a hub of activity for the promotion of atheism, humanism, and social change. After the death of Gora in 1975, the Atheist Centre's activities are undertaken under the able guidance of Mrs. Saraswathi Gora, the cofounder of the Centre. She was assisted by a dedicated team of people who are engaged in the promotion of atheism as a way of life. The Atheist Centre is also actively engaged in secular social work activities for comprehensive rural development and rendering assistance to the people to develop an alternate way of life along secular and humanist lines. The Atheist Centre gives the highest priority to fighting the evil practices of untouchability and caste distinctions. In the face of severe opposition, the Atheist Centre has taken up programs of intercaste dining and intercaste marriages (marriages among different castes), in order to fight the heinous custom of untouchability. Gora made it a point to stay in an untouchable locality whenever he was invited to address a meeting at any village. Intercaste dining programs were also organized in villages on many occasions. It was a deliberate attempt to usher in modern social change in a traditional society. The Atheist Centre is at the forefront of promoting intercaste and casteless marriages; more than five hundred such marriages have taken place at the Centre and other parts of the state. Members of the Atheist Centre present an example before others by breaking the barriers of untouchability. It is an example that inspires others in the efforts for social equality. In addition to the casteless marriages, it also organizes socially mixed programs where food is cooked in different homes, but eaten together, transcending the barriers of caste. It organizes gatherings of the intercaste and casteless couple and honors them. It also encourages marriages under the Special Marriage Act, which is a secular method without reference to caste and religion. Inter-religion marriages between Hindu–Muslim, Hindu–Christian, and Hindu–Sikh are held at the Centre, strengthening secular values.

Dispelling superstitions is an important work of the Atheist Centre. The superstitious mind that believes in miracles is a bane to Indian society and prevents its forward progress. Hence, Gora and Saraswathi Gora started fighting superstition right from the 1920s; they publicly viewed eclipses, defying the superstitious taboo that pregnant women should not do so. They also lived in so-called haunted houses and exploded the myths surrounding the public's fears of such places. The Atheist Centre takes up programs to promote the scientific outlook and rational thinking. Fire walking demonstrations are organized in the villages. Many so-called miracles are exposed. God-men are challenged to prove their so-called supernatural abilities. When Sai Baba visited Vijayawada, the Atheist Centre questioned him to prove his miracles. Scores of people were arrested in this connection. It also exposed the hoaxes of rebirth.

In a traditional society where people are still steeped in superstition, the belief in witchcraft and sorcery wrecks havoc on many innocent lives. It leads to feuds and even murders in the villages, with allegations and accusations of sorcery. In the Hyderabad State, the belief in witchcraft and sorcery is still deeply entrenched in the minds of the people. In 1983, leaders in the district administration in Medak invited the Atheist Centre to help dispel such superstitions. A team of doctors, social workers, psychiatrists, and scientists, headed by Dr. Samaram, visited Medak District to study the mass hysteria that had reached epidemic proportions. Similar assignments were undertaken in Nalgonda district to educate the people about the nonexistence of witchcraft. In exposing and debunking witchcraft and sorcery, the Atheist Centre receives the cooperation of the Indian Medical Association, the police and the government departments, and other social organizations.

With a view to promoting literacy and education along secular and humanist lines, the Atheist Centre also organizes education and awareness programs. Adult and women's education are important ingredients of these activities. Substantial work has been done by the Atheist Centre in the field of social and adult education. Gora's books for adult literacy and scientific and social outlook are widely read. In a traditional society like India, championing sex education is an uphill task. Undaunted by the hurdles, the Atheist Centre is championing sex education. Dr. Samaram of the Atheist Centre has been writing on sex science in the most popular Telugu daily newspaper *Eenadu* for more than five years. His five volumes *Sex Science* have become very popular. So far, Dr. Samaram has published more than 150 books on health education, family planning, and popularizing medical science. The books are widely read. For the last thirty years, Dr. Samaram has been contributing every week in the dailies and weeklies on various aspects of health and his column of questions and answers on sex problems receives wide attention. Dr. Samaram is not only a medical science writer, but also a practicing doctor. He and Dr. Maru are helping in the organization of health camps and AIDS awareness programs on a wider scale.

GORA (1902–1975)

One of the shining lights of southern India's unbelief movement was Gora, or Goparaju Ramachandrarao. He was a Brahmin who stood against the supremacy of Brahmins and hence was excommunicated from the caste. He came from Andhra Pradesh and was closely associated with M. K. Gandhi in the freedom fight against the British. Gora never compromised on the principle of atheism. His wife Saraswati (died 2006), who also came from an orthodox Brahmin family, was an active participant, and together they led the atheist movement. In 1940, Gora established an atheist center in Vijayawada, a coastal town in Andhra Pradesh and spread secular ideas through magazines, literature, and meetings. Gora toured many countries of the world and was in contact with world atheist leaders such as Madalyn Murray O'Hair. Gora organized beef and pork dinners for Hindus and Muslims, who consider both dishes as sacrilegious. He wanted party-less democracy, simple living, and the spread of positive atheism, which asserts ethical life. His entire family is still promoting his ideas. Gora also conducted several intercaste and interreligious marriages, and both his son and daughter married spouses who came from the untouchable castes, showing by example what their father preached. The international atheist center established by Gora and managed by his family is well known throughout India as well in rationalist circles around the world for its path-breaking activity. Mr. Lavanam, Dr. Vijayam, Dr. Samaram, Vikas Gora, Hemalatha Lavanam, the late Saraswathi Gora, Maaru, Chennupati Vidya (once elected to Parliament of India), and several family members are working hard to spread the atheist philosophy. They conduct science exhibitions, organize international conferences, and publish books and monographs regularly. They run two monthly journals: *Atheist* (in English) and *Naastika patrika* (in Telugu). Their social service to reform former criminal tribes and rehabilitation of the tsunami-affected people in coastal areas is well appreciated. Dr. Samaram exposes the fraudulent claims of alternative medicines, bogus god-men, and their divine powers to safeguard the gullible public. Andhra Pradesh's atheist movements spawned several splinter groups, often with their own magazines and literature. For example, Mr. Ravipudi Venkatadri is editing a monthly Telugu magazine *Hetuvadi* to spread rationalist theories. He has published several books and monographs in Telugu. He heads the Rationalist movement in Andhra Pradesh.

Other southern and western Indian states of Kerala, Karnataka, and Maharastra also saw a surge in rationalist activity in the early twentieth century with skeptical and agnostic ideas. Abraham Kovoor electrified the skeptics' movement with his speeches and demonstrations, touring several states in India as well as Sri Lanka to spread the movement. His books—debunking astrologers and god-men—were very popular. Another active member of the rationalist movement in Kerala was Govindan (late, poet), who edited the magazine, *Sameeksha*. The father and son duo of Joseph and Sanal Edamaruku were also instrumental in challenging god-men and exposing fraudulent "miracles," touring intensively to demonstrate the falsehood of miracles. Sanal Edamaruku shifted to Delhi where he started an international rationalist organization with a Web site, journals, books, and an active publicity campaign. He exposed god-men constantly through demonstrations and media. Sanal Edamaruku is the president of the Rationalist International and edits the Internet publication *Rationalist International*, which appears in English, French, German, Spanish, and Finnish. He has convened three International Rationalist Conferences in 1995, 2000, and 2002. Mr. Sreeni Pattathanam is a Malayalam writer who has ten books and many investigative reports to his credit. He was born in Kollam, Kerala State. He began his career in the police department, which helped him to recognize the unjustifiable alliance between the state and religion. Mr. Sreeni Pattathanam was instrumental several years ago in exposing the "miracle" of the divine Makarajyoti light, which appears during the annual Ayyappa pilgrimage in Kerala on a remote hill. Having resigned from the police service, Mr. Pattathanam became a teacher in a government school. The investigative mind of a police officer and the analytical mind of a schoolteacher gave Mr. Pattathanam a charming presentation of his topic, which reflected in his writings as well. He traveled a lot in the nooks and corners of Kerala. He had been the editor of *Ranarekha*, a rationalist monthly, published in Malayalam. He was also the state general secretary of the Indian Rationalist Association (IRA) of which Mr. Sanal Edamaruku is its national general secretary. Currently he is the chief editor of *Yukthirajyam*, the Malayalam rationalist monthly and the general secretary of Bharatiya Rationalist.

Meanwhile, skeptic groups began working in states such as West Bengal, Orissa, Bihar, Punjab, Gujarat, Andhra Pradesh, Karnataka, Maharashtra, and Tamil Nadu. B. Premanand arranged for a federation of all the groups and conducted several meetings at the national level, personally training several people in magic so that faith healers and god-men and -women could be easily exposed. The state level federation in Andhra Pradesh (FARA) actively fought against fraudulent claims of god-men, alternative medicines, and supernatural claims under the coordinator N. Innaiah. The Rationalist Association, which started in Mumbai during 1930s, slowly picked up the momentum. Abraham Solomon, Lokhandawala, M. N. Roy, M. V. Ramamurhty, R. Venkatadri, Avula Gopalakrishna Murthy, and Innaiah Narisetti were all active participants and advocates of the movement.

BIHAR STATE

The Bihar Buddhiwadi Samaj (Bihar Rationalist Society, BRS) was founded in 1985 by Ms. Kawaljee and Dr. Ramendra as a nonparty, nonprofit, educational society for the promotion of rationalism. Kiran Nath Datt, Shivendra, Manavendra, Ramanand Mandal, and Rahul

Prasad were the other founding members of the organization. In the beginning they used the name "Bihar Buddhiwadi Samaj." Gradually they have started using Bihar Rationalist Society. According to the BRS, blind faith in God and organized religions are big hurdles obstructing the growth of human knowledge and a rational morality.

"Why I Am Not a Hindu" is the only English publication of the BRS, and it was published in 1993. Its second edition titled "Why I Am Not a Hindu" and "Why I Do Not Want Ramrajya" were published in 1995. Besides publishing such works, BRS has also organized meetings, seminars, and letter-writing campaigns. It has organized and supported miracle-busting campaigns, intercaste dining, and intercaste marriages. One of the highlights of the activities of the BRS has been the establishment of contact and cooperation with organizations having broadly similar or complementary aims. Cooperation with like-minded organizations has included the exchange of articles, journals, and literature, as well as help in publicizing one another's works.

MAHARASTRA STATE

In Maharastra, a big campaign was organized to convert the Hindus into Buddhists so that they could get rid of inequality, untouchability, and attain human rights with dignity. B. R. Ambedkar led this movement, though without much success. In 1983 Dabholkar started working in the field of superstition eradication. After helping form MANS in 1989, he helped it grow to more than 170 branches in nearly all districts of Maharashtra. He has been the executive president (*Karyadhyaksha*) of MANS since its founding. He has written eleven books on various aspects of superstitions and their eradication. In the past decades he has confronted many Babas, Buas, Tantrics, and Mantrics, among others, and has led many agitations against various forms of superstitions, water pollution, and animal sacrifice. Inculcation of the scientific outlook is one of the main functions of MANS, a mobile van named "Scientific Attitude Promotion Van" or "Vidnyan Bodh Vahini." It has helped spread a scientific attitude in school children, especially in rural areas. Since its inception, MANS has carried out more than 1,200 programs in different schools all over Maharashtra. MANS workers travel in this well-equipped van, visiting schools and presenting a four-hour program; in this program they teach basic principles of science by using scientific toys and other aids. There is also a program for imparting sex education wherein films made for adolescent boys and girls are shown separately. Posters about astronomy are displayed to develop interest in students about the universe. Books promoting scientific and a moral ethical outlook are displayed and sold at affordable prices. A mini-science festival-like atmosphere is created whenever this van—the Vidnyan Bodh Vahini—conducts a four-hour program in any school.

The vehicle is equipped with a small kitchen, toilet, and bath and boarding accommodations for five people. Three sides of the rear portion of the van can be opened and can be used as a bookshop as well as a stage. It is also equipped with a big screen and a projector to show educational films to many people at a time. The new custom-made van providing for the stay of MANS workers will surely help us further our mission—Promotion of Scientific Attitude.

The Moral Rational Movement or Vivek Vahini is a movement initiated by MANS for teachers and colleges students. It aims at making students into thoughtful, discerning, judicious, ethical, principled, civilized, honorable, rational, wise, and cultured citizens, enabling them to put their rational thinking into practice through concrete programs for the betterment of themselves and society. This organization has gained accreditation from the education department of the government of Maharashtra State and works under the chairmanship of the lecturers and professors of the respective colleges. Study Circle and some novel programs are a few of its activities.

TRUTH SEEKERS MARRIAGE CEREMONY OR "SATYASHODHAK" MARRIAGE CEREMONY

Maharashtra Andhashraddha Nirmoolan Samiti (or the Maharashtra Superstition Eradication Committee) helps and propagates the "Satya Shodak" marriage ceremony to prevent huge amounts of money being wasted by many people in unnecessary pomp and show in conventional marriages. Many people from all strata of society get entrapped in debt, leading to untold hardship. Mahatma Jotirao Phule, from Maharashtra the great social reformer of the twentieth century, propagated this marriage ceremony that was simple and inexpensive and made the Brahmin priest's services redundant. Mahatma Phule started Satyashodhak Samaj, the Society of "Truth Seekers." Hence the marriage ceremony adopted by this society is called Satyashodhak Marriage.

WEST BENGAL

Prafulla Kumar Naik, with the help of local humanists and rationalists, questioned the claims of miracles by Mother Theresa. In Andhra Pradesh and Kerala, focus has been against god-men and -women who claim to provide miracle cures. Andhra rationalists opposed unscientific alternative medicines (homeopathy), exposing the bogus claims of Alex Orbito (psychic surgery), the swallowing of live fish for asthma cures, the hugging of Matha Amrithananda Mayi in order to obtain prosperity, and geomancy (*Vaastu*).

Mr. Manoj Datta, Mr. Subhankar Ray, Mr. Ajit Bhattacharya, Bhaskar Sur, and others are continuing to spread the Humanist message. Prof.

Amlan Datta, former vice chancellor of Viswabharati and Prof. Shib Narayan Ray are the veterans in West Bengal who constantly inspire the humanists through their writings and speeches. Several books have been published with documentation about fraudulent god-men, the truth about the Bible, the falsehood of geomancy, the unscientific nature of astrology, critiques of Hinduism, and the general need to spread skeptical thinking. Basava Premanand, Sanal Edamaruku, Innaiah Narisetti, Ramanamurthy (editor, *Vijaya Viharam* Telugu magazine), and G. R. R. Babu continue to question the authenticity of holy persons and have taken their message to an international level, drawing considerable media attention to what is going on inside India. *Charvaka*, a Telugu magazine edited by Mr. Thotakura Venkateswarlu from Vijayawada had a great impact on the youth in early 1970s.

Increasingly, the movement is also getting help from Indians who are now living abroad, people such as Aramalla Purnachandra and Nirmal Mishra, and Jyothi Sankar (who died in 1998) in the United States who are providing key intellectual backing to India's small number of humanists, skeptics, and rationalists. Despite their efforts, these miracle cures continue to draw thousands of believers, many of whom are conned into making financial donations in the hope of curing their ills.

Punjab Rationalist Activity

Founded in 1984 under the leadership of Megh Raj Mitter, the Tarksheel Society aims to disseminate rationalist ideas and scientific thinking among the Indian people in order to eradicate religious fanaticism, communalism, the caste system, untouchability, and superstition. Affiliated to Federation of Indian Rationalist Associations, the Tarksheel Society advocates the separation of religion and education. The society has units in almost all the villages and towns of Punjab.

Orissa Rationalist Activity

The Orissa Rationalist Society (ORS) functions under the leadership of Prof. D. N. Padhi and Prof. D. Sahoo Md Sukur. Dr. A. K. Patra, a scientist of the Orissa University of Agriculture and Technology, extends his help and cooperation. Dr. N. Patel, A.D.M.O., Kalahandi, and Dr. B. C. Panda, a noted gynecologist, extend their help in secular activitities. Dr. A. K. Patra gave some action programs to dispel superstitions of the masses.

ANDHRA PRADESH

Andhra Pradesh has the Atheist Society of India, the Radical Humanist Centre, Inkollu, Chirala, the Renaissance Institute, two Rationalist

Associations of Andhra Pradesh, the Humanist and Ethical Association of Hyderabad, and the Institute for Advancement of Women, to name a few. They publish ten journals in Telugu and English, including *Hetuvadi, Rationalist Voice, Nastika Margam,* and *The Atheist.* A recent catalogue showed nearly 450 Humanist book titles available for sale in the Telugu language.

Several universities include M. N. Roy's Humanist philosophy as part of their philosophy and political science curriculum. The Atheist Centre, an associate member and recipient of IHEU's International Humanist Award for pioneering social reform activities, and in memory of whose founder, Gora, the government of India issued a commemorative stamp in 2002, is based in Vijayawada. The Atheist Centre's activities stand as an internationally recognized monument to atheist and Humanist social action. Not very far from Vijayawada is the independent Charvaka School run by (the late) B. Ramakrishna who died in 2007 in Nidamarru, with its own textbooks on atheist morality for children. Bringing together many of these diverse Humanist activities to create a strong and powerful profile and unified identity for Humanism in the state is FARA: the Federation of Rationalist, Atheist and Humanist organizations of Andhra Pradesh. It is headed by veteran journalist and Humanist and chair of the IHEU Committee on Religious Abuse of Children, Dr. Innaiah. Under Dr. Innaiah's leadership, humanism and rationalism have received prominent publicity in the media. Jana Vigyana Vedika, a science popularization organization, is a close collaborator. The rationalist and Humanist movement has the active support of Dr. P. M. Bhargava, a distinguished biochemist, and Professor Balasubramanyam, the 1997 winner of UNESCO's Kalinga Award for Popularization of Science. Justice Sambasiva Rao, a respected ombudsman, and the feminist Malladi Subbamma are both closely associated with humanism. With such support and leadership, but also facing the growth of Hindu nationalism, the movement has great strengths but many challenges as well.

CENTER FOR INQUIRY INDIA

In 2005, the Center for Inquiry India commenced its work with Hyderabad as its headquarters. The activities include publications of books by Paul Kurtz, M. N. Roy, Richard Dawkins, and Sam Harris (all translations in Indian languages), the writings of Dr. N. Innaiah, and the translations of Venigalla Komala. Research projects undertaken include a survey of scientists on their belief systems, child abuse, and the spread of the scientific method among youths and students. National seminars have been conducted on the population problem, child abuse by religions, women, and equality. Dr. N. Innaiah is the chairman of the center with directors from various walks of life.

Additional Organizations

The Social Development Foundation (SDF) in Uttar Pradesh works under the leadership of Mr. V. B. Rawat to uplift the untouchables. It holds humanist workshops regularly. Projects are undertaken to educate and train girls. The Goa Science Forum is a well-known group of science and rationalist activists based in Goa, India. Affiliated to the Federation of Indian Rationalist Associations (FIRA), it conducts workshops on various issues with a view to spreading scientific points of view, humanism, rationalism, and a spirit of inquiry and reform. The Forum also encourages the critical investigation of paranormal and fringescience claims from a scientific point of view. Its current president is R. G. Rao, and under the leadership of Manavatavadi, secular activities are taken up in the state of Haryana.

REFERENCES

The following are general references for information of secularism in India:

Magazines and Journals

The Atheist: monthly magazine, Vijayawada, India
Buddhiwadi: Hindi quarterly journal published by the Buddhiwadi Foundation, Patnar, Bihar, India
Humanist Outlook: quarterly magazine, Delhi, India
The Indian Skeptic: monthly journal of the Indian Society for the Investigation of Claims of the Paranormal, Podanur, Tamilnadu, India
Modern Rationalist: monthly magazine, Chennai, Delhi
The Secularist: bimonthly magazine, Mumbai, India
Radical Humanist: monthly magazine, Meerut, UP, India

Web Sites

Rationalist International of Sanal Edamaruku. http://www.rationalistinter national.net/ (accessed August 31, 2009)
Ramendra Buddhiwadi Samaj. http://www.geocities.com/brs_patna/ (accessed August 31, 2009)
Vidya Bhushan Rawat. http://www.blogger.com/profile/11765166843439006384 (accessed August 31, 2009)

Books

Karnik, V. B. 1960. *Indian Trade Unions: A Survey*. Bombay, India: Manatalas.
Karnik, V. B., and M. N. Roy. 1967. *Strikes in India*. Bombay, India: Manatalas.
Narayan Ray, Shib, ed. 1987. *Selected Writings of M. N. Roy*. 4 volumes. New Delhi: Oxford University Press.

Ramendra, Nath. 1992a. *Dr. Ambedkar ne Hindu Dharma ka tyag kyon kiya* (*Why Dr. Ambedkar renounced Hinduism*). Patnar, Bihar, India: Buddhiwadi Foundation.

———. 1992b. *Sampoorna Kranti aur Buddhiwad* (*Total Revolution and Rationalism*). Patnar, Bihar, India: Buddhiwadi Foundation.

———. 1996. *Hindutva, Sangh Pariwar aur Fascism, in Cooperation with the Indian Renaissance Institute*. Patnar, Bihar, India: Buddhiwadi Foundation.

———. 1997. *Buddhiwad aur Manavtavadi Dristikone* (*A Secular Humanist Declaration*). Hindi translation of A. Solomon's Rationalist and Humanist Outlook 1997. Patnar, Bihar, India: Buddhiwadi Foundation.

Roy, Manavendra Nath. 1985. *Kya Ishwar Mar Chuka Hai?* (*Is God Dead?*). Patnar, Bihar, India: Buddhiwadi Foundation.

———. 1986a. *Buddhiwadi Ghoshna-patra* (*Rationalist Manifesto*). Patnar, Bihar, India: Buddhiwadi Foundation.

———. 1986b. *Roy ka Nav Manavatavad* (*New Humanism*). Patnar, Bihar, India: Buddhiwadi Foundation.

Roy, Samaren. 1970. *The Restless Brahmin: Early Life of M. N. Roy*. Bombay: Allied Publishers.

Chapter 8

Atheism and Secularity in the Netherlands

Loek Halman

Dutch society is quite exceptional in terms of religion. In no other European country are there so many people not belonging or no longer belonging to a religious denomination. On the other hand, of those who are (still) members of religious denominations, a large part should be characterized as core members in the sense that they not only are members, they also attend religious services frequently and are also otherwise strongly involved in religious activities and organizations. This polar situation, with high levels of unchurched people on the one hand and relatively many core members on the other hand, appears to be typically Dutch (Halman and de Moor 1994; Halman, Luijkx, and van Zundert 2005, 72).

Religion in the Netherlands appears to be a particular case in Europe also from another perspective. A few decades ago, Dutch society was still pillarized, and although other countries also have experienced pillarization such as Austria, Switzerland, Belgium, West Germany, and France (Hellemans 1988; Righart 1986), the degree of pillarization seems to be an unique feature of Dutch society. Belonging to a pillar had far-reaching consequences for everyday life. Being a Catholic, for instance, implied to attend a Catholic school, vote for a Catholic political party, be subscribed to a Catholic newspaper, belong to a Catholic broadcasting company, be a member of a Catholic trade union, receive medical treatment in a Catholic hospital, and so on. Processes of modernization rapidly decreased the former ideological isolation of the various social groups in Dutch society and made people aware of other systems of meaning. Since the 1960s, Dutch society witnessed a process of depillarization, which meant at the individual level that identification and mass support for and membership of pillarized organizations decreased and that the once strong links between religious preferences and political orientations became substantially weaker. This is reflected in the already mentioned large share of the Dutch population that does not belong to one of the denominations. The number of unchurched people in the Netherlands is unparalleled in Europe. According to the most recent European Values Study (EVS), only the percentages of unchurched people in Estonia and Chech Republic exceed the Dutch percentage (Halman, Luijkx and Van Zundert 2005, 71). Indeed, the Dutch appear to be a particular case in Europe! This raises questions such as whether this evolution from severely pillarized into unchurched society implied that Dutch people have turned into nonreligious people and have become atheists. And who are these nonreligious people and atheists? Do they have specific characteristics in terms of sociodemographics such as age, level of education, or gender?

Another question deals with the implications of such a development. It is often argued that modern people are individualized people and to a large extent independent of society. They are no longer forced to accept a public order of standards and evaluations. As Wilson wrote, because God is dead or has become rather silent "man is adrift on an unchartered sea, left to find his moral bearings with no compass and no pole star, and so able to do little more than utter personal preferences, bow to historical necessity, or accept social conventions" (Wilson, 1997, 5). Religious control over individual actions has diminished severely and people's moral convictions are increasingly based on people's own ideas and personal values, or as Martin (2005, 23) writes, "as far as morality was concerned people grew less inclined to accept rules, and began to dissolve the sense of obligation into a utilitarian calculus of happiness." It is argued that contemporary people are too narrowly focused on pure self-interest, which is considered a severe threat for the respect for human rights and human dignity, liberty, equality, and solidarity. The "good" values are assumed to have declined or even vanished, while the wrong, "bad" values triumph in today's highly individualized society. In particular so called Communitarians have expressed their concern for the ultimate consequences of this development toward hedonism, privatism, consumerism, and the "I" culture. In their view, there is a trend toward radical individualism and ethical relativism and the withdrawal of the individual from community life, and in order to stop this downward spiral they suggest the reestablishment of a firm moral order in society by (re-) creating a strong "we" feeling and the (re-) establishment of a "spirit of community" (Etzioni 1996, 2001).

However, the idea that secularization not only means religious decline but also moral decline is widespread, not only among Communitarians. Many of our political leaders, politicians, and church leaders argue along such lines. The question is: Are they correct? Do we really have to be afraid of the atheists and secular people? If atheists and nonreligious people do not regard the church and church leaders as their moral guides, what implications will this have on the moral state of a nation? Can we find evidence that nonreligious people are more individualistic and more permissive or even in favor of an ethos of anything goes? To address such questions, we explore the moral convictions of the unchurched, the atheists, and nonreligious people in Dutch society and compare them with the morals of the Dutch churched and religious people.

We start this chapter with an overview of the trends with regard to religion in Dutch society using data from a long-term survey project on God in Dutch society (God in Nederland; see Bernts, Dekker, and de Hart 2007; Dekker, de Hart, and Peters 1997; Goddijn, Smets, and van Tillo 1979). This data set enables us to look back in recent Dutch history and to investigate the trends since 1966. The further exploration of the characteristics of atheists in Dutch society is based on survey data from the EVS (Halman 2001; www.europeanvalues.nl). This data set is also analyzed to investigate the moral consequences of the trends.

THE DUTCH RELIGIOUS LANDSCAPE

If one thing is clear, secularization understood in terms of declining levels of religious adherence has obviously occurred in the Netherlands. The numbers of unchurched people steadily has increased since 1966. In 1966, one in every three Dutch people was not affiliated with one of the denominations; by 2006 this had almost doubled: 61 percent. Such figures are unparalleled in Western Europe, even in the Nordic secular countries. Only in some former communist countries that most strongly experienced social repression during Soviet domination and its secular ideology show similar or higher levels of nonaffiliation (Halman 2001, 74; Halman, Luik, and van Zundert 2005, 71).

In particular, the adherence of the Catholic Church dropped sharply; it halved, from 35 percent in 1966 to 16 percent in 2006. The reduction of adherents of the Protestant churches cannot be shown so easily. The recent merging of the Dutch Reformed Church and various Re-Reformed Churches into one church, the Protestant Church in The Netherlands (PKN) complicates a straightforward comparison of figures over time. It seems, however, that the decline is mainly caused by Dutch Reformed people leaving their church. Between 1966 and 1996, the adherence of Re-Reformed Churches remained more or less the same: about 8 percent of the Dutch people, whereas the adherence of the Dutch Reformed Church declined by 6 percentage points from 20 percent in 1966 to 14 percent in 1996 (Dekker, de Hart, and Peters 1997, 12). So, the recent increase in numbers of unchurched people in

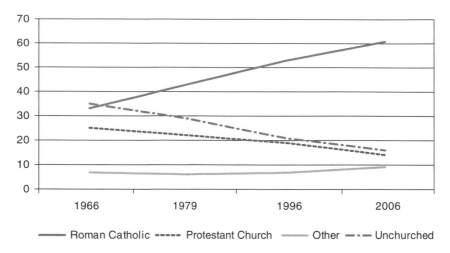

Figure 8.1. Denominational affiliation in the Netherlands
Source: Bernts, Dekker, and de Hart (2007).

the Netherlands is to a large extent the result of Catholic people leaving their church.

As can be seen in Figure 8.1, the adherence of other religious groups is confined to less than 10 percent. This group of people of other religions is very diverse and includes Jews, Hindus, Buddhists, and Muslims. At this moment about 6 percent of the Dutch population is Muslim (Bernts, Dekker, and de Hart 2007, 15).

Worship is one thing, religious practice another. For instance in the Nordic European countries, large majorities of the people consider themselves a member of the Lutheran church. This phenomenon of high levels of church membership may be understood from the strong connection between church and state in these countries where "citizenship implied church membership" (Gustafsson 1994, 21). Church membership is considered almost a citizen's duty in these cultures and as such church membership can be seen as a way of expressing solidarity with society and its basic values (Hamberg 2003, 50). However, because the level of actual participation is rather low in the Nordic countries, membership in these countries will be less meaningful religiously than in other countries. Davie (2000, 3) depicted this situation as belonging without believing.

Church attendance has also steadily declined in the Netherlands. Although half of the Dutch people in 1966 reported attending religious services at least once a week, in 2006 this had declined to 16 percent.

It appears that among Catholic people in particular, church attendance is low. One in every four Catholics claims to go to church frequently, while among adherents of Protestant churches it is 40 percent. If, using the Dutch data from the most recent EVS in 1999, the Protestant church

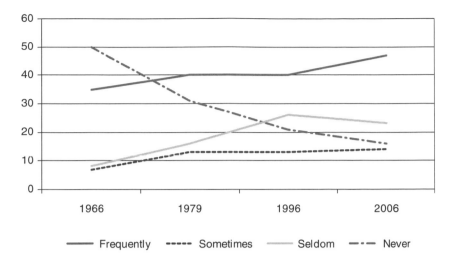

Figure 8.2. Church attendance in the Netherlands
Source: Bernts, Dekker, and de Hart (2007).

is further divided into Dutch Reformed and Re-Reformed adherents, church attendance is higher among the latter group (49 percent) than among Dutch Reformed (32 percent). Unchurched people, the majority in the Netherlands, never (80 percent) or rarely attend a religious service.

Combing the characteristics of church adherence and church attendance provides a clear picture of the religious landscape of the Netherlands. The landscape appears to be bipolar: on the one hand, a majority (54 percent) of Dutch people do not belong to a church and never or hardly ever go to church, and on the other hand, a large minority (20 percent) are members and attend religious services frequently. This minority can be considered core churchmembers! Also in this respect, the Netherlands is unique in Europe (Halman, Luijkx, and van Zundert 2005, 72). Having such a large group of non-affiliated people who rarely go to church makes the question whether or not Dutch society is not only secular but also has become atheist even more interesting.

ATHEISM AND SECULARITY

There is little research on religion and atheism in the socioscientific literature. "Systematic attempts to understand Atheism as a social or psychological phenomenon, employing rigorous theory and quantitative research methods, have been rare" (Bainbridge 2005, 3). One obvious problem to investigate atheists using quantitative research methods is the limited number of atheists in most countries. As we will see, the Netherlands is not an exception in this regard. Further, the category of atheists remains unclear for in many empirical studies they are often lumped together with agnostics, religious "indifferents," and the broader category of unchurched people.

The same is of course true for the term secularity. This concept is as unclear as the category of atheists is. Does secularity denote nonreligiosity? Are secular people not religious people, or is religion not important (anymore) to them? Does secularity refer to people who may still feel religious but who are not or are not any longer willing to be connected to a church? Their once-strong ties between belief and practices may have diminished, and although people who go to church are likely to be more religious than those who do not go to church, it does not necessarily mean that religious people go to church. Why should they? Bainbridge argues that those who are "healthy, prosperous, and untroubled in their personal relations might have little or no need for specific compensators" (Bainbridge 2005, 6) as provided by most religious traditions. However, does that make them atheists or just believers without belonging, as suggested by, among others, Davie (2000, 2002)? She argued that the "marked fall-off in religious attendance (especially in the Protestant North) has not resulted, yet, in a parallel abdication of religious belief" (Davie 2002, 5; 2000, 8). Therefore, instead of speaking of secular Europe, she regards it more appropriate and accurate to speak of *unchurched* Europe because of the discrepancy between religious practices and actual beliefs.

Among others, Inglehart (1997, 80) argued that the emergence of a sense of security among people in economically more advanced societies has reduced the need for "the reassurance that has traditionally been provided by absolute belief systems, which purport to provide certainty and the assurance of salvation, if not in this world at least in the next." However, the decline in traditional religious beliefs is "linked with a growing concern for the meaning and purpose of life" (Inglehart 1997, 80). What has happened is that the social significance of religious institutions has declined, but also Bryan Wilson (1982, 150) wrote that it does not mean "that most individuals have relinquished all their interest in religion, even though that may be the case. It maintains no more than that religion ceases to be significant in the working of the social system" (see also Dobbelaere 1981, 2002). It is the individual who has become the main point of reference in the shaping of values, attitudes, and beliefs. Increasingly, people believe in whatever they themselves want to believe in, which is not necessarily what the Churches tell them to believe. In other words, traditional dogmatic beliefs have been replaced by a more modern, personalized way of believing. Some analysts have emphasized this development, which they regard "as a shift away from the traditional churches . . . with larger numbers of people defining and practicing their religiosity in non-traditional, individualized and institutionally loose ways" (Berger 2001, 447). Institutional religion is assumed to have become marginalized and, consequently, to have lost much of its influence on people's lives. As such, it seems that the decline in religiosity is mainly confined to institutional decline and does not indicate a decline in religious beliefs. In many European countries, this has resulted in a situation that Davie characterized as "believing without belonging" (Davie 2000, 3). This would mean that people in contemporary advanced society are no longer in need of a church, but can still be religious. Religion has become privatized, meaning that it has become a matter of individual choice and preferences and it remains to be seen if and to what extent people have turned into atheists.

But what are atheists? In most, if not all, empirical studies, atheists are those people who declare themselves atheist. Also in the data set used by Bainbridge this was the case: "Those individuals who do not have a religious preference were asked to describe themselves using the responses Non-religious, Agnostic, Atheist or none of these" (Bainbridge 2005, 12). In other surveys, such as the EVS (Halman 2001), the World Values Surveys (Halman, Inglehart, Díez-Medrano, Luijkx, Moreno, and Basáñez 2007; www.worldvaluesurveys.org), the International Social Survey Programme (www.issp.org), the European Social Survey (http://www.europeansocial survey.org), and various issues of the Eurobarometers (see http://ec.europa. eu/public_opinion/index_en.htm), similar questions are included to tap the degree to which people are religious or are convinced atheists.

In data sets from Dutch repeat surveys on God in the Netherlands (God in Nederland), not such a direct question was asked, but the number of atheists was determined by the response to the question of what comes closest to your own conviction. The response categories were (1) there is a personal God, there must be some kind of ultimate power; (2) I do not know if God exists or if there is an ultimate power; and (3) there is no God or ultimate power (Bernts, Dekker and de Hart 2007, 217). The latter response item was considered to indicate the category of atheists and asked in this way, 14 percent of the Dutch people in 2006 could be classified as such (Bernts, Dekker, and de Hart, 2007, 40). About one in every three respondents said to believe in something supernatural, whereas for one in every four respondents it appears less certain. They said that they did not know if God or a supernatural power existed. A more or less equal number of people in the Netherlands said they believe in a personal God (theists).

Since 1966 the percentages of theistic believers has been halved, whereas the number of atheists doubled. Percentages of people who believe in the existence of an ultimate power increased slightly, and the percentage of agnostic people increased by ten percentage points, from 16 percent in 1966 to 26 percent in 2006. The trends are shown in Figure 8.3.

However, when asked in a more direct way, the number of convinced atheists appears to be much lower. A direct question is available in the EVS and World Values Surveys. In these surveys,

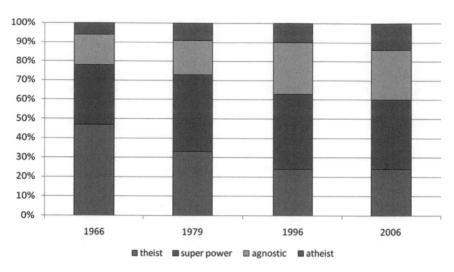

Figure 8.3. Percentages of Dutch people who say they believe in a personal God (theist), in a supernatural power, who do not know if a God or supernatural power exists (agnostic), and people who deny the existence of God or a supernatural power (atheist)
Source: Bernts, Dekker, and de Hart (2007).

respondents were asked: "Independently of whether you go to church or not, would you say you are: A religious person; Not a religious person; A convinced atheist." Asked in this way, it appeared that in 2005 only 7 percent of the Dutch population considered themselves a convinced atheist. This percentage has slightly increased since 1981. Although the time span of the EVS is more limited than the time span of the God in Nederland project, the trends are more or less the same. In 1981 about 4 percent declared themselves convinced atheists; in 1990 it was 5 percent, and in 1999 6 percent. Not a very sharp increase, yet a steady one. In Figure 8.4 these trends are displayed. The figure also reveals the slight decline in the number of religious people and also the slight increase in the number of people who claim not to be religious. If the latter category is indicative of secularity, a trend of growing secularity is visible in Dutch society.

The results from these two different data sources in the number of atheists can likely be attributed to the indirect way atheism is tapped in the God in Nederland project and the direct way of asking used in the EVS and World Values Surveys. Only 25 percent of the people who claim not to believe in any sort of spirit, God, or life force consider themselves an atheist! The majority of them (69 percent) indicate that they are not a religious person. It seems as if the rejection of God or the existence of an ultimate power cannot be equated with being a convinced atheist. If the two responses are combined and we consider

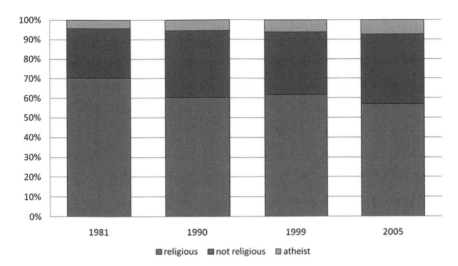

Figure 8.4. Percentages of Dutch people who claim to be religious, not religious, or convinced atheist in 1981, 1990, 1999, and 2005
Source: EVS 1981–1999 and WVS 2005

those respondents who claim to be atheist and also claim that they do not think that there is any spirit, God, or life force, the percentage of atheists in Dutch society would only be three! For 55 percent of the Dutch respondents, being religious seems to imply either belief in a personal God or belief that there is some kind of spirit or life force. Six percent consider themselves religious but do not really know what to think.

What is clear from such figures is that a majority of Dutch people still claim to be religious and that atheism is a phenomenon that applies to a very small or even negligible minority of the Dutch population. The figures also reveal that since the '90s not much change can be reported. The main changes took place before and during the '80s and boil down to an increasing number of nonreligious people at the cost of the number of religious people. However, this increase in the number of nonreligious people does not reveal a trend toward disbelief or unbelief. Even nonreligious people appear to "believe in something." More recently, the situation seems to have stabilized and hardly any changes can be reported.

ATHEISTS AND DISBELIEF?

Although there exists ambiguity and controversy about what atheism exactly is and how it emerged and developed, a common understanding of atheism is the abandonment of all religious claims, beliefs, and convictions. Does it mean that the atheist denies all beliefs and faiths, or do atheists deny the existence of God, and thus can atheism

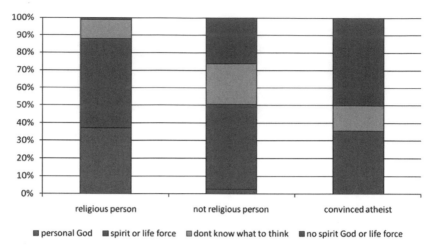

Figure 8.5. The "beliefs" of the religious, not religious, and atheists in the Netherlands
Source: EVS 1999

best be described as disbelief in God? As Silvia Berti (1995, 562) pointed out, "he who asserts, however courageously, that he does not believe in God, in the end does nothing more than say, 'I believe that God does not exist.'" This is not the place to enter into the philosophical or theological discussions and for the purpose of this chapter it seems sufficient to regard atheists as not simply unbelievers, but to further explore the beliefs, convictions, and practices of those who claim to be convinced atheists.

In order to explore this, we analyze data from the most recent EVS in the Netherlands (Halman 2001). Half of the convinced atheists does not think that there is any sort of spirit, God, or life force, which means that also half of them is less certain. Fourteen percent of the convinced atheists are hesitant and do not really know what to think. So, one in every seven convinced atheists shares the agnostic view, whereas, as shown in Figure 8.5, one in every three convinced atheists states that there is some sort of spirit or life force.

Thus, despite the fact that they claim to be convinced atheists and the majority of them deny the existence of a personal God, a rather large minority of the Dutch convinced atheists believe in a supernatural power! What other beliefs do they share?

They do not believe in God, hell, and heaven, but many of them believe in telepathy and reincarnation! In Table 8.1, these data are displayed.

Belief in hell is also not widespread among Dutch people in general, neither religious nor nonreligious people. The majority of the religious people do believe in God, life after death, heaven, sin, and telepathy,

Table 8.1
The religious beliefs of the religious, not religious, and atheists in the Netherlands

	Belief in (% yes)						
	God	Life after death	Hell	Heaven	Sin	Telepathy	Reincarnation
Religious person	87.1	70.2	21.6	56.5	55.4	51.9	23.9
Not religious person	16.6	20.9	1.9	10.4	14.7	48.2	18.1
Convinced atheist	1.6	13.3	0	1.6	13.1	41.1	21.3

Source: EVS 1999

whereas among atheists only one in every seven admits to believe in life after death and heaven. However, with regard to belief in telepathy the differences between religious people and atheists is not so strong, whereas as many religious people as nonreligious people and convinced atheists claim to believe in reincarnation!

Thus, convinced atheists in the Netherlands do indeed differ from Dutch religious people, mainly with regard to the dogmatic faith or traditional convictions in the sense that in general they report they do not believe in these. They resemble each other, however, with regard to belief in telepathy and reincarnation. All this seems to demonstrate the decline of traditional institutional religiosity in favor of a more personal way of believing.

This can also be demonstrated from the obvious differences between atheists and nonreligious people on one side and religious people on the other with regard to church related activities, such as church attendance and the importance of religious services at significant life events. Nonreligious people and atheists hardly ever go to church, and they do not consider it important to have religious services at the occasion of birth, marriage, and death. However, a small minority of the Dutch atheists takes some moments of prayer, meditation, or contemplation or something like that. Fewer atheists (55 percent) than religious people (81 percent) take such moments, and although religious people may have answered "yes" because they actually pray to God, whereas atheists were thinking of moments of contemplation when they answered this question, it seems clear that prayer, contemplation, or meditation is not an activity that is solely reserved for religious people. Perhaps it is also an indication that the quest for meaning remains and is not exclusive for religious people.

WHO ARE THE ATHEISTS AND SECULAR PEOPLE?

It turns out that atheists differ from religious people in terms of traditional institutional beliefs and behaviors that are more adhered to by the latter than the former. In many ways atheists do not differ much from people who claim to be not religious persons. But who are the atheists in terms of sociodemographic characteristics? Do they have typical characteristics or can they be found among all categories of the Dutch population? And because atheists no longer believe in the religious dogmas and convictions, are they also more modern in other aspects? The latter may be assumed because atheism is often connected to secular ideology that emerged from the Reformation, the Enlightenment, and expanding role of science in society and increasing levels of personal autonomy (Berti 1995, 556). If atheism is indeed the ultimate consequence of modernization in general and secularization and individualization in particular, it can be expected that atheists are among the most modern people in society. Of course, it can be doubted that atheism is a modern phenomenon and did not exist in premodern times. There always have been people who denied the idea of God or did not believe in a God, and atheism or unbelief seem to have been in all times. Whether or not they share more "modern," that is, less traditional views beyond the religious domain remains to be seen.

In order to address these questions, a number of simple analyses were performed. More sophisticated analyses (e.g., regression analyses) cannot be used here because of the limited number of atheists (N = 62). However, applying multinominal logistic regression techniques reveals that atheists differ from religious persons mainly in terms of level of education and gender. Atheist differ from nonreligious people only with regard to the level of education. Included in these regression analyses as independent variables were—apart from level of education and gender—age, income, and degree of urbanization.

Atheists are more often found among men than among women, who appear to be more often religious than men. These differences are often attributed to differential socialization (Miller and Stark 2002) but also to the more family-oriented attitude of women. It is argued that because of such an attitude, women pray more than men, and they pray for the well-being and happiness of their families (Dobbelaere and Voyé 1992, 131, 160; 2000, 139). Proponents of the work-force theory use time constraints as the main argument to explain why women are more religious than men. Participation in the work force not only means that people have less time to be engaged in other activities and thus also in church activities but "work force participation can provide alternative sources of identity, interests, values, legitimations, and commitments so that religion simply becomes less important" (De Vaus and McAllister 1987, 473). Although female participation in the labor force has increased sharply in the last decades, also and especially in the Netherlands, more than in other countries Dutch women are mainly involved in part-time jobs. Eurostat figures on employment reveal that in the Netherlands 68 percent of employed women are in part-time jobs. Because more men than women are engaged in paid full-time employment, men are less involved in church or religious activities and are likely to be less religious. That women will be more religious than men can also be argued from yet another perspective. Women are, more often than men, employed in "caring jobs," e.g., nursing activities, childcare, and school-teaching, which, owing to the historical link between the caring activities of deaconesses in Lutheran churches and women who are religious, are often associated with higher levels of religiosity. We are not going to elaborate on these findings, but these arguments make it understandable that fewer women than men appear to be atheist.

That more highly educated people appear more often to be convinced atheists may also not come as a big surprise. As can be argued, education implies increasing cognitive skills and being more critical toward authorities, including the religious ones. Highly educated people, more than less educated people, emphasize individual autonomy and personal judgment. Hence, people with more education will display lower levels of religiosity. This hypothesis is based on Weber's idea of the absolute incompatibility of religious and scientific orientations. It is argued that people are either scientific or religious, but not both (Johnson 1997, 232). Although the relationship may be more complex (see, e.g., Johnson 1997, 233), most empirical evidence indicates a negative association between level of education and degree of religiosity. The higher level of education also seems to imply that people do not have to escape into vague terminology, such as being nonreligious, but they are able to define themselves as atheists.

Are atheists more modern than religious people, and do atheists also differ in terms of modernity from nonreligious people, or is it justified to lump these two categories together as is done so often in empirical analyses? There is not much empirical evidence that atheists are indeed more modern than religious people. Modernity is understood as rejecting traditional women's roles and authorities, emphasizing individual freedom, and being more rational. In Figure 8.6 the differences between religious and nonreligious people and atheists on a few dimensions of modernity are shown.

The traditional female role as housewife is indeed slightly less accepted by atheists than by religious people, but atheists resemble nonreligious people in this respect. The same applies for single parenthood, which is slightly more accepted by atheists and nonreligious people than by religious people. Contrary to what could be expected, religious people stress emphasis on the individual more than atheists and nonreligious people, and they also put more emphasis on technology than

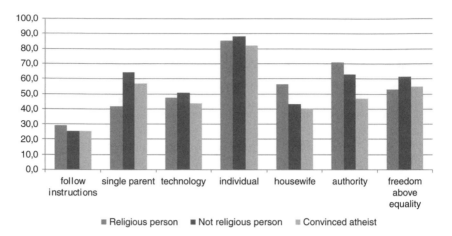

■ Religious person   ■ Not religious person   ■ Convinced atheist

Figure 8.6. Traditional and modern orientations among religious, not religious, and atheist persons in the Netherlands
Source: EVS 1999

atheists and nonreligious people. However, the differences are rather modest. When it comes to authority, atheists more than religious people and nonreligious people reject greater respect for authority, and atheists appear to be more independent than religious and nonreligious people. More than these latter categories, atheists indicate having control over their lives. Because having control over your life seems to generate higher levels of happiness and life satisfaction, it appears strange that atheists are not happier and more satisfied than religious people. As such, these results confirm what Andrew Clark from l'École de Economie in Paris and Orsolya Lelkes from The European Centre for Social Welfare Policy and Research have demonstrated earlier. Using two large-scale European data sets, they showed that the religious people enjoy higher levels of life satisfaction and that religion does seem to insure against the effects of some adverse life events. They concluded that Christian beliefs affect the lives of Europeans positively (Clark and Lelkes 2006), and it also applies to the Dutch. Religious people in the Netherlands appear slightly more happy and satisfied with their lives than atheists. The differences are statistically, however, not significant.

CONSEQUENCES?

The waning of the dominant position of religion in modernizing society fostered the establishment of a "new morality" or "permissive morality" (Wilson 1982, 86). Since the moral guidance of the churches and religion is less self-evident and under heavy pressure, it can be assumed that people's religious orientations are no longer, or less strongly, linked to their moral views. In traditional societies, individual belief systems and religious practices were assumed to be strongly dependent on the beliefs of the community and on the prescriptions of the churches. Cultural and social differentiation resulted in people increasingly participating in different universes of meaning, each governed by its own set of values. Within each institutional sphere, norms and values have become functional, rational, and, above all, autonomous. In this interpretation, secularization can be seen as "the repercussion of these changes on the religious subsystem. It denotes a societal process in which an overarching and transcendent religious system is reduced to a subsystem of society alongside other subsystems, the overarching claims of which have a shrinking relevance" (Dobbelaere 1995, 1; see also Dobbelaere 2002, 166). The processes of differentiation, specialization, and professionalization made each social sphere in life increasingly autonomous and a specialized unit in society with its own set of values and rules (Münch 1990, 443). The churches have lost several of their traditional functions such as schools, hospices, social welfare, registry of births, marriages, and deaths, culture, and organization of leisure (Dogan 1995, 416). Institutional domains have become segmented in the sense that within each institutional sphere norms and values have become functional, rational, autonomous, and withdrawn from the religious sphere. The "sacred canopy is more and more restricted" (Dobbelaere 2002, 23). As a consequence, religion became marginalized and lost much of its influence on people's lives. In other words, religion has lost its societal and public functions, and religion has become privatized and marginalized within its own differentiated sphere (Casanova 1994, 19). The emancipation of the individual, the growing emphasis on personal autonomy and individual freedom, the deunification of collective standards, and the fragmentation of private pursuits seem advantageous to "a declining acceptance of the authority of hierarchical institutions, both political and nonpolitical" (Inglehart 1997, 15). Thus, citizens are increasingly questioning the traditional sources of (religious) authority and no longer bound by common moral principles. All in all, it seems reasonable to assume that moral and sexual choices are increasingly based on personal decisions and lifestyle preferences and less on prescriptions by the church and church leaders. It implies a weakened impact of religious beliefs and values on people's moral choices and convictions. The moral guidance of the churches and religion is no longer self-evident and under heavy pressure. Particularly secular people will not take for granted the prescriptions and rules of the church. Religious people are much likelier to adhere to the moral teachings and guidelines of the church, and as such it can be expected that religious people will be more strict than less religious people, in particular with regard to condemning (deviant) sexual behaviors. The latter is to be expected because religion,

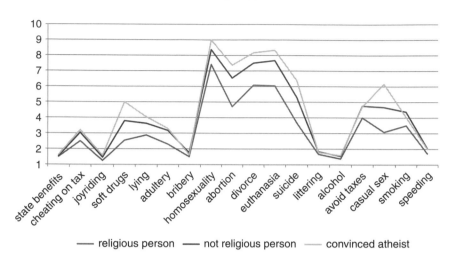

Figure 8.7. Acceptance of various behaviors by religious, not religious, and atheist people in the Netherlands
Source: EVS 1999

churches, and church leaders have always and still do condemn(ed) sexual behaviors strongly.

The data from the EVS surveys does support these ideas. In the EVS surveys, a list of items covering a wide variety of moral issues and particular behaviors "which an adult living in the twentieth century might have to confront in his or her life, or might at least be expected to have an opinion about" (Harding et al. 1986, 7) was presented, and respondents were asked to indicate whether or not the behaviors could always be justified (p. 10), never be justified (p. 1), or something in between. Eighteen statements were presented, ranging from cheating on taxes and claiming state benefits illegally and paying cash for services to avoid taxes, to homosexuality, euthanasia, and having casual sex. In Figure 8.7 we have displayed the mean scores on these 10-point scales for each of the issues mentioned and for the religious, nonreligious, and atheist people in the Netherlands.

Figure 8.7 reveals, first of all, that the acceptance of issues such as claiming state benefits illegally, joyriding, bribery, littering, driving under the influence of alcohol, and speeding over the limit, are in general not accepted by Dutch people. These activities are illegal and seem demonstrations of disrespect for laws and rules.

Cheating on taxes, the use of soft drugs, lying in your own interest, avoiding taxes, adultery, and smoking in public buildings are issues that the individual gains personal benefits from. These are slightly more accepted by Dutch people in general. Most accepted are behaviors that are strongly associated with the private, personal life sphere, including corporeality. Homosexuality, abortion, euthanasia, divorce, and casual sex are acceptable by larger numbers of the people in the Netherlands.

Figure 8.7 also reveals that when it comes to such issues of civicness (such as joyriding and speeding over the limit) and issues of personal interest (avoiding taxes), the differences between religious, nonreligious people, and atheists are negligible. Atheists and nonreligious people resemble the religious Dutch respondents in rejecting these behaviors, but when it comes to sexual issues and micro-ethical questions, religious people appear far more strict than nonreligious and atheist people. It is clear that the moral guidance of the churches has come under strong pressure, particularly in the realm of sexuality and morality. On issues like divorce, homosexuality, abortion, and euthanasia, people no longer rely solely on the judgments and prescriptions of the Church. Increasingly, individuals are deciding for themselves. As Taylor once put it, "masses of people can sense moral sources of a quite different kind, ones that don't necessarily suppose a God" (Taylor 1989, 312–13). Dogmatic ethical (religious) rules are not taken for granted anymore, but are dependent on the situation and private interpretations and evaluations of these situations. The data from the EVS surveys seems to confirm the suggestion that moral and sexual choices are thus increasingly based on personal decisions and lifestyle preferences.

The data seem to demonstrate that the institutional, religion-dominated morality has been marginalized. People have not become amoral, but instead their morality is based more on personal considerations and convictions. In other words, a personal morality has developed, but there is not much evidence that an ethos of anything goes has developed. Most people, religious and nonreligious as well as atheists, are very reluctant in accepting all kind of "indecent" and "uncivic" behaviors.

There are also not much differences between religious and nonreligious people and atheists in the Netherlands when it comes to degrees of solidarity. The fear that the marginalized role of religion for some will eventuate in a loss of solidarity is ungrounded. We cannot find evidence that supports that view.

In the EVS, solidarity was tapped by two questions. One asked the degree to which people were concerned about the living conditions of groups of people in the sociospatial sphere. These groups varied from your immediate family and people in your neighbourhood, the region, and fellow countrymen, to Europeans and humankind. The other asked the degree to which people were concerned about the living conditions of four welfare target groups: the elderly, the unemployed, immigrants, and sick and disabled people. Answer categories ranged from 1 = not at all concerned to 5 = very much concerned. In Figure 8.8, the mean scores on these items for the religious and nonreligious people and atheists in the Netherlands are shown.

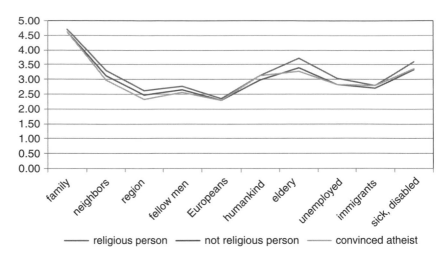

Figure 8.8. Solidarity among religious, not religious, and atheist people in the Netherlands
Source: EVS 1999

It is obvious that there are no big differences in the degree to which atheists are in unity with the various groups in society compared with religious and nonreligious people. True, religious people are overall more unified than nonreligious people and atheists, but the differences are only modest and concern solidarity with people in the neighborhood, people in the region, and the elderly, sick, and disabled (all $p < 0.000$). However, it cannot be concluded that atheists are not unified with these groups in society and that low levels of solidarity can be attributed to being atheist or not religious!

CONCLUSIONS

Writing about Dutch atheists is not so easy because in surveys the number of atheists is rather limited and often too limited to justify statistical analyses. Although many people in the Netherlands are not (any longer) affiliated with one of the religious denominations, it does not imply that Dutch society has turned into an atheist society or into a society of nonbelievers. There is a decline in the number of religious people and thus an increase in the number of people who claim not to be religious, but the number of people in the Netherlands who consider themselves atheist is modest and has hardly increased in the last decades. That atheism has not increased is not a result of certain policies in the Netherlands. In Dutch society, church and state have been separated for a long time, and there is freedom of religion and of atheism. Being an atheist is not a hindrance to becoming a minister! It is not an issue in Dutch politics although there are some Christian and even Orthodox Christian political parties, and representatives of them are in the Parliament and current government.

The Dutch atheists appear not to have special characteristics in terms of sociodemographic features. They do not appear as being the most modern or postmodern group in society. In fact they appear to be a very diffuse group, and in many respects they resemble nonreligious people. Both the nonreligious group and the atheists can together be differentiated from religious people. Atheists appear slightly more tolerant when it comes to the acceptance of all kinds of sexual and ethical behaviors. The behaviors that are more acceptable to them all relate to the private sphere that is increasingly regarded as a sphere in which traditional authorities are not allowed to interfere. Also religious people in Dutch society are more lenient toward these sexual behaviors than to accepting indecent behavior. As such, neither in the religious group, nor among atheists, is an ethos of anything goes developing. Civic morality was and remains high throughout Dutch society.

The conclusion therefore is simple: Dutch atheists are as ordinary and common as religious people in the Netherlands. Apart from the fact that they do not believe in the existence of God, they have no typical characteristics that makes them special. They can be found among all layers in Dutch society. They are as moral and responsible as religious and nonreligious people, but they remain a small minority. Although in the Netherlands the number of people that claim to be not religious has increased, and the number of unchurched people exceeds the number of religious-affiliated people, most people remain believers and have not become atheists. Apart from belief in God, most Dutch people believe in "something."

REFERENCES

Bainbridge, W. S. 2005. Atheism. *Interdisciplinary Journal of Research on Religion* 1, no. 1 (Article 2): 1–26.

Berger, P. L. 2001. Reflections on the sociology of religion today. *Sociology of Religion* 62:443–454.

Bernts, T., G. Dekker, and J. de Hart. 2007. *God in Nederland 1996–2006.* Kampen: Ten Have.

Berti, S. 1995. At the roots of unbelief. *Journal of the History of Ideas* 56:555–575.

Casanova, J. 1994. *Public religions in the modern world.* Chicago: University of Chicago Press.

Clark, A., and Lelkes, O. 2006. Deliver us from evil: Religion as insurance. Paper number 06/03 in Papers on Economics of Religion of the Department of Economic Theory and Economic History of the University of Granada. http://ideas.repec.org/p/gra/paoner/06-03.html (accessed September 1, 2009).

Davie, G. 2000. *Religion in modern Europe.* Oxford: Oxford University Press.

———. 2002. *Europe: The exceptional case.* London: Darton, Longman and Todd.

Dekker, G., J. de Hart, and J. Peters. 1997. *God in Nederland 1966–1996*. Amsterdam: Anthos.

De Vaus, D. A., and I. McAllister. 1987. Gender differences in religion: A test of the structural location theory. *American Sociological Review* 52:472–481.

Dobbelaere, K. 1981. Secularization: A multidimensional concept. *Current Sociology* 29:1–213.

———. 1984. Godsdienst in België. In *De Stille Ommekeer*, ed. J. Kerkhofs and R. Rezsohazy, 67–112. Tielt: Lannoo.

———. 1995. Religion in Europe and North America. In *values in western societies*, ed. R. de Moor, 1–29. Tilburg: Tilburg University Press.

———. 2002. *Secularization: An analysis at three levels*, Bern, Brussels: Publishing Group Peter Lang.

———, and L. Voyé. 1992. Godsdienst en kerkelijkheid. In *De Versnelde Ommekeer*, ed. J. Kerkhofs, K. Dobbelaere, L. Voyé, and B. Bawin-Legros, 115–162. Tielt: Lannoo.

———, and L. Voyé. 2000. Religie en kerkbetrokkenheid: Ambivalentie en vervreemding. In *Verloren Zekerheid*, ed. K. Dobbelaere, M. Elchardus, J. Kerkhofs, L. Voyé, and B. Bawin-Legros, 117–152. Tielt: Lannoo.

Dogan, M. 1995. The decline of religious beliefs in western Europe. *International Social Science Journal* XLVII:405–418.

Etzioni, A. 1996. *The new Golden Rule. Community and morality in a democratic society*. New York: Basic Books.

———. 2001. *The monochrome society*. Princeton: Princeton University Press.

European Commission. Public opinion. Eurobarometers http://ec.europa.eu/public_opinion/index_en.htm (accessed September 1, 2009).

European Social Survey. http://www.europeansocialsurvey.org (accessed September 1, 2009).

Goddijn, W., H. Smets, and G. van Tillo. 1979. *Opnieuw: God in Nederland*. Amsterdam: de Tijd.

Gustafsson, G. 1994. Religious change in the five Scandinavian countries, 1930–1980. In *Scandinavian values*, ed. T. Pettersson and O. Riis, 11–58. Uppsala: Acta Universitatis Upsaliensis.

Halman, L. 2001. *The European Values Study: A third wave*, Tilburg: EVS, WORC, Tilburg University. http://www.europeanvalues.nl (accessed September 1, 2009).

———, and R. de Moor 1994. Religion, churches and moral values. In *The individualizing society*, ed. P. Ester, L. Halman, and R. de Moor, 37–66. Tilburg: Tilburg University Press.

———, R. Inglehart, J. Díez-Medrano, R. Luijkx, A. Moreno, and M. Basáñez. 2007. *Changing values and beliefs in 85 countries. Trends from the values surveys from 1984 to 2004*. Leiden, Boston: Brill. http://www.worldvaluesurveys.org (accessed September 1, 2009).

———, R. Luijkx, and M. Van Zundert. (2005). *The atlas of European values*. Leiden: Brill.

Hamberg, E. 2003. Christendom in decline: The Swedish case. In *The decline of Christendom in Western Europe, 1750–2000*, ed. H. McLeod and W. Ustorf, 47–62. Cambridge: Cambridge University Press.

Harding, S., D. Phillips, and M. Fogarty, 1986. *Contrasting values in western Europe*. London: Macmillan.

Hellemans, S. 1988. Katholicisme en verzuiling in België, Duitsland, Nederland en Frankrijk. *Tijdschrift voor Sociologie* 9:351–393.

Inglehart, R. 1997. *Modernization and postmodernization*. Princeton: Princeton University Press.

International Social Survey Programme. http://www.issp.org (accessed September 1, 2009).

Johnson, D. C. 1997. Formal education vs. religious belief: Soliciting new evidence with multinominal logit modelling. *Journal for the Scientific Study of Religion* 36:231–246.

Martin, D. 2005. *On secularization. Towards a revised general theory*. Aldershot, Hants: Ashgate.

Miller, A. S., and R. Stark. 2002. Gender and religiousness: Can socialization explanations be saved? *The American Journal of Sociology* 107:1399–1423.

Münch, R. 1990. Differentiation, rationalization, interpretation: The emergence of modern society. In *Differentiation theory and social change*, ed. J. F. Alexander and P. Colomby, 441–464. New York: Columbia University Press.

Righart, H. 1986. *De katholieke zuil in Europa*. Meppel: Boom.

Taylor, C. 1989. *Sources of the self*. Cambridge: Harvard University Press.

Wilson, B. 1982. *Religion in sociological perspective*. Oxford: Oxford University Press.

Wilson, J. Q. 1997. *The moral sense*. New York: Free Press Paperbacks.

Chapter 9

Atheism and Secularity: The Scandinavian Paradox

Peter Lüchau

Depending on how one interprets the concept of secularization the Scandinavian countries, Denmark, Norway, and Sweden, are either the three most secularized countries in the world or among the least secularized. In general the Scandinavian countries are considered among the most secularized in the world. According to most surveys the Scandinavian populations rank among the least religious when compared to the rest of Europe.[1] According to data from the International Social Survey Program (ISSP) 1998, about 11 percent of the Danes attend church at least once a month; for Norwegians it is about 10 percent, and among Swedes it is about 8 percent. Compare this to Germany where about 26 percent attend church at least once a month or Portugal where the number is about 47 percent.[2] With regard to the belief in central tenets of the Christian faith such as God, an afterlife, heaven, hell, and sin, both Danes and Swedes exhibit some of the lowest scores in Europe, scoring lower than even the French and much, much lower than the Greeks.[3] The comparably weak religiosity of the Scandinavians is contrasted by their strong support of their national majority churches: the formal membership rates are above 80 percent in the Scandinavian countries. Religiosity is low but formal church membership rates are very high, comparable to those of southern Europe.

The combination of low levels of Christian religiosity and high rates of formal church membership is puzzling, but the question is what consequences it has for the number of atheists in the Scandinavian countries. This depends on how an atheist is defined. For the purpose of this chapter a distinction will be made between an a-religious individual and an atheist. The a-religious are individuals who are simply not religious according to any of the measures applied here: Someone who does not believe, does not attend church, and generally claims not to be religious when asked directly. A-religious individuals are people for whom religion makes very little sense. They have no need for religion, and in their minds religion is basically irrelevant. An atheist on the other hand is someone who is actively a-religious or maybe it would be better to say actively antireligious. They share with the a-religious a lack of belief and religious activities and can be considered a subgroup of the a-religious. What separates the atheists from the a-religious is their interest in religion. The a-religious do not care about religion one way or the other, whereas atheists actively try to curb the influence of religion. They care about religion but in a negative sense. Using the word atheist about oneself is not a neutral description but rather a way to signal a set of particular values regarding religion. It is a way for individuals to show their surroundings that they find religion a threat to their own way of life. Either the threat is confined to the public sphere and the atheist could live with the existence of privatized religion, or the threat is all encompassing as religion is seen as a threat to rational thought itself. Since what the atheists are engaged in is a power struggle, their prime targets should tend to be organized religion, particularly established majority churches. It is also very likely that behind the atheists' skeptical attitude toward religion lies a comprehensive worldview much like that of a trained theologian. Atheists fight religion both outside as well as inside themselves. They need an all encompassing, well thought through worldview to show themselves (and the world) that religion is not needed in order to explain the human condition. The a-religious are much more likely not to think too deeply about life in general. They do not need religion nor a humanistic answer to it.

As mentioned above, comparatively few Scandinavians attend church and believe in central tenets of the Christian faith. This means that the number of a-religious individuals in Scandinavia could be quite high, maybe as high as 38 percent.[4] If the above description of atheists is true, then it is highly unlikely that athiests would be members of an established church. They would most likely make it a point to be unaffiliated. Because formal membership rates are high in the Scandinavian countries, the potential number of atheists should be lower than 16 percent of the population.[5] Hence the potential number of atheists in the most secularized countries in the world is potentially rather small, which is somewhat surprising.

To find an explanation for this contradictory situation it is prudent to look at exactly how the process of secularization has run its course in the Scandinavian countries. Since a theoretical discussion of secularization is outside the scope of this chapter, the definition proposed by Dobbelaere will be used here. According to Dobbelaere secularization is a process that happens at three different levels. At the societal level secularization is a process whereby the values of church religion lose their relevance for the integration and legitimization of everyday life in modern society.[6] Because society is divided into autonomous spheres, e.g. the political, the economic, the scientific, and the religious, the religious values of the church can no longer function as an overarching value system for the whole of society. At the organizational level secularization entails the accommodation of the doctrine of religious organizations to the outside world.[7] As society becomes secularized, religious organizations must come to terms with the fact that they can no longer expect to influence society as a whole nor control their own religious adherents. Instead they narrow the scope of the religious while at the same time loosening any demand that their values be taken over completely by their adherents. Theological arguments become less important while nonreligious arguments become more important in legitimizing what the churches do. In this sense organizational secularization is a reaction to societal secularization. At the individual level secularization is a decline in church involvement, such as church attendance and church membership.[8] It is not necessarily the decline of individual religiosity as such but a change in what kind of religiosity is prevalent.

Dobbelaere suggests that there are links between the three types of secularization in that societal secularization promotes organizational secularization,[9] and individual secularization is influenced, though not solely, by societal secularization.[10] The relationship between societal secularization and church involvement has an intervening component: compartmentalization. Societal secularization influences compartmentalization, which again influences individual church involvement. Compartmentalization is secularization-in-mind of the individual, which means that individuals in their minds separate the religious from the political, the medical, the scientific, and others.[11] It can be argued that there is a subjective as well as objective aspect to compartmentalization.[12] The subjective aspect is that individuals feel that religion should be separated from politics, science, and economics. This could also be termed secularism, a conscious attempt at promoting societal secularization. The objective aspect of compartmentalization is that the statistical correlation between religious values and nonreligious values (e.g., political values) disappears at the individual level. Compartmentalization is the product of societal secularization, and once it has taken hold in the individual, it leads to lower levels of church involvement. Hence one interpretation of Dobbelaere could be that societal secularization leads to compartmentalization, which again leads to lower church membership rates, which finally raises the potential number of atheists.

It has been observed above how the Scandinavian countries are considered highly secularized, but this is based on observations at the individual level. If the societal level is taken as the starting point, things look very different. At the societal level none of the Scandinavian countries can be said to be secularized to any noteworthy degree compared to the rest of Europe or the United States.

Denmark has an established church, the Danish People's Church ("Den danske folkekirke"), the existence of which has been established in the Danish constitution since 1849.[13] The Danish People's Church is a state church in the sense that it is controlled by the Danish parliament through both constitutional and common law administered by the state bureaucracy. According to Espersen, the Danish parliament has the power to control both administrational matters as well as strictly religious matters, for example, liturgy and matters of faith.[14] The Danish People's Church is part of the state bureaucracy in that all newborn babies must be registered as new citizens by contacting the local parish office of the Danish People's Church regardless of the religious heritage or religious affiliation of the parents. The information on the newborn is then sent on to the central registration bureau, which has information on all Danish citizens. Being registered here is the key for gaining the benefits of the comprehensive Danish welfare state. According to the Danish constitution, the monarch is obliged to be of the Evangelical Lutheran faith although not necessarily a member of the Danish People's Church.[15] The Danish People's Church is financed through a church tax collected by the tax authorities and through a direct subsidy from the state, neither of which are available to other religious entities in Denmark. Only members of the church pay church tax, but all citizens contribute to the direct state subsidy. Most official holidays in Denmark are Christian (in name), and the Danish People's Church is represented at many official ceremonies, including the opening of parliament and royal weddings. Christianity is taught in public schools but is claimed to be nonconfessional. It is however possible to be exempted from these lessons on religious grounds.

The Church of Norway ("Den norske kirke") is the established church of Norway, connected to the state through the constitution.[16] The constitution also states that members of the Church of Norway are obliged to raise their children in the faith of the church. The king of Norway is obliged by the constitution to profess the Evangelical Lutheran religion. It is also stipulated that the Council of State consisting of the prime minister and at least seven members of the government must have at least half of its members professing the official religion of the state. This is usually interpreted as half the members of the Council of State must be members of the Church of Norway. The Church of Norway is funded primarily by a state grant. This grant is not tied to church taxes and is paid for by all inhabitants of Norway. In order not to discriminate on religious grounds, any officially registered religious community or (beginning 1981) ethical association is entitled to a state grant approximately equivalent to the sum given to the Church of

Norway based on the number of members of said religious or ethical association. If a registered religious community has one hundredth of the members of the Church of Norway, it will be entitled to a grant one hundredth the size of the grant awarded to the Church of Norway each year. Religious education (RE) in Norwegian public schools is considered (by the authorities) neutral, but exemption is possible nonetheless. Education in Norway, including day care institutions, has as a goal to give the pupils a Christian and moral upbringing. This applies to all curriculum in public schools and is not restricted to RE.[17]

Sweden abolished the constitutional ties between the Swedish state and the Church of Sweden (*Svenska kyrkan*) in 1999/2000. The Church of Sweden is still an established church in the sense that it is mentioned by name in common law, though no longer in the Swedish constitution.[18] This special section of common law defines certain aspects of the inner workings of the Church of Sweden. This means that there is still an intimate relationship between church and state just as there is in Denmark and Norway. The state is not free from the church and the church is not free from the state. The Church of Sweden is funded primarily through a church tax that is collected by the state. Collection of church tax by the state is, however, also open to other religious organizations, and several have taken advantage of this offer. Those individuals who are not members of a state-approved religious community do not pay church taxes. There is RE in public schools, and it is not possible, as in Denmark and Norway, to be exempt from this education. The reason is that RE is considered neutral, and therefore the lack of exemption is not considered to contradict the European Convention on the Exercise of Children's Rights by the Swedish authorities.[19]

Summarizing the current relationships between religion and state in the three Scandinavian countries, it is difficult to argue that they are secularized at the societal level. In all three countries there is an established church that has special privileges vis-à-vis the state and other religious communities. It could be argued that the tight integration of the majority churches and the state in the three Scandinavian countries means that the values of the churches do indeed play a role the integration and legitimization of society. Even if societal integration through religion is not possible in a modern society,[20] it does not prevent politicians from trying to accomplish this goal through the formulation of laws and often through RE in the public schools. At least at the societal level the Scandinavian countries cannot be said to be secularized, and hence they should not be secularized at the other levels. As has already been established, the Scandinavian countries are secularized at the individual level, even though they are not secularized at the societal level. This is what the Scandinavian paradox is. The question is what consequences this has on the organizational level and what consequences it has for the actual numbers of atheists in the Scandinavian countries.

It is difficult to ascertain whether secularization has occurred at the organizational level in the Scandinavian countries. One would either have to do it by analyzing the official stances of the Scandinavian churches on particular issues or by analyzing the range of services they offer their members. This is beyond the scope of this chapter, but suffice it to note that such an analysis would be made highly complicated by the legal integration of church and state in the Scandinavian countries. Sometimes the churches can speak for themselves[21] whereas at other times parliamentary politicians do it for them. At the organizational level secularization is an organizational accommodation of the changed conditions of the church. Because it is difficult to analyze if and how the established Scandinavian churches have responded to secularization, maybe it would be more telling to analyze other organizational responses to secularization. Because the topic is atheists, it could be interesting to look at nonchurch organizations that demand external changes in the majority churches, particularly the relationship between church and state. Basically there are two types of nonchurch organizations that are opposed to the established churches (and religion in general). One type is organizations that are defined by being atheistic or nonreligious; the latter usually term themselves humanistic. Another type is organizations that oppose organized religion as one of many political viewpoints. The Scandinavian countries have had a tradition for leftwing political parties and labor unions, some of which (i.e., the communist parties) have been opposed to religion as part of their general political goals. Here the focus will be the former type of organizations and not the latter. Unfortunately very little has been written on atheism in Scandinavia and even less on atheistic and humanistic organizations. This means that the following is far from an exhausted list of atheistic and humanistic organizations in Scandinavia. It does however encompass some of the more high-profile and vocal organizations.

There has not really been any tradition for atheistic organizations in Denmark. Even though there has been an established church since 1849, the current atheistic organizations are rather recent. The largest atheistic organization in Denmark is the Atheistic Society (*Ateistisk Selskab*), which was founded in 2002. They currently have about 900 paying members,[22] and according to their Web site their main goal is the separation of church and state in Denmark.[23] They communicate through a newsletter and by sending written materials to parliamentary politicians and newspapers. The Atheistic Society has a sister movement of sorts in the Internet-based debate forum, Atheistic Forum (*Ateistisk Forum*). The forum started in 2002 and became a society in 2006. According to their Web site they have 730 members, since they consider registered users of the Internet-based forum as members.[24] There is no membership fee and chances are that many of the users of Atheistic Forum are also members of the Atheistic Society, even though the society has its own Internet-based debate forum. The Atheistic Society has managed to get some news coverage, but beyond that they have little power. There has not been any serious discussion about the separation of church and state in Danish parliamentary politics, and there seems to be little debate in parliament on the intricacies of the tight integration of church and state in Denmark in general. This leaves little room for any initiatives on the part of the Atheistic Society as they have to raise the discussions all on their own. Whether the Atheistic Society would be invited if there were for instance an official government report on the relationship between church and state is anyone's guess.

The largest atheistic or humanistic organization in Norway is the Norwegian Humanist Association (*Human-Etisk Forbund*). Founded in 1956, they currently have, according to their own account, more than 72,000 members.[25] The large number of members is not the product of a steady increase over the years but the result of a combination of aggressive campaigning beginning in the mid-seventies and state and municipal subsidies. The Norwegian Humanist Association started as an association consisting mainly of academics in the Norwegian capital with only 256 members.[26] In 1976 the Norwegian Humanist Association had only accumulated 1,768 paying members, adding up to a net increase in membership of a little over 1,500 people in 20 years.[27] Under new leadership the association managed to increase the membership rate dramatically during the late 1970s, and in 1979 the Norwegian Humanist Association had more than 5,000 members.[28] In 1986, thirty years after it was founded, the association reached 30,000 members.[29] While increasing their membership, the association also expanded geographically and established local branches in most of Norway, changing from a big city phenomenon to a true national association.[30] To finance their activities, the Norwegian Humanist Association started to obtain municipal grants beginning in the latter half of the 1960s,[31] and in 1981 the Norwegian Humanist Association managed to become the first, and to this day only, nonreligious organization to get a grant from the state proportionately equal to that received by the Church of Norway each year.[32] This was the product of the association's lobbying parliamentary politicians, but it would not have been possible had the association not grown to a considerable size during the late seventies.[33]

The size of the grant from the Norwegian state depends on the number of members the Norwegian Humanist Association has, but since adult members still have to pay a yearly fee (members between 15 and 24 years of age are exempt) chances are that the association's membership rate of 72,000 is not particularly inflated. The Norwegian Humanist Association runs a string of secular services. They perform rites in connection with birth, coming of age, and death and can perform legally binding marriages. They run a number of nonreligious support groups ranging from crisis support as well as drug rehabilitation. The Norwegian Humanist Association publishes a periodical and runs a publishing house focusing on debate books about the relationship between church and state and other issues of religion in the public sphere. The most telling aspect of the Norwegian Humanist Association, however, is not their impressive array of activities nor their large membership rate. The most telling aspect is their integration into the fabric of public space. As already mentioned they receive a state grant as the only nonreligious organization in Norway, but more importantly they participate in the preparation of government reports. A government report on the future relationship between church and state in Norway was published in 2006, and the group behind the report included members of the Church of Norway, the Norwegian parliament, the Council of Free Churches, and the Norwegian Humanist Association.[34] This means that in Norway the Norwegian Humanist Association is deemed to be an organization to be reckoned with in matters of the state.

In Sweden the main humanistic organization seems to be the Humanists (*Humanisterna*) which was founded in 1979 as the Humanistic-Ethical Society (*Human-Etiska Förbundet*). They later changed their name after an internal organizational schism in 1999. The Humanists currently have about 5,000 paying members,[35] and their main goal is making Sweden a secular society.[36] To disseminate their views, the Humanists publish a periodical and a newsletter and generally try to make themselves heard in the media. The Humanists have members who are entitled to perform legally binding marriages, and the Humanists offer secular rituals for birth, marriage, and death. Before the formal separation of church and state in Sweden in 1999/2000 a number of government reports were prepared to suggest how to handle the separation. The Humanists were not invited to participate in this work,[37] probably because of their comparatively small membership rate. This means that the Humanists cannot be said to be as influential as the Norwegian Humanist Association is in Norway.

Comparing atheistic/humanistic organizations in the Scandinavian countries, they have developed rather differently with regard to size and influence. In Denmark they are a late and for now somewhat irrelevant phenomenon because of their very small membership and range of offers (basically an Internet-based debate forum), though this may change with time. In Sweden at least one organization is somewhat established in that it has a decent membership rate, can perform legally binding marriages, and offers a wide range of secular ceremonies. It is however less influential in that it was not involved in the government report regarding the separation of church and state in Sweden. In Norway the Norwegian Humanist Association has managed to grow to an organization of some size and is integrated into the fabric of public life, particularly through its legal privileges (the state grant and the ability to perform legally binding marriages) and its role in the formulation of state reports. Even if it is difficult to ascertain whether the established Scandinavian churches have accommodated to the surrounding society and its secularization at the societal level something can be said about the organizations most likely to press for reforms of the churches and their stance vis-à-vis society as a whole. It could be argued that pressure for secularization at the organizational level is most evident in Norway and rather weak in Denmark and Sweden. In Norway there is a major organizational demand for reforms of the way church and state interact. This demand has not gone unheard as the participation of the Norwegian Humanist Association in the preparation of the government report demonstrates. In neither Denmark nor Sweden has the organizational pressure been so big as to be officially noted.

One way to interpret the differences in size and influence of the atheistic/humanistic organizations in the Scandinavian countries could be that the very tight integration between church and state in Norway has produced a strong response from organized atheists, whereas the less tight integration in Denmark and Sweden has not. Because church and state have been formally separated in Sweden under a social democratic government, it could be that Swedish atheists have found an organizational outlet for their atheism through existing political organizations rather than specifically atheistic/humanistic organizations. It may also have been important that Norway has been home to a very conservative interpretation of Protestantism (including belief in demons as late as the 1970s), which the Norwegian Humanist Association managed to capitalize on to get the attention of the mass media. This would fit well with the assumption that atheists are actively nonreligious people. They act when provoked and need an object at which to direct their anger. An established church that is highly integrated with the state through the constitution seem the perfect focusing point for such anger. However, the stark differences in the sizes of the Scandinavian atheistic/humanistic organizations suggest that it is not just a question of the degree to which church and state are integrated. Even though the integration of church and state may be the tightest in Norway, church and state are still very tightly integrated in both Denmark and Sweden. This suggests that part of the explanation for the relative sizes of the atheistic/humanistic organizations in Scandinavia could be the number of atheists in each country. If so, then it could be expected that the number of atheists will be largest in Norway, much smaller in Sweden, and almost minimal in Denmark.

From the short discussion of who atheists are assumed to be, several indicators could be used to delineate atheists in surveys. To cut the operationalization of atheists short, the easiest thing to do is to let the respondents decide for themselves. This means that in the following, atheists are individuals who when faced with the choice are willing to define themselves as atheists. The European Values Study (EVS) was conducted in 1981, 1990, and 1999, and in all three waves an item asked the respondents the following: "Independently of whether you go to church or not, would you say you are . . . A religious person, Not a religious person, or A convinced atheist." All those respondents who chose the latter option will be considered atheists. Both Denmark and Sweden participated in the EVS 1999, and hence data from the EVS 1999 will be used for Denmark and Sweden. The EVS has a sister survey called the World Values Survey (WVS), which is based on the EVS 1981 and contains many of the same questions as the EVS. For most intents and purposes the two surveys are interchangeable. The WVS is conducted at different intervals from that of the EVS. In Norway it was conducted in 1996 and again in 2007, although data were not publicly available at the time of this writing. Hence the data from the WVS 1996 will be used for Norway, because Norway does not take part in the EVS. Using survey data to analyze atheism will accomplish two things. It will establish the approximate number of atheists in the three Scandinavian countries and it will allow for an analysis of who the atheists are vis-à-vis the rest of the population.

The number of atheists in Scandinavia is rather small. According to the EVS 1999 and the WVS 1996 about 5 percent of the Danes are self-proclaimed atheists, and it is about 4 percent among the Norwegians and about 7 percent among the Swedes (Table 9.1). Looking at the combined data set (with the appropriate weights applied) about 6 percent of the Scandinavians or a little over one million people out of a population of over 18 million people could be said to be atheists at the time of the surveys. The differences between the countries are small, so small in fact that there is no significant difference in the number of atheists in Denmark and Sweden and in Denmark and Norway.[38] There were, however, significantly more atheists in Sweden than in Norway, but the difference is still rather small. Because the percentage of atheists in the Scandinavian countries was so small, it would appear

Table 9.1
Atheists (in percent)

	[a]Denmark	[b]Norway	[a]Sweden
Atheists	5	4	7
Non-Religious	18	49	54
Religious	77	47	39

Design weight applied
[a] EVS 1999
[b] WVS 1996

that the number of atheists follows the level of secularization at the societal level rather than at the individual level. It would also appear that the size and influence of atheistic/humanistic organizations in the Scandinavian countries has little relationship with the actual number of atheists. Strictly speaking Norway has the smallest number of atheists compared to Sweden, whereas the opposite should have been the case.

The large difference in the proportions of religious and nonreligious respondents (Table 9.1) is most likely the product of differences in translation. In Sweden and Norway "religious" was translated literally (into *religiös* and *religiøs*, respectively), while in Denmark it was translated into something akin to the English "believer" (*troende*). Hence in the following, the variable on being religious will be collapsed into two categories: atheist and other.[39]

The repeated nature of the EVS and the WVS makes it possible to compare the number of atheists in Scandinavia from 1981 to 1999, a time period of 19 years. There are some minor differences because the latest data from Norway is from 1996 and the first wave of the EVS was not conducted in Norway and Sweden until 1982. Nevertheless it can be concluded that the number of atheists in Scandinavia has remained unchanged since the beginning of the 1980s (table not shown). For Denmark, Norway, and Sweden the proportion of the population that identify as atheists has not changed significantly in the time period in which the EVS and WVS has been conducted. This suggests that being an atheist is not something taken lightly but is rather a stabile, general disposition just like religious beliefs in general. It is something that changes slowly and gradually. Most likely as the result of generational changes rather than life cycle stages or historical events. The slowly changing nature of the number of atheists also suggests that using data that are almost ten years old is less of a concern.

Because the Scandinavian countries are very similar with regard to structural factors (all three are stable democracies with comprehensive welfare systems) and secularization at the societal level, they will be analyzed as a whole. A population weight will be applied as well as a design weight because of a slightly skewed sampling in Sweden. To avoid the worst pitfalls of simplification, separate analyses will also be done for each country, but the results will only be mentioned if they contradict or correct the results of the main analyses, and the tables will not be shown.

Starting with demographics and education the atheists differ from the rest of the population on all variables (Table 9.2). Atheists are significantly more likely to be males than the rest of the population, and more than 70 percent of the atheists are male compared to about 48 percent among the rest of the population.[40] Atheists are also generally younger than the rest of the population. The average age of the atheists is 37 years old compared to an average age of 45 among the

Table 9.2
Demography and education (in percent)

	Atheist	Other
Female	29	52*
Male	71	48
Age (mean)	37	45*
Size of Town		
< 100,000	45	65*
100,000+	55	35
Education		
Less	50	59*
Secondary+	50	41

Design and Population weights applied
* Statistically significant at 5 percent level

rest of the population.[41] Atheists are significantly more likely to live in a large city (100,000 citizens or above), which is about 55 percent of them compared to about 35 percent among the rest of the population. Finally atheists are slightly but significantly more likely to have completed secondary school than the rest of the population. Among the atheists about half have completed secondary school compared to about 41 percent among the rest of the population.

Before any conclusions are reached it is important to note that the pattern found for the entire sample does not necessarily hold for the three national samples separately. The difference in gender composition and mean age holds in all three Scandinavian countries. The atheists tend to be male and younger. The tendency for atheists to live in larger cities on the other hand only holds for the Swedish sample. In neither Denmark nor Norway is there a significant difference between the atheists and the rest of the population on this variable. Regarding the difference in education, it only holds for the Danish sample. In Sweden and Norway atheists are not more likely to have completed secondary school than the rest of the population. With the differences between countries being what they are, it can be concluded that atheism in Scandinavia is only a structural phenomenon to the extend that it is more prevalent among males and those who are younger. That atheists are more likely to be male is not surprising, taking into consideration that males are generally less religious than females when measured using traditional Christian beliefs and practices. Because males are less likely to believe, there are more of them who could potentially take their unbelief to the next level and declare themselves atheists. If being an atheist, like being religious in general, is a generational phenomenon, then the younger mean age of the atheists suggests that atheism only started to make sense for the Scandinavians somewhere in the middle of the twentieth century, probably in the post-World War II years. It cannot, however, be concluded that atheism, like Christian religiosity in general, follows urbanization and education. Living in a large city and having a high level of education, two variables that generally predicts a lower level of Christian religiosity, do not seem to promote atheism in the Scandinavian countries in general.

Since the differences between atheists and the rest of the population are not entirely demographic nor educationally related a good second candidate is politics. There is a strong tendency for atheists to be more left leaning politically than the rest of the population. If a scale on left-wing/rightwing political self placement is reduced to only three categories then about 35 percent of the atheists can be considered left wing compared to about 17 among the rest of the population (Table 9.3). Generally speaking the atheists seem to be more polarized than the rest of the population as there are fewer center-oriented atheists than there are center-oriented in the rest of the population. Atheists seem generally more likely to take an extreme stance. If they have a political stance, then they do not compromise but instead tend to seek the extreme position unlike regular people. By combining five items on participation or likelihood of participating in petitions, boycotts, demonstrations, strikes, and occupations of buildings, an eleven-point index of political participation ranging from 0 to 10 can be constructed from the data.[42] Even though the median score on the index is the same for atheists and the rest of the population, there is a significant relationship between the two variables in that atheists are much more likely to participate in political activities outside voting. This combined with their political polarization suggests that in Scandinavia atheists are a special kind of people who tend to have strong political views and act

Table 9.3
Politics and trust (in percent)

Pol. Orientation	Atheist	Other
Right wing	11	17*
Centre	55	67
Left wing	35	17
Pol. Part. (median)	5	5*
Social Trust		
Trusting	68	66
Careful	32	34

Design and Population weights applied
* Statistically significant at 5 percent level

on them. It must be noted that in Norway and Sweden atheists tend to be more left wing than the rest of the population, whereas in Denmark they are as likely to be right wing as is the rest of the population but less likely to be center oriented. This does not change the conclusion because the point was not that atheists are more left wing but that they are more clear cut in political matters and go for the outlying positions on the political scale. In all three countries atheists are significantly more likely to score higher on the political participation index.

The lack of large atheistic/humanistic organizations in Denmark and Sweden becomes a little more puzzling taking the participatory tendencies of the atheists into consideration. If the atheists tend to take the extreme political view and act on it, they should be more active. Because the Scandinavian countries all have established churches and can hardly be said to be secularized at the societal level, there should be more than enough motivation for atheists to act. Only in Norway has there been a large organizational response to the established church. The most likely explanation for the apparent lack of activity among the Danish and Swedish atheists could be that atheists, because of lack of large and influential atheistic/humanistic organizations, have tended to find outlets for their (anti-)religious sentiments through established political organizations like the several left-wing parties that have existed at various points in the Scandinavian countries throughout the past decades.

Religion and the community it can create is related to the production of social trust particularly through church attendance.[43] Because the Scandinavian atheists have had little opportunity for social outlet through organizations, except in Norway, it could mean that they have less social trust than others. Social trust as a variable is important as it tend to predict trust in general, not to mention xenophobia (at least in Denmark). The idea that atheism should promote less social trust is rejected by the numbers (Table 9.3). There is no significant difference with regard to social trust between atheists and the rest of the population. Being actively nonreligious does not diminish one's general trust of others. This means that atheism in itself is not a threat to society in the sense that it could lower levels of civic participation or undermine the parliamentary system.[44]

With the proportion of atheists being about 6 percent in the Scandinavian countries there is ample room for the atheists to be religiously unaffiliated, even though the established churches of the Scandinavian countries have more than 80 percent of their populations as members. It is assumed that being an atheist is not the same as being a nonbeliever. If it were, the number of atheists should be much higher, maybe about 30 to 40 percent. Instead the Scandinavian countries have a large proportion of nonreligious or nonbelievers. The most likely scenario then is that the atheists are the ones who have left the established church, whereas the nonreligious are those who have stayed for whatever

Table 9.4
Church membership (in percent)

	Atheist	Other
National Church	47	80*
Other/None	53	20

Design and Population weights applied
* Statistically significant at 5 percent level

reasons they may have. Atheists are, after all, more likely to act (at least politically) and hence theoretically more likely to leave the established church. Surprisingly this expectation is contradicted by the survey data. Among the atheists about 47 percent are members of an established church compared to about 80 percent among the rest of the population (Table 9.4). This means that there are about half a million atheists in the Scandinavian countries who are also members of an established church. Even though they are ready to declare themselves atheists (rather than just nonreligious or nonbelievers), almost half the atheists for some reason are still members of an established, and state supported, Christian majority church. This is very puzzling indeed as the tendency for political activity does not seem to readily translate into religious action on the most basic level. There is of course a marked difference between atheists and the rest of the population with regard to membership in an established church as atheists are much more likely not to be members, but many of them still retain their membership regardless of the fact that they claim to be atheists.

Traditionally the Christian churches have promoted a specific kind of morality that their adherents were expected to follow. It could be argued that secularization has undermined the church-sponsored morality as the churches can no longer influence society as a whole. It could on the other hand be argued that this is not necessarily a problem in the Scandinavian countries as they are not particularly secularized at the societal level. Even with this caveat it could still be argued that in the Scandinavian countries atheists should be less inclined to adhere to a strict moral code because they are actively nonreligious and hence should not be particularly bound by whatever moral guidelines the established churches may promote. In fact their antireligious stance may even motivate them to choose a moral standpoint that is exactly the opposite of that of the churches. Using the EVS/WVS morals can be divided into civic moral and private moral, the latter often being referred to as permissiveness.[45] Here civic moral is whether respondents think it can be justified to claim state benefits one is not entitled to, cheat on one's taxes, or accept a bribe. It is a moral that relates to the individual's role

Table 9.5
Morals (median)

	Atheist	Other
Civic	25	26*
Private	12	19*

Design and Population weights applied
* Statistically significant at 5 percent level

as a citizen and to the individual's relationship to civil society. Private moral are whether the following can be justified: homosexuality, abortion, divorce, euthanasia, and suicide. It is a moral that relates to things that are basically private and do not readily impact society as a whole. In both cases responses have been combined into indexes.[46]

With regard to civic moral, atheists tend to be slightly less strict than the rest of the population (Table 9.5). On an index ranging from 0 to 27, where 0 is morally lax and 27 is morally strict, atheists have a median score of 25 compared to a median score of 26 among the rest of the population. The difference is rather small but significant nonetheless. Regardless of the minor difference between the two groups the table shows that the Scandinavians regardless of religiosity have a very strict civic moral. This is undoubtedly rooted in the comprehensive welfare systems that have helped promote a view of the nation-states of Scandinavia as bottom-up constructs rather than top-down. The state is there to help its citizens and not vice versa. Checking for differences in civic moral for each sample separately reveals that there is only a difference between the atheists and the rest of the population in Norway. In both Denmark and Sweden atheism makes no impacts on civic morals. This only supports the notion that civic morals in the Scandinavian countries are a product of nation-state building rather than individual preferences, religious or not.

The picture is different with regard to private morals. Here atheists are much more morally permissive than the rest of the population. On an index ranging from 0 to 45, with 45 being the morally strictest, the median score of the atheists is 12 compared to a median score of 19 among the rest of the population. This means that the atheists are generally more accepting of sexual and marital mores that the Christian churches have traditionally opposed. It would seem that the atheists, in their active and outspoken nonreligiousness, have rejected the moral mores of the Christian churches. They may still be members to a high degree, but they insist on ignoring the moral rules of the church. Regardless of the marked difference between the atheists and the rest of the population with regard to private morals, the table also shows how morally permissive the Scandinavians are. Even the median score of 19 for the nonatheists is still far from the maximum score of 45.

Compare this to the median score of 25 and 26 on the civic moral index, with its maximum score of 27. The Scandinavians regardless of whether they are atheists or not have very strict civic morals combined with comparatively lax private morals.

In the end, with the data available, a picture is painted of atheists in Scandinavia as a group that is in some instances unique and in others indistinguishable from the rest of the population. A Scandinavian atheist is characterized by being a younger male with relatively extreme political viewpoints and a general inclination toward political action. Probably as a consequence of their nonreligious standpoint atheists are more often not members of a church and reject the morals the church has traditionally preached. Their appreciation of other people and their respect for society in general and their fellow man is the same as their nonatheist fellow Scandinavians. In this sense it could be argued that atheists are secularized individuals to the point where their (non-) religious viewpoints have lost their impact on the values of other life-spheres. Their rejection of religiosity has an impact only on those areas which are related to traditional Christian church religiosity: church membership and private morals. Being a self-declared atheist does not seem to entail a comprehensive philosophy of life but is rather a narrow concept that is only related to the strictly religious. Outside the religious sphere a Scandinavian atheist is just like every other Scandinavian. Or maybe it is the other way round.

Secularization in Scandinavia is not a straightforward phenomenon. At the societal level it would, in many respects, be most correct to state that Scandinavia is not secularized. Large established churches with special legal privileges and strong popular support in the form of membership rates rival those of the Catholic Church in southern Europe. At the individual level, on the other hand, the Scandinavians seem highly secularized; in fact they seem like the most secularized people in the world. Very low church attendance rates are combined with weak support for central tenets of the Christian faith. This is the Scandinavian paradox: strong churches and a-religious citizens. Secularization is a societal phenomenon that has the power to create the structural possibility for atheism, but the question is whether it is secularization at the societal or individual level that is conducive to atheism in Scandinavia: societal secularization seem to leave rather little room for atheism because Scandinavia is not particularly secularized, and individual secularization leaves rather more room for atheism because the low levels of religiosity make for a large group of potential atheists. There are rather few atheists in Scandinavia. Only about 6 percent of the populations of the Scandinavian countries can be said to be atheists as defined here. This suggests that it is (the lack of) secularization at the societal level that sets the limits for atheism in Scandinavia. Somehow the presence of established churches tightly integrated in the state has helped hold back what could have been a much larger number of atheists. There is a large group of nonreligious Scandinavians; how many depends on how they are defined, but for some reason they do not seem to be attracted by being self-described atheists. If atheism is seen as a reaction of nonreligious people to the presence of religion in the public sphere and particularly an opposition to the traditional Christian majority churches of Europe, then it is plausible that it is the combination of the Scandinavians' bottom-up relationship to the state and the relationship between the state and the established churches that is the cause of the low number of atheists in Scandinavia. Even though many Scandinavians are de facto a-religious, they do not feel resentment toward nor threatened by the established churches because they see them as part of the comprehensive welfare system. Without an "enemy" at which to direct their resentment of religion, atheists are unlikely to materialize. Because the established churches are seen as part of the welfare states, they are part of something that all Scandinavians regard very highly. The established churches may be the cause of the low levels of religiosity in Scandinavia,[47] but it would seem that they are also the cause of the low number of atheists in Scandinavia.

NOTES

1. Loek Halman et al., eds., *Traditie, secularisatie en individualsering. Een studie naar de waarden van de Nederlanders in een Europese context* (Tilburg: Tilburg University Press, 1987); Peter Ester et al., eds., *The Individualizing Society: Value Change in Europe and North America,* 2nd ed. (Tilburg: Tilburg University Press, 1994); Loek Halman et al., "The Religious Factor in Contemporary Society. The Differential Impact of Religion in the Private and Public Sphere in Comparative Perspective," *International Journal of Comparative Sociology* 40, no. 1 (1999): 141–60; Christian Albrekt Larsen et al., *Danskernes forhold til religionen—en afrapportering af ISSP 1998* (Aalborg: Institut for Økonomi, Politik og Forvaltning, 2002).

2. Larsen et al., *Danskernes forhold til religionen—en afrapportering af ISSP 1998,* 33.

3. Peter B. Andersen and Peter Lüchau, "Tro og religiøst tilhørsforhold i Europa," in *Danskernes særpræg,* ed. Peter Gundelach (København: Hans Reitzels Forlag, 2004).

4. According to data from the EVS 1999 and the WVS 1996 less than 70 percent of the Danish and Norwegian samples believe in God, and in the Swedish sample it is less than 55 percent. For the combined (and weighted) sample about 62 percent claim to believe in God. If belief in God is considered a minimum of belief for someone to be considered religious in a Christian sense, then the number of a-religious could be as high as 38 percent. Those who are religious but not Christians would have to be subtracted from the 38 percent, but it is difficult to ascertain how many religious non-Christians there are in Scandinavia because the current surveys have very few items on non-Christian religiosity.

5. According to data from the EVS 1999 and WVS 1996 about 90 percent of the Danes and Norwegians claim to be members of a church or other religious

organization. The number for Sweden is more than 75 percent. For the combined (and weighted) sample about 84 percent claim to be members of a church or other religious organization. If atheists are unaffiliated on principle, then they would have to be among the 16 percent unaffiliated.

6. Karel Dobbelaere, *Secularization: An Analysis at Three Levels* (Brussels: P.I.E.-Peter Lang, 2002), 19.

7. Ibid., 21–22.

8. Ibid., 140.

9. Ibid., 134.

10. Ibid., 167–168.

11. Ibid., 169.

12. Peter B. Andersen et al., "Religion in Europe and the United States: Assumptions, Survey Evidence, and Some Suggestions," *Nordic Journal of Religion and Society* 21, no. 1 (2008): 61–74.

13. Inger Dübeck, "State and Church in Denmark", in *State and Church in the European Union*, 2nd ed., ed. Gerhard Robbers (Baden-Baden: Nomos Verlagsgesellschaft, 2005).

14. Preben Espersen, *Kirkeret. Almindelig del.* (København: Jurist og Økonomforbundets Forlag, 1993), 76.

15. Hans Gammeltoft-Hansen, "§6", in *Danmarks Riges Grundlov med kommentarer*, ed. Henrik Zahle (København: Jurist- og Økonomforbundets Forlag, 1999). Gammeltoft-Hansen does however argue that it would not be very practical for the monarch to be member of a church other than the Danish People's Church, and it has in fact never been the case since 1849 when the Danish constitution was established.

16. Njål Høstmælingen, "The Permissible Scope of Legal Limitations on the Freedom of Religion or Belief in Norway," *Emory International Law Review* 19, no. 2 (2005): 989–1032.

17. Ibid., 1003.

18. Lars Friedner, "State and Church in Sweden", in *State and Church in the European Union*, 2nd ed., ed. Gerhard Robbers (Baden-Baden: Nomos Verlagsgesellschaft, 2005).

19. Rune Larsson, "Rätten till befrielse från skolans religionsundervisning i Sverige," in *Religion, skole og kulturel integration i Danmark og Sverige*, ed. Peter B. Andersen et al. (København: Museum Tusculanums Forlag, 2006).

20. Richard K. Fenn, "Toward a New Sociology of Religion," *Journal for the Scientific Study of Religion* 11, no. 1 (Spring, 1972): 16–32.

21. This is not possible in Denmark because the Danish People's church does not have a synod, church council, or any kind of official organ to decide an official stance of the church.

22. The secretary of the Atheistic Society; e-mail message to author, August 14, 2008.

23. See http://www.ateist.dk (accessed September 1, 2009).

24. See http://www.ateist.net (accessed September 1, 2009). Being a society is a Danish legal construct that basically makes the society a legal person with the rights and duties inherent in such a status.

25. See http://www.human.no (accessed September 1, 2009).

26. Paul Knutsen, *Livet før døden. Human-Etisk Forbund 1956–2006* (Oslo: Humanist Forlag 2006), 10. The book is a history of the Norwegian Humanist

Association written by a professor of history. It was published by the publishing house of the Norwegian Humanist Association.

27. Ibid., 243.

28. Ibid., 250.

29. Ibid., 253.

30. Ibid., 255.

31. Ibid., 258.

32. Høstmælingen, "The Permissible Scope of Legal Limitations on the Freedom of Religion or Belief in Norway," 1001.

33. Knutsen, *Livet før døden. Human-Etisk Forbund 1956–2006*, 261–262.

34. "Staten og Den norske kirke," *Norges offentlige utredninger* 2006, no. 2 (2006):9.

35. The Humanists' press service, e-mail message to author, August 14, 2008.

36. See http://www.humanisterna.se (accessed September 1, 2009).

37. See "Staten och trossamfunden," *Statens offentliga utredningar* 1994, no. 42 (1994), 3–4. The members of the committee were either politicians or employees of the Church of Sweden.

38. Difference of proportions test used.

39. Using the original variable in the analyses does not change the overall conclusions. The results from the combined sample are the same although there are some minor differences when the national samples are analyzed separately.

40. Gamma tests have been used to test for statistical significance. In the one case where a Student's t-test has been used it is mentioned in a note.

41. Student's t-test used.

42. The items conform to a Mokken model with a Loevinger's H of 0.50 for the entire sample, which means that the items form a strong scale.

43. Robert D. Putnam, *Bowling Alone: The Collapse and Revival of American Community* (New York: Simon & Schuster, 2000).

44. See Gabriel A. Almond and Sidney Verba, *The Civic Culture: Political Attitudes and Democracy in Five Nations* (Princeton: Princeton University Press, 1963).

45. See Peter Ester and Loek Halman, "Empirical Trends in Religious and Moral Beliefs in Western Europe," *International Journal of Sociology* 24, no. 2–3 (1994): 81–110.

46. A factor analysis with Varimax rotation conducted on the eight variables shows that they belong to two different factors. The index on private moral tests well for scalability (Cronbach's Alpha = 0.77), while the index on civic moral does not (Cronbach's Alpha = 0.47). Since the factor analysis showed that the items on civic moral were related, both indexes will be used.

47. See Mark Chaves and David E. Cann, "Regulation, Pluralism, and Religious Market Structure. Explaining Religion's Vitality," *Rationality and Society* 4, no. 3 (1992): 272–90; Rodney Stark and Laurence R. Iannaccone, "A Supply-Side Reinterpretation of the 'Secularization' of Europe," *Journal of the Scientific Study of Religion* 33, no. 3 (1994): 230–252.

Chapter 10

Atheism and Secularity in China

Liang Tong

Before we discuss the term *atheism*, it is necessary to distinguish two kinds of meaning of the word "atheism" (*Wu Shen Lun* in Chinese). One refers to the doctrine that God does not exist and the belief in the existence of God is false (Jones et al. 2005, 576), whereas the other is connected with the Chinese character "*Wu* (negation) *Shen* (god)," which generally means a negative assertion of the faith or belief held by different tribes or villages.

In the early time of which there are archaeological records (Chang, K.C., 130–134), the Chinese character *Shen* (god) refers to a divine being, which is regarded as the powerful dominator of the world by people living in a certain tribe or village. The mysterious power of divine being derives from the unpredictable heaven. The divine beings vary with tribes or villages; however, the people who belong to one tribe (or village) usually admit faith or belief in their own *Shen*, but negate that in others.

Nevertheless, the focus of this chapter is on the first meaning of atheism occurring within a particular context of religious institution generally comprising institutional and diffused religion. In Yang's opinion, the institutional religion refers to universal religions such as Buddhism and Taoism, and other religious groups or organizations, which play relatively independent parts in the social system of China. And the diffused religion embedded in the ideas, rituals, and structure of secular life of the Chinese people has theological theories, worshipped objects, and adherents whose constitution is looser than the former (Yang 2007, 268–270). However, atheism in ancient China developed in such circumstances as those mentioned above. On that account, atheism is usually conditioned by the surrounding circumstances in which it develops, and thus is consequently accompanied with certain emphases or omissions that constitute the characteristics of the atheism. So it is necessary to give a brief account of the background of the Chinese society and civilization.

Until today, it was known to many Western people that the Chinese people were less concerned with religion than other people elsewhere. For example, Professor Bodde thinks that Chinese people "are not a people for whom religious ideas and activities constitute an all-important and absorbing part of life. . . . It is ethics (especially Confucian ethics), and not religion (at least not religion of a formal, organized type), that provided the spiritual basis in Chinese civilization. . . . All of which, of course, marks a difference of fundamental importance between China and most other major civilizations, in which a church and a priesthood have played a dominant role" (Bodde 1942, 293).

The statement of Bodde brings out the situation of Chinese religion, but leaves more questions about religion in Chinese culture in the meantime. The reason why Chinese people have less concern with religion is that they have so much concern with the transcendent dimension of secular life. Chinese people are not as religious as those of the West because the former are self-cultivated or neighborhood-moralized in the family system. The family system constitutes the mainstay of social system of China and provokes the patriarchal clan system, which has kept up for more than two thousand years (Jin 1984, 30–37). For economic reasons, the members of a family, including descendants must live together. Thus there developed the Chinese family system, which was undoubtedly one of the most complex and well organized in the world. In the *Erh Ya*, which is the oldest dictionary of the Chinese language, dating from before the Christian era, there are more than one hundred terms for various family relationships, most of which have no equivalent in the English language.

A great amount of Confucianism, including Confucian ethics, became the rational justification or theoretical expression of the social system of China. With their secular life integrated with Confucian ethics, Chinese people became used to the homiletics of the patriarchal clan system and fulfilled themselves through their daily practice in pursuit of the elevation of mind—a reaching out for what is beyond the present actual world and for values that are higher than moral ones.

It is quite different for ordinary people to fulfill themselves. Under the guidance of teachers, men have to study "Six Classics" which consist of the *Book of Changes*, the *Book of Odes* (or *Poetry*), the *Book of History*, the *Rituals* (or *Rites*), the *Music* (no longer preserved as a separate work), and the *Spring and Autumn Annals*, a chronicle history of Confucius' state of Lu extending from 722 to 479 BCE, if they could fortunately secure an opportunity of disciple in the private capacity. Furthermore, the outstanding students among those men in the study had to be well prepared so as to try their best in the imperial examinations. Women, on the other hand, have to scrupulously abide by the cardinal guide "husband guides wife"[1] and diligently tackle domestic chores in perfect order. It can be regarded as a form of fulfilling oneself whether to prepare for the imperial examinations or tackle the domestic chores.

Moreover, following along with the principle *Chung* (the golden mean)[2] (Yang 1980, 64), which means neither too much nor too little, i.e., just right, and doing common and ordinary things with understanding of their full significance, one can gain the harmony of inner heart and outer world, which represents the Confucian way of elevating the mind. In this way one can achieve other-worldliness, yet at the same time not lose this-worldliness. Nevertheless, Western readers may feel puzzled about the coexistence of incompatible this-worldliness and other-worldliness based on their cultural inheritance of knowledge. The inheritance of knowledge of Western culture emphasizes the articulate concepts, cogent arguments, and valid reasoning so as to draw a clear dividing line between different things. However, the Confucian way of elevating the mind in Chinese culture strives for the synthesis out of such antitheses as this-worldliness and other-worldliness. It doesn't mean that antitheses are to be abolished; on the contrary, they are still there. They have been made into a synthetic whole (Mu 1997, 101–103). So what the Confucian way pursues is not either wholly this-worldly nor wholly other-worldly, yet both of this world and of the other world, that is, very practical though not superficial.

While fulfilling oneself, one must also see that others are likewise fulfilled. One cannot fulfill oneself while disregarding the fulfillment of others. The reason is that one can develop one's nature to the utmost only through the human relationships, that is, within the social system, especially the family system. To fulfill oneself is to develop to the utmost what one has received from heaven, and to help others is to assist the transforming and nourishing operations of heaven and earth according to Confucius ethics. By fully understanding the significance of these things, one is enabled to form a unity and harmony of heaven, earth, and human beings.

In terms of elevation of mind, Chinese people gain a good deal of enlightenment and inspiration from an immense number of ancient Chinese books. Those books are accustomed to expressing ideas in the form of aphorisms, apothegms, or allusions and illustrations, which perhaps gives the reader an impression of briefness and disconnectedness of the sayings and writings of their authors. The whole book of *Lao-tzu* consists of aphorisms, and most of the chapters of the *Chuang-tzu* are full of allusions and illustrations. Even in writings such as *Confucian Analects* and *Mencius*, both of which have a good few systematic reasoning and arguments, there are still so many aphorisms, allusions, and illustrations in contrast to writings of the West, which are full of elaborated reasoning and careful arguments. In general, aphorisms sound very brief, and allusions and illustrations sound disconnected.

Aphorisms, allusions, and illustrations are thus not articulate enough, but their insufficiency in articulateness is compensated for by their suggestiveness. Articulateness and suggestiveness are certainly incompatible. The more an expression is articulate, the less it is suggestive—just as the more an expression is narrative, the less it is poetic. The phrasing and wording of ancient Chinese books are so inarticulate that their suggestiveness is almost boundless (Hall and Ames 2005, 201–206). Given the language barrier, an intelligent reader should learn to read not only what is inside the book, but also what is between the lines.

FORMATION AND FORERUNNERS OF ATHEISM IN ANCIENT CHINA

Transitional Views toward the Ghosts and Spirits

Given less concern with religion, it doesn't mean that Chinese people are not religious whether in ancient or present time. The religious belief system of China has usually been regarded as beginning in ancestor worship, but this is not totally true. Ancestor worship was present from the early time before the Xia dynasty, for which there are archaeological records (Chang, K. C., 130–134), but only as one element in Chinese religion. The other element is the worship of the spirits of nature, which is based on naturalism (Sivin 1995, ch. IV, 1–2). The naturalism brings about the nurturing of atheism during the Spring and Autumn period extending from 770 to 476 BCE (Li 2002, 121–137), which will be discussed in the following paragraphs.

Chinese people approached the riddle of human life by supposing that a person has two souls: the *po* (animal soul or life soul), and the *hun* (spiritual soul or personality soul). Both souls become separated from the body at death, and both can be kept alive by sacrifices upon which they feed. The life soul (*po*), however, gradually decays with the body, whereas the personality soul (*hun*) survives as long as it is remembered and receives due sacrifices from the living. It can become a deity of power and influence, can respond in divination to the questions and requests of its descendants, and can even postpone their deaths. If the *po* is neglected, it may become a *gui* (demon) and haunt the living, whereas the neglected *hun* in a similar case will become a pitiable ghost but also is capable of working harm. Hence it is of paramount importance for male descendants to perform the family ancestral sacrifices so as to comfort both souls of ancestors.

In fact, the family ancestral sacrifices are correlated with the *pao* (response or return) probably coming from the deity of deceased ancestors or spirits of nature. Here the *pao* is regarded as a form of reciprocity of actions between people and supernatural beings, and therefore the person who bestows favors on ancestors normally anticipates a response or return from them in the future. Favors done for others are often considered what may be termed "social investments," for which handsome returns are expected. The more a certain ancestor who is esteemed by his worshipers wins offerings, the more he will potentially reciprocate favors (Yang 1976, 357–358). The interaction between worshipers and ancestors with reference to *pao* can be looked on as a vivid example of the special Chinese "relation-faith pattern" (Li 2006, 80–81) and as a theoretical explanation for the principle of Chinese ancestor worship.

Since the Shang dynasty, there are formal and systematic rituals of family ancestral sacrifices, which are classified as communicative behaviors or magic ones (Leach 1966, 403), and the Chinese characters *zu* and *zong* (ancestors), which are originally two ritual names, eventually combined into the general name of family ancestral sacrifices (Li 1998, 172). With the development of patriarchy, the rituals of family ancestral sacrifices seem to focus on the legitimacy of the orthodoxy and orthopraxy of a religious belief system (Watson 1988, 9–11). It can be inferred that old male members, particularly admired or respected ones, are linked more and more closely with sacrifice rituals of the family system. Thus there develops the ancestor worship, which lasts several thousand of years and maintains the consistency and integrality of Chinese culture.

Besides the ancestor worship, certain spirits of nature also receive worship in ancient China. In the Shang dynasty, there is mention of a series of spirits of nature, such as the Eastern Mother, the Western Mother, the Ruler of the Four Quarters, the Dragon Woman, the Snake Spirit, and the Wind, who were reverenced deities (Strassberg 2002, 48–49). Mention of these names is in honor of nature spirits and deities of fertility. The loess soil of north China is quite fertile on the condition that it receives sufficient rainfall. On the other hand, the Yellow River flowing through loess country has historically deposited silt, which built up its bed above the surrounding land in such a way that, when floods did occur, the damage was enormous and widespread. Hence the balance of nature, between too little rain and too much, is obviously regarded as a delicate one, and it is necessary for the chieftain of a certain tribe or village to preserve the balance of nature by due sacrifices not only to heaven but also to the gods of the earth (Granet 1989, 168–170).

Crude and primitive as the forms of worship of ancestor and spirits of nature are, the presence of the above worship with an emphasis on fertility is clearly attested in China, as elsewhere in the world. The characters for *zu* (ancestor) and *she* (god of the soil) both contain a phallic symbol that honors reproductive humans (Fan et al. 1998, 472) or grain (Yuan 1985, 18–19, 209). The before-mentioned forms of worship enjoy equal concern, with shrines placed east and west of the entry to the palace, as if designed to ensure good crops of sons to the ancestors and of grain in the fields.

In the ancient classics and inscriptions of the Shang dynasty (c. 1750–1100 BCE), there are frequent references to a supreme dominator in heaven known as *shang-ti*. This god is not known as the creator, but he was undoubtedly a divine supervisor over human society, whose decrees determine the course of events on earth (Chang 2002, 192–193). When the Shang dynasty was supplanted by the Zhou dynasty (c. 1100 BCE), the name *T'ien* appeared alongside of *Shang-ti* as a designation for the supreme dominator in heaven. However, the word *t'ien*, rendered as either "heaven" or "sky" and sometimes as "nature," gradually lost the connotation of a personal being and came to suggest the more universal conception of a cosmic rule that impartially determines the affairs of people on earth by their conformity to a moral order. Closely related to *t'ien*, the ultimate ordering principle of things, was the completely impersonal *Tao*, literally "way" or "road." By extension it means the way to go, the truth, the normative ethical standard by which to govern human life. In the famous book *Lao-tzu*, which in later time was also known as the *Tao Te Ching* (*Classics of the Way and Power*), it brings forward a belief that the metaphysical principle *Tao* governs the world. *Tao* cannot be described in words, but can be dimly perceived within the complicated balance and harmony of nature. *Tao*, which is not understood as God or as a god, is the law or order of nature identified with nature itself. Thus the belief of *Tao* brings about the rise of naturalism and atheism.

Forerunners of Atheism and Humanistic Enlightenment

Before Confucius put forward his skeptical arguments of theism,[3] a senior official of the state of Zheng named Tzu Chan (c. 580–522 BCE), brought forth the famous statement, "the will of God is remote while the humanism is close at hand" (Li 1998, 1087), when he was asked whether to perform the sacrifice for keeping fire away (Fang et al. 1994, 57–58). Though it cannot be inferred the religion faith of Tzu Chan only from one statement of his, Tzu Chan does make his valuable step out of prevalent theistic conceptions of his era. Tzu Chan's statement places more emphasis on humanism than mysterious conceptions of heaven, which separates ordinary life from the constant sacrifices to the God or gods. As a forerunner of atheism, Tzu Chan also has an insight into the ascription of some diseases. One day, Tzu Chan was sent to ask after a high official of state Jin who fell ill. When he inquired about the symptoms of the high official, Tzu Chan ascribed the cause to disorders between work, rest, and diets, whereas the witch doctor insisted on spirits working harm (Li 1998, 915–916). In the era full of magic and superstition, Tzu Chan manifests the humanism by his words and actions, which objectively sing higher praise for the rationality of human than the god's will. And there comes the trend of skepticism of the existence of God or gods. Consequently the atheism comes into being.

Confucius is the latinized name of the person who has been famous in China as K'ung Tzu or Master K'ung. His family name was K'ung, and his personal name Ch'iu. He was born in 551 BCE in the state of Lu (Fang et al. 1994, 170), in the southern part of the present Shandong province in eastern China. His ancestors had been members of the ducal house of the state of Sung, which was descended from the royal house of Shang, the dynasty that had preceded the Chou. Because of political troubles, the family had lost its noble position and migrated to Lu before the birth of Confucius (Kuang 1990, 18–23).

Confucius was impoverished in his youth, but entered the government of Lu, and by the time he was fifty had reached high official rank. On account of political intrigue, he was soon forced to resign his post and leave his homeland. For the next thirteen years he traveled from one state to another, invariably hoping to seek an opportunity to realize his ideal of gradual political and social reform. However, nowhere did he succeed, and finally as an old man he returned to Lu, where he died three years later in 479 BCE (Kuang 1990, 86–88).

So far as modern scholarship can determine (Kuang 1990, 286–268), Confucius was the first person in Chinese history to teach large numbers of students in a private capacity, by whom he was accompanied during his travels in different states. In regard to tradition, he had several thousand students, of whom several tens became famous thinkers and scholars. The former number is obviously a gross exaggeration, but there is no question that he was a very influential teacher, and what is more important and unique, China's first private teacher (Wu 1997, 55–56). His ideas are best known through the *Lun Yü* (*Analects*), a collection of his scattered sayings and apothegms that was compiled by some of his disciples.

As the founder of the *Ju* school (Confucian School), Confucius was more than a *ju* (literatus) in the common sense of the word. Confucius wanted his disciples to be "rounded men" who would be useful to state and society, and therefore he taught them various branches of knowledge based on the different classics especially on "Six Classics." In the eyes of Confucius, his primary function as a teacher was to interpret to his disciples the ancient cultural heritage. That is why, in his own words as recorded in the *Analects*, he was "a transmitter and not an originator" (Yang 1980, 66). By teaching the ancient classics, Confucius and the descendant *Ju* School inherit the ancient cultural legacy and carry forward the skeptical soul of rationalism and necessary intellect resources for atheism as well.

On the other hand, while transmitting the traditional institutions and ideas, Confucius gave his disciples interpretations derived from his own moral concepts, which are involved with the transcendent dimension of secular life. It is by reason of Confucius' interpretation and persistence that Confucian ethics infiltrate step-by-step into the explanation system of the secular life in ancient China. For example, Confucius adopted the suspension standpoint[4] and made no comment on ghosts and spirits in his interpretation of the prevalent custom of the sacrifices to ancestors. In the book *Analects*, as the saying goes:[5]

> He sacrificed [to the dead], as if they were present. He sacrificed to the spirits, as if the spirits were present.
> The Master (Confucius) said, "I consider my not being present at the sacrifice, as if I did not sacrifice." (Legge 1870, 21)

Confucius ingeniously avoided clarifying his standpoint on ghosts and spirits by using "as if," which can be regarded as an elucidation of his suspension standpoint. Some scholars straightforwardly by claim that Confucius takes the theistic stand to vindicate the slave-owning system (Ji 1951, 5), whereas others infer that Confucius is no more than a halfway theist, for he presents himself at the sacrifice, while he doesn't acknowledge his theistic belief straightforward (Guo 1981, 61–62). But I think that whether Confucius is a halfway theist or not cannot merely depend on the saying quoted above. Anyway, there are other pivotal sayings in *Analects* that can help us to deal with the question about Confucius' suspension standpoint:

> Tzu-lu (one disciple of Confucius) asked about serving the spirits [of the dead], the Master said, "While you are not able to serve men, how can you serve [their] spirits?"[6] [Tzu-lu added], "I venture to ask about death?" He was answered, "While you do not know life, how can you know about death?"[7] (Legge 1870, 57–58)

Instead of serving the spirits of the dead, Confucius told his disciples to show concern for secular business of the living, which seems to foster the filial piety of young generations (Ya and Wang 1992, 67). Thus the essentials of sacrifice were replaced on the quiet by the Confucian idea of self-cultivation. Atheist as Confucius may not be, he risked universal condemnation to ingeniously carry out his humanistic propositions in the era of prevalent theistic conceptions. If Confucius did not take the suspension stand, he would hardly be a teacher in the midst of a long career during the turbulent but worshipful Spring and Autumn period.

Generally by speaking, Confucius scarcely talked of supernatural beings in terms of his disciples' recordation because he acknowledged the inevitability of the world as it exists, and so to disregard his external success or failure (Lao 2005, 102–103). Suppose one does his duty, which is normally done through his very act, regardless of the external success or failure of his action. The subjects on which the Master did not talk, were extraordinary things, feats of strength, disorder, and spiritual beings[8] (Legge 1870, 39).

On the whole, Confucius believed that people could cultivate their moral character with the practice of human-heartedness (*jen*) and righteousness (*yi*). Human-heartedness means "loving others," whereas righteousness means the "oughtness" of a situation in correlation with a categorical imperative (Lao 2005, 106). For instance, the father acts according to the way a father should act who loves his son; the son acts according to the way a son should act who loves his father. Hence Confucius says: "Human-heartedness is to love [all] men."[9] (Legge 1870, 67).

The person who really loves others is the one able to perform his duties in society. Consequently, the word *jen* in some sayings of the *Analects* denotes not only a special kind of virtue, but also all the virtues combined, so that the term "man of *jen*" becomes synonymous with the man of all-round virtue. However, it is not practicable to be a "man of *jen*" if straying from the daily life even trifles. Human-heartedness and righteousness is so concrete that everyone has to learn and exercise in life with regard to Confucius' view, because the value of learning and exercising what he ought to do lives in the doing itself, but not in the external result (Lao 2005, 101–102).

It is necessary for everyone to eat and drink at regular physiological intervals. Hence eating and drinking are the common and ordinary activities of mankind. They are common and ordinary exactly because they are so important that no one can live without them. The same is true of human relations and moral virtues. They appear to some people as so common and ordinary as to be of little value, yet they are, quite simply because they are so important that no one can live without them, especially in an agrarian country during the less developed era. To eat and drink and to maintain human relations and moral virtues is to follow the nature of man. It is nothing else but the Way (*Tao*). What is called spiritual culture or moral instruction is nothing more than the cultivation of this Way. The function of spiritual culture is to give people an understanding that they are all, more or less, secularly following the Way so as to incite them to be conscious of what they are doing. For a better understanding of the conception of Way, it is necessary to discuss the Chinese pattern of thought that is key to go into the development of atheism in Ancient China.

ANCIENT CHINESE PATTERN OF THOUGHT AND DEVELOPMENT OF ATHEISM IN CHINA

It is unwise to talk about the development of atheism in China without considering the conception of Way. Though the two main schools of Chinese thought, Taoism (Taoist School) and Confucianism (Confucian School), have different arguments in various doctrines; they agree on a theory concerning both the sphere of nature and that of

Human. It is called "reversal is the movement of Tao." The theory tells us when the development of anything brings it to one extreme, a reversal to the other extreme takes place. In other words, everything involves its own negation,[10] which is one of the major theses of Lao Tzu's philosophy and also that of the *Book of Changes* as interpreted by the Confucianists. The theory probably draws inspiration from the movements of the sun and moon and the succession of the four seasons, to which peasants must pay special heed in order to carry on their own work in the agrarian country (Liu 2000, 11–18).

In the Appendices of the *Book of Changes*, it is said: "When the cold goes, the warmth comes, and when the warmth comes, the cold goes." (Zhou 1991, 260) and further: "When the sun has reached its meridian, it declines, and when the moon has become full, it wanes." (Zhou 1991, 195). Such movements are regarded as "returning" in the Appendices. Thus the first volume of the Appendix says: "In returning we see the mind of Heaven and Earth." (Zhou 1991, 86). Analogously in the *Lao-zu* we discover the words: "Reversal is the movement of the *Tao*."[11] (Zhu 1984, 165). According to Lao Tzu, the theory is the most fundamental one among all the laws that govern the changes of thing. It means anything that develops extreme qualities will invariably revert to the opposite qualities (Guo and Wang 2002, 171).

This theory has had stupendous influence on the Chinese people and has contributed a lot to their success in overcoming the various difficulties that they have encountered in the long history of China. Convinced of this theory, they remain cautious even in time of prosperity and hopeful even in time of extreme danger (Wan 1989, 141–143). In the decades of civil war, the concept provided the Chinese people with a sort of psychological weapon, so that even in their darkest period, most people lived on the hope that was expressed in the phrase: "The dawn will soon come." It was this "will to believe" that helped the Chinese people to go through the war.

This theory has also provided the principal argument for the doctrine of the golden mean, favored by Confucianist and Taoist alike. "Never too much" has been the maxim of both. For according to it, it is better for one to be wrong by having too little, than to be wrong by having too much, and to be wrong by laving things undone, than to be wrong by overdoing them. For by having too much and overdoing, one runs the risk of getting the opposite of what one wants. As an old Chinese proverb says: "Humility often gains more than pride."[12]

Ancient Chinese Pattern of Thought: Everlasting and Dynamic Holism

The conception of Way provides the thread for tapping into the Chinese pattern of thought, yet that does not mean we count on the conception only. However, it is quite necessary to make reference to *Wu Hsing, Yin-yang,* and *Ch'i,* which comprise the Chinese pattern of thought. Working as the naturalistic explanation mechanism of natural and social changes (Sivin 1995, ch. IV, 29), they are put at a premium in the ancient society of China. Deeply embedded as they are in antique classics or scriptures that last hundreds of years, *Wu Hsing, Yin-yang,* and *Ch'i* remain fascinating to those who are eager to learn the essentials of the development of Chinese atheism.

The *Wu Hsing* theory

The term *Wu Hsing* is usually translated as the Five Elements (Benedict and Heller 1999, 55–56; Li-Ling 2003, 993–94), i.e., five fundamental constituents of the universe. However, they are not static elements, but rather as five dynamic and interacting forces. Historically, *Wu Hsing* emerged as an analogous set of fivefold divisions, also complementary, of configurations of processes. "Phase" is an elegant English counterpart of the *hsing* in *Wu Hsing,* a concept that occurs in the *Springs and Autumns of Master Lü* and thereafter. It reflects the common, nontechnical sense of "phase", i.e., "any one aspect of a thing of varying aspects; a state or stage of change or development" (Lloyd and Sivin 2002, 197). Thus "Five Phases" can be regarded as the appropriate translation of the term *Wu Hsing.*

Further, the first really authentic account of the term *Wu Hsing* is found in the *Hung Fan* ("Great Plan" or "Grand Norm") section (Wang 1982, 115–129) of the *Book of History.* Traditionally, the "Great Plan" is said to be the record of a speech delivered to King Wu of the Chou dynasty by the Viscount of Chi, a prince of the Shang dynasty, which King Wu conquered at the end of the twentieth century BCE. In this speech, the Viscount of Chi in turn attributes his ideas to Yü, traditional founder of the Xia dynasty who is said to have lived in the twenty-second century BCE. These traditions are mentioned as examples of the way the writer of this treatise tried to give importance to the *Wu Hsing* theory. As to the actual date of the "Grand Plan," modern scholarship inclines to place it within the range of the early period to the middle one of the Western Zhou dynasty, i.e., the tenth or ninth centuries BCE (Chen 2003, 91; Li 2004, 82).

In the "Great Plan" we are given a list of "Nine Categories." "First [among the categories] is that of the *Wu Hsing.* The first [of these] is named Water; the second, Fire; the third, Wood; the fourth, Metal; the fifth, Soil. [The name of] Water is to moisten and descend; of Fire, to flame and ascend; of Wood, to be crooked and straighten; of Metal, to yield and to be modified; of Soil, to provide for sowing and reaping." (Wang 1982, 118–119).

In the "Great Plan," the conception of the *Wu Hsing* is still crude and naive. With reference to them, its author is still thinking in terms of the actual substances, such as water and fire, instead of abstract forces bearing these names, as the *Wu Hsing* came to be regarded later on. During the third century BCE, *Wu Hsing* became vaguer in its meaning because the Chinese character *hsing* had acquired its transferred meaning "to act" or "to do." Therefore the term *Wu Hsing*, literally translated, would mean the Five Activities, or Five Agents. They are also known as the *Wu Te*, which means Five Powers (Needham 1990, 260–262).

According to the well-known ancient Greek figures Aristotle and Hippocrates, everything in the world consists of four fundamental elements: earth, air, fire, and water. Similarly, the ancient Chinese considered metal, wood, water, fire, and earth to be fundamental. There are two important differences between the theory of Five Phases and that of Four Elements in ancient Greece. First, the Five Phases were considered as the basic components of the universe, yet they did not apply to exploring the substantial constitution of particular things because of the unfavorable technical and social conditions. Nevertheless, the Five Phases are five basic categories[13] for classifying things according to their properties and relationships to other things. Second, the Five Phases are not independent of one another, but have significant relationships and laws of transformation among them. The ancient Chinese showed much concern for the relationships and laws among five phases rather than five phases themselves, which was inspired by the concept of nature in the organic philosophy (Needham 1990, 311–312).

There are two basic kinds of relation or sequence among the five phases: Mutual Promotion (production or *Sheng* in Chinese) and Mutual Subjugation (conquest or *Ke* in Chinese). The principle of Mutual Promotion says that five phases may activate, generate, and support each other. It is through these promotions of the substances that five phases continue to survive, regenerate, and transform. The sequence of Mutual Promotion is as follows: wood promotes fire, fire promotes earth, earth promotes metal, metal promotes water, water promotes wood, and wood again promotes fire.

However, the principle of Mutual Subjugation, concerns relations such as restraining, controlling, and overcoming. Mutual restraint keeps the dynamic and conditional balance and harmony among the five phases. Wood subdues earth; earth subdues water; water subdues fire; fire subdues metal; metal subdues wood; wood in its turn acts on earth. Figure 10.1 shows the mutual promotion and mutual subjugation relationship among the five phases.

The meaning of the above principles comes from experience yet not merely experience. Fire is created when wood is burned. Ash (earth) is left after burning. All metals come from earth and liquefy on heating, while water is indispensable for growing trees and vegetation. These relations support the principle of Mutual Promotion (Production). On the other hand, the ancient Chinese noticed that trees grow on earth,

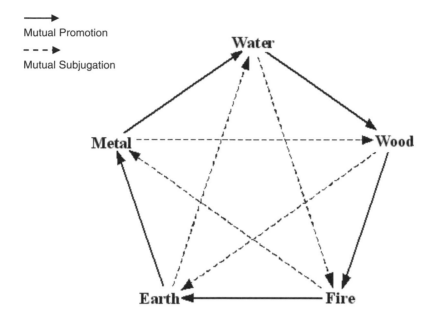

Figure 10.1. Mutual Promotion and Mutual Subjugation relations among five phases

impoverishing the soil. To prevent floods, dams and channels are built with earth. Water puts out fire while metals can be softened and melted by fire. A sword or ax made of metal can be used to fall a tree. These relations are summarized in the principle of Mutual Subjugation (Conquest). In addition, five phases have their origin in the observation and recordation of breadthways, apparent motions of five planets including Venus, Jupiter, Mercury, Mars, and Saturn, in contrast with the lengthways ones of twenty-eight Chinese *hsiu* (constellations; Liu 1991, 197–199). Thus it seems that more than experience can account for the meaning of mutual relationships of the Five Phases.

Most things in the world can be classified into one of the five basic categories according to their properties, function, and relations with others. Table 10.1 shows some objects relevant to nature, human, and their secular relations. For example, the liver is similar to wood with respect to its mild features, and the heart warms the whole body so it is analogous to fire. The spleen is responsible for assimilation of nutrients and corresponds to the earth. The lung is clear, analogous to metal. The kidney is similar to water by virtue of its responsibility of regulating fluids in the body. On the whole, the classification and correspondence in terms of the Five Phases illustrate the mutual relationship between the human body, the seasons, climate factors, senses, and emotions.

Table 10.1
The five phases as five categories and their correlations adapted from *science and civilisation in China* (Needham 1990, 285)

Heaven (Nature)							Five Phases			Human (Society)			
Yin-Yang	*Taste*	*Colors*	*Development*	*Weather*	*Cardinal Points*	*Seasons*		*Viscera*	*—*	*Sense organs*	*Body*	*Affective State*	*Dynasty*
Less Yang	Sour	Green	Birth	Wind	East	Spring	**Wood**	Liver	Gall	Eyes	Muscles	Anger	Xia
Yang	Bitter	Red	Growth	Heat	South	Summer	**Fire**	Heart	Small intestine	Lingua	Pulse (blood)	Joy	Zhou
Equilibrium	Sweet	Yellow	Change	Wet	Center	Later summer	**Earth**	Spleen	Stomach	Mouth	Flesh	Think (desire)	Yellow Emperor
Less Yin	Acrid	White	Reaping	Dry	West	Autumn	**Metal**	Lungs	Large intestine	Nose	Skin & Hair	Sorrow	Shang
Yin	Salt	Black	Storing	Cold	North	Winter	**Water**	Kidneys	Bladder	Ears	Bones (marrow)	Fear	Qin

The Yin-yang theory

The theory of the Five Phases interpreted the structure of nature, human, and society, but did not explain the origin of the world. This was provided by the theory of the *Yin* and *Yang*.

The word *yang* originally meant sunshine, or what pertains to sunshine and light; that of *yin* meant the absence of sunshine, i.e., shadow or darkness. Both words have come into use in ancient works of Chinese philosophy no earlier than fourth century BCE (Needham 1990, 296). In their later development, the *Yang* and *Yin* came to be looked on as two cosmic principles or forces, representing masculinity, activity, heat, brightness, dryness, hardness, etc., for the *Yang*, and femininity, passivity, cold, darkness, wetness, softness, etc., for the *Yin*. Through the interaction of these two primary principles, all phenomena of the world are produced.

This concept has remained dominant[14] in Chinese cosmological speculation down to recent times. An early reference to it can be found in the *Kuo Yü* (*Discussions of the States*). The historical work noted that when an earthquake occurred in the year 780 BCE, a savant of the time explained: "When the *Yang* is concealed and cannot come forth, and when the *Yin* is repressed and cannot issue forth, then there are earthquakes." (Xu 2002, 26).

The *Yin* and *Yang* are complementary to and independent on each other, even though they are opposites. For every individual object, the *yin* and *yang* it contains do not remain in a static state, but are constantly in a dynamic equilibrium affected by the changing environment. Like everything else, the human body and its functions are all governed by the principle of *Yin* and *Yang*. Remaining healthy and functioning properly require keeping the balance between the *yin* and *yang* in the body. Diseases appear when there is in equilibrium of *yin* and *yang* inside the body. This principle is central to traditional Chinese medicine, and its application dominates the diagnosis, treatment, and explanation of diseases. In light of *Inner Canon of the Yellow Emperor: Basic Questions* (*Huang-ti Nei Ching Su Wen*), one of the most significant and original classics of traditional Chinese medicine, "the principle of *yin* and *yang* is the way by which heaven and earth run, the rule that everything subscribes, the parents of change, the source and start of life and death." (Wang 1963, 31).

The integration of Ch'i

Another fundamental concept in Chinese culture is *Ch'i*, which plays a pivotal role in the theoretical background to integration of the *Wu Hsing* and the *Yin* and *Yang*. In the ordinary Chinese language, the term *Ch'i* refers mostly to air or gas, and sometimes is also used to indicate a kind of emotion—anger. But as for its general academic connotation, *Ch'i* means the material and energetic basis of things and their transformations. Further, there are three points worth consideration. First, *Ch'i* is not a type of substance and has no fixed shape or constitution. Second, it is indispensable for explaining the dynamic changes or transformations that take place among nature, human, and society. Third, it is responsible for the resources of the function and operation of the organic whole, i.e., the vivid human body or balanced ecosystem. *Ch'i* has variously been interpreted in terms of the Greek *pneuma*, vital force, or energy (Lloyd 1996, 8, 65, and 110), and therefore it serves a dual purpose of spirituality and materiality.

Ch'i seems to become a philosophical concept no earlier than the publication of the book *Mencius* (Onozawa 1990, 37). Mencius thinks that *Hao Jan Chih Ch'i* (Great Morale) is a matter concerning humans and the universe and therefore is a super-moral value. It is the morale of the man who identifies himself with the universe, so that Mencius says of it that "it pervades all between Heaven and Earth" (Yang 1960, 62). As the bridge of understanding correlations between heaven, human beings, and earth, *Ch'i* integrated with *Wu Hsing* and *Yin* and *Yang* offered ancient Chinese people an efficient and rational pattern of thought instead of a theistic and teleological one as in other nations. Whatever confronted them—the natural phenomena, secular life or social institution, the ancient Chinese pattern of thought provided people with correlative, coherent, and conditional explanations in spite of its disadvantages (Schwartz 2004, 363–368). Hence, in virtue of everlasting and dynamic holism inspired by the pattern of thought, atheism sprang up vigorously in ancient China.

An Outline of the Development of Atheism in China

In the history of atheism in China, there are so many distinguished figures[15] who broach various statements of merit that we cannot introduce to readers one by one in this chapter. However, we can still provide an outline of the development of atheism in China from the following discussion.

Several important figures need to be recognized in the development of atheism in China (Wang 1999, 3–4). First is Confucianist Hsün Tzu. He interpreted the human as one power of the three of the universe: Heaven, Earth and Human, each of which has its particular vocation. And the vocation of Human is to utilize what is offered by Heaven and Earth, hence creating his own culture and forming a unity and harmony with Heaven, Earth, and himself (Chao 2001, 16–17). Hsün Tzu attributed the highly active character to the human, which imperceptibly diminished the status of God or gods at the same time.

The second figure is Eastern Han thinker Wang Ch'ung. In his masterpiece *Discourses Weighed in the Balance* (*Lun Heng*), Wang Ch'ung

Table 10.2
The latest survey data of Chinese religious affiliation (Grim 2008)

Chinese Religious Affiliation	2007 %	2006 %	2005 %
Total Religious Believers	14	18	16
Buddhist	12	16	11
Christian	2	1	4
Protestant	1	1	2
Catholic	1	<1	2
Muslim	<1	1	1
Taoist	<1	<1	<1
Other	—	<1	<1
None	81	77	77
Refuse or DK	5	5	7
Total respondents	4,104	2,180	2,191
Sampling error	+/− 1.6	+/− 2.3	+/− 2.3

Question wording: What is your religious faith?
Note: The differences in the three estimates may be due to sampling error and the cities sampled rather than significant shifts in religious adherence among years.
Source: For 2007, Horizon survey reported by C100; *Source:* For 2005 and 2006, Horizon survey reported by the Pew Global Attitudes Project.

proposed the vitality theory to maintain that everything in the world develops on the basis of the natural law rather than the teleological or theistic explanation (Zeng 2001, 116 119). Most of all, he achieved the task of theorizing of atheism based on the study of his predecessors.

Finally, Fan Tzen, the thinker of Liang era of Southern dynasties, is famous for his harsh criticism on the doctrine of eternal soul claimed by Buddhism. He wrote a thesis, *Refutation of Doctrine of Eternal Soul (Shen Mie Lun)*, to argue against the existence of the soul separated from the body. He regarded the relation between body and soul as that of substance and function (Zhao 2003, 103–104) to demonstrate that the soul cannot live without body. Fan Tzen's theory and stand against eternality of soul were followed by the successors Liu Ts'ung-yuan and Liu Yü-hsi, thinkers of Tang dynasty.

Chinese Religious Affiliation

Brian J. Grim, from the Pew Forum on Religion & Public Life, reports data on Chinese religious affiliation compiled by the Horizon Research Consultancy Group's self-sponsored survey "Chinese People View the World" (Grim 2008). Table 10.2 shows the number of people who belong to China's five main recognized religions: Buddhism, Protestantism, Catholicism, Islam, and Taoism. The proportion of nonbelievers in China showed a considerable increase of 4 percent from 2006 to 2007. As for the doctrine of religious belief in the Party Constitution, the members of the Chinese Communist Party (CCP) formally hold communist beliefs, i.e., atheism, instead of the other religious ones. However, quite a few nonbelievers may not be authentically atheists but general skeptics of religious belief, and thus we should take cautiously the reported value of 81 percent in the 2007 survey.

ATHEISM INTERACTED WITH LIFE AND SOCIETY IN CONTEMPORARY CHINA

Since the CCP established the People's Republic of China in 1949, atheism has been emphasized and elevated theoretically in the national ideology because of the consideration of uniting people and their thought. In the ideological dictionary of the CCP, atheism is a basic doctrine that manifests in two major forms: scientific atheism and militant atheism. Scientific atheism as the outcome of the European Enlightenment Movement, regards religion as illusory or false consciousness, nonscientific, and backward, so that atheist's propaganda is necessary to cripple religion with the advancement of science and education. In contrast, militant atheism, as advocated by Lenin and the Russian Bolsheviks, treats religion as the dangerous opium and narcotic of the people, a wrong political ideology serving the interests of the antirevolutionary forces; thus force may be necessary to control or eliminate religion. Scientific atheism is the theoretical basis for tolerating religion while carrying out atheist propaganda, whereas militant atheism leads to antireligious measures (Dai 2001, 38–57). Militant atheism is so radical and left-leaning that it merely lasted 30 years or so (i.e., 1949–1979) and dwindled away with the launch of "economic reforms and open-door policies" at the end of 1978.

Scientific atheism had been flourishing in the New Culture Movement (1915–1923),[16] which was incited by Enlightenment thinkers like Chen Du-hsiu (1879–1942), Hu Shih (1891–1962), and Lu Hsun (1881–1936). In the opinions of Enlightenment thinkers at that time, "Te Hsian-hseng (Sir Democracy)" and "Hsai Hsian-hseng (Sir Science)" were two hot issues in that movement because the Chinese people had become used to the sophisticated homiletics of the patriarchal clan system and quite a few unjustified conceptions from mysticism or superstition.

The New Culture Movement encouraged people to use vernacular Chinese frequently rather than classical Chinese. Under the efforts of Hu Shih et al., what children at the stage of elementary education needed to learn was no longer "Six Classics," which their ancestors had to study well under the guidance of teachers, but was Chinese literature (*Yu Wen* in Chinese), mathematics (*Shu Xue* in Chinese), English learning, physical education, arts education, nature study and ideology, and morality lessons instead.

The ideology and morality lessons have their special function in passing on the basic ideas, including the general knowledge about human life, social morality, local custom or tradition, and scientific atheism. The basic ideas of scientific atheism are, for example, respect for knowledge and science but resistance to ignorance and superstition; also other doctrines such as devoting one's love to the homeland, faithfulness to the people, and loyalty to the Party now are taught to children in the primary schools. There is no particular order from the local or central authority to indoctrinate children with detailed rules of scientific atheism.

In China, there is easy of access to scientific atheism not only from the slogans in the streets, the popular readings, and academic books or journals, but also from the popular media including TV programs, radio broadcasts, and Internet resources. The China Central Television Station (CCTV), which is the only official TV institution and is subsidized by the central government of China, has established a special channel, CCTV-10, for broadcasting programs concerning popular science, science education, and scientific atheism. The government clearly knows that there will be no better means of crippling religion than by showing the advantages of science and scientific atheism, rather than showing its disadvantages.

The legitimate rights and interests of religious adherents today are protected by the Chinese Constitution, which means that any official or unofficial institutions and groups cannot persecute religious adherents ad arbitrium. The first constitution of People's Republic of China clarified that every Chinese citizen has the right and freedom of religious belief (The First Session of the 1st National People's Congress 1954, 29).

During the "Cultural Revolution" (1966–1976), even the little freedom for writing about religious studies vanished. From 1967 to 1974, not a single article on religion was published in journals, magazines, or newspapers in the People's Republic of China (Huang 1998, 102). It was during this period of time when the American observer Donald MacInnis visited China in 1973, reporting a totally secularized society with empty churches and temples and willing atheist young people. What he saw was only on the surface, which was maintained by a terrifying dictatorship (Strong and Strong 1973, 321–330):

> During the Cultural Revolution, under the slogans of "class struggles are the guiding principle" and "completely break up with conventional ideas," religion was listed as part of the "four olds" [old ideas, old culture, old customs, and old habits] and of "feudalism, capitalism and revisionism" that should be eradicated. Religious beliefs of the great masses were said to be reflections of class struggles in the sphere of ideology

and signs of political backwardness and reaction; religious believers were cracked down as "ox-monsters and snake-demons," resulting in many framed and fabricated cases. Religion was a realm of heavy catastrophes. The Religious Affairs Administration was dissolved; religious affairs cadres were censured for their crime of following "the wrong political line." All religious venues were closed. Many religious artifacts were destroyed. Religious research completely halted. The "criticism of theism" quickly became in practice the theoretical declaration for struggling and eliminating religion in society. (Dai 2001, 43)

Though the religious adherents were treated in an illegal and abnormal way, they have been depurged and redressed by the government since Deng Xiaoping emerged as the paramount leader of the CCP and brought order out of chaos derived from the Cultural Revolution.

In light of the past unjust and painful treatments, religious adherents won't set their hearts at rest until the report *To build a modernized, democratic and law-based country: the general theory of the study report of China's politics reform* (The Studying Team of "Studies of China's Politics Reform" 2007, 52) was published in late 2007. The report sings high praise for the positive function of religion and calls for the comprehensive participation of all forces and quarters of the society comprising not only nonreligious believers but also religious adherents. It will be of good prospect for religious people to advance in Chinese society with the wise and considerate leadership of the latest generation of CCP.

NOTES

1. "Husband guides wife" is one of the three cardinal guides that belonged to the moral laws in olden times of Chinese society, and the other two are "ruler guides subject" and "father guides son." Moreover, women had to obey the three obediences: (1) to father before marriage, (2) to husband after marriage, and (3) to son after the death of husband, and the four virtues consisting of morality, proper speech, modest manner, and diligent work. The three obediences and four virtues are spiritual fetters that were imposed on women in the patriarchal society (Fairbank 1958, 30–32).

2. The famous ancient Greek philosopher Aristotle has made a point of "mesotees (moderation)." He said, "For both temperance and bravery are destroyed by excess and by defect, and are preserved in perfection by moderation" (Williams 1869, 39). The "moderation" of Aristotle and the "golden-mean" of Confucius are different in approach but equally satisfactory in result.

3. In the case of Confucius' attitude toward theism, most scholars hold that Confucius is a theist, some even think that he is a pantheist, and a few scholars insist on the atheistic stand of Confucius (Lü 1987, 184–85). However, I maintain that Confucius takes a skeptical stand in theism and gives neither affirmative nor negative comments on the existence of God or gods. However, it doesn't mean Confucius takes no account of sacrifice to ancestors. Confucius thinks highly of the moral value of rituals (*li* in Chinese) in sacrifice to ancestors

instead of the divine connotation. Moreover, Confucius and other Confucian scholars endow the antique sacrifice rituals with their new interpretations in transmitting the traditional institutions and ideas, because nothing other than sacrifice to ancestors can shed light on the veneration of elder members of a family (Hall and Ames 1996, 64–65).

4. "The suspension standpoint" is quite similar to the research method of phenomenology founded by Edmund Husserl (1859–1938), the well-known German philosopher in modern phenomenology. Husserl uses "phenomenological epoché" (suspension) and "parenthesizing" to investigate the objective world (Husserl 1960, 20–21).

5. The saying of Confucius quoted above has another English translation by Arthur Waley, whose translation is also popular as one of the *Analects* in the West. In the following quotations of sayings of *Analects*, Waley's translation will be given as well as Legge's so that readers can make comparisons between them:

> Of the saying, "The word 'sacrifice' is like the word 'present'; one should sacrifice to a spirit as though that spirit was present", the Master said, if I am not present at the sacrifice, it is as though there were no sacrifice. (Waley 1998, 31).

Waley's translation has a little difference from Legge's in the connotation of "spirit." In Waley's translation, the "spirit" seems to denote ghosts, some of which originates from the deceased, and spirits including nature gods. In contrast, Legge's translation distinguishes the ghosts and the spirits, since "the dead" suggests not only those ghosts originating from the departed people but also deceased ancestors, and "the spirits" refer to spirits of nature and other deities.

6. The word "spirits" here refers to the *hun* (spiritual souls or personality souls) rather than spirits of nature and other deities.

7. Waley's translation is as follows: "Tzu-lu asked how one should serve ghosts and spirits. The Master said, 'Till you have learnt to serve men, how can you serve ghosts?' Tzu-lu then ventured upon a question about the dead. The Master said, 'Till you know about the living, how are you to know about the dead?'" (Waley 1998, 133).

8. Hereinafter is Waley's translation: "The master [Confucius] never talked of prodigies, feats of strength, disorders or spirits" (Waley 1998, 87).

9. Waley translates the saying into "the Good (ruler) loves men" (Waley 1998, 157). Waley regards the saying as Confucius' illustration of the proper way that a ruler treats his subjects.

10. Similar philosophical expression can be found in Hegel's works. The German philosopher Hegel says: "though in determinate being there is involved an element of negation, this element is at first wrapped up, as it were, and only comes to the front and receives its due in Being-for-self" (Hegel 1980, 203).

11. The saying has an English version of liberal translation from Chinese original text by Paul Carus: "Homeward is Reason (*Tao*)'s course" (Carus 1903, 118).

12. The English translation for the proverb can also be "Pride leads to loss/ downfall while modesty brings benefit" (Wang et al. 1996, 248).

13. Five Phases (fivefold divisions) emerged as one kind of several analogous sets for classifying things. Besides, there were fourfold and sixfold divisions that were less popular than the fivefold one (Liu 1998, 144–146).

14. Besides the dichotomy of the *Yin* and the *Yang*, there were other division methods such as trichotomy and quartation in the ancient history of China (Pang 2003, 174–194). The trichotomy cited in ancient Chinese classics was no less than dichotomy.

15. Anyone who is interested in their statements or remarks on atheism in the history of China can read the book *The History of Atheism in China* (Ya and Wang 1992) for further acquaintance.

16. For additional reading to learn more about the New Culture Movement, please browse the Web page: New Culture Movement, Wikimedia Foundation, 2008. http://en.wikipedia.org/wiki/New_Culture_Movement (accessed September 2, 2009).

REFERENCES

Benedict, Martha, and Lyra Heller. 1999. The enduring elements of traditional Chinese medicine. *Total Health* 21 (2): 54–57.

Bodde, Derk. 1942. Dominant ideas in the formation of Chinese culture. *Journal of the American Oriental Society* 62 (4): 293–299.

Carus, Paul, trans. 1903. *The canon of reason and virtue (Lao-tze's Tao Teh King): translated from the Chinese by Paul Carus*. Chicago: Open Court Publishing Company.

Chang, Kwang-chih. 1999. *Collected essays on Chinese archaeology*. Beijing: SDX Joint Publishing.

———. 2002. *Shang civilization*, trans. Zhang Liangren, Yue Hongbin, and Ding Xiaolei. Shenyang: Liaoning Education Press.

Chao, Fulin. 2001. The vocations of heaven and human in Hsün Tzu's theory. *Guan Zi Journal* no. 2: 13–18.

Chen, Puqing. 2003. "Hongfan (Great Plan)" was written during the early Zhou dynasty. *Journal of Social Science of Hunan Normal University* 32 (1):90–96.

Dai, Kangsheng. 2001. 50 years of religious research in New China. In *Annual of Religious Research, 1999–2000*, ed. Cao Zhongjian, 38–57. Beijing: Religious Culture Press.

Fairbank, John K. 1958. *The United States and China*. Cambridge: Harvard University Press.

Fan, Minsheng, et al., ed. 1998. *The dictionary of sexology*. Shanghai: Shanghai Lexicographical Publishing House.

Fang, Keli et al., ed. 1994. *The dictionary of Chinese philosophy*. Beijing: China Social Sciences Press.

The First Session of the 1st National People's Congress. 1954. *The Constitution of People's Republic of China*. Beijing: People's Press.

Granet, Marcel. 1989. *Festivals and songs of ancient China*, trans. Zhang Mingyuan. Shanghai: Shanghai Literature and Arts Publishing House.

Grim, Brian. 2008. Religion in China on the eve of the 2008 Beijing Olympics. The Pew Forum on Religion & Public Life. http://pewforum.org/docs/?DocID=301 (accessed September 2, 2009).

Guo, Ruixiang. 1981. The standing and influence of Confucius in the history of atheism of China. *Jianghan Tribune* no. 1: 58–63.

Guo, Shangxing, and Wang Chaoming, ed. 2002. *A dictionary of Chinese philosophy with English annotations*. Kaifeng: Henan University Press.

Hall, David L., and Roger T. Ames. 1996. *Thinking through Confucius*, trans. Jiang Yiwei and Li Zhilin. Nanjing: Jiangsu People's Publishing House.

———. 2005. *Anticipating China: Thinking through the narratives of Chinese and Western Culture*, trans. Shi Zhonglian et al. Shanghai: Academia Press.

Hegel, Georg Wilhelm Friedrich. 1980. *Logic: Part One of the encyclopedia of the philosophical sciences*, trans. He Lin. Beijing: The Commercial Press.

Huang, Xianian. 1998. Buddhist studies in 20th century China. In *Annual of Religious Research, 1996*, ed. Cao, Zhongjian, 95–113. Beijing: China Social Sciences Press.

Husserl, Edmund. 1960. *Cartesian meditations: An introduction to phenomenology*, trans. Dorion Cairns. The Hague: Martinus Nijhoff Publishers.

Ji, Wenfu. 1951. The progressive and conservative aspects of Confucius' thought. *Journal of Historical Science* no. 6: 4–5.

Jin, Guantao. 1984. *Behind the appearance of Chinese history*. Chengdu: Sichuan People's Publishing House.

Jones, Lindsay, et al., ed. 2005. *Encyclopedia of religion*. 2nd ed. Woodbridge: Macmillan Reference USA.

Kuang, Yaming. 1990. *A critical biography of Confucius*. Nanjing: Nanjing University Press.

Lao, Sze-Kwang. 2005. *A new history of Chinese philosophy*, Vol. 1. Guilin: Guangxi Normal University Press.

Leach, E. R. 1966. Ritualization in man in relation to conceptual and social development. *Philosophical Transactions of the Royal Society of London, Series B, Biological Sciences* 251 (772): 403–408.

Legge, James, trans. 1870. *The Chinese classics: A translation by James Legge*. New York: Hurd and Houghton.

Li, Junjing. 2004. Investigation of the written time of the book *Hongfan: The Grand Law*. *Journal of Zhengzhou University (Philosophy and Social Sciences Edition)* 37 (2): 79–83.

Li, Mengsheng, trans. 1998. *The translation and annotation of Master Tso's tradition of interpretation of the Spring and Autumn annals*. Shanghai: Shanghai Ancient Books Publishing House.

Li, Shen. 2002. *Philosophy and natural sciences in Ancient China*. Shanghai: Shanghai People's Publishing House.

Li, Xiangping, 2006. *Faith, revolution and power order: A social study of religion in China*. Shanghai: Shanghai People's Publishing House.

Li, Yih-yuan. 1998. *Analects of religion and mythology*. Taipei: New Century Publishing Company.

Li-Ling, Jesse. 2003. Human phenome based on traditional Chinese medicine: A solution to congenital syndromology. *American Journal of Chinese Medicine* 31 (6): 991–1000.

Liu, Qiyu. 1998. The origin of Wu Hsing (Five Phases) and brief introduction to its transition. In *The ancient Chinese pattern of thought and inquiries into the Yin-yang and Wu Hsing theory*, ed. Sarah Allan, Wang Tao, and Fan Yuzhou, 133–160. Nanjing: Jiangsu Ancient Books Publishing House.

Liu, Qiyu. 1991. *A continued differentiation of ancient history of China.* Beijing: China Social Sciences Press.

Liu, Wenying. 2000. *The space and time conceptions of ancient China* (Enlarged Version). Tianjin: Nankai University Press.

Liu, Xiaohong. 1994. *The mysterious Five Phases (Wu Hsing): A study of Five Phases theory.* Nanning: Guangxi People's Publishing House.

Lloyd, Geoffrey E. 1996. *Adversaries and authorities: Investigations into ancient Greek and Chinese science.* Cambridge: Cambridge University Press.

Lloyd, Geoffrey E., and Nathan Sivin. 2002. *The Way and the word: Science and medicine in early China and Greece.* New Haven: Yale University Press.

Lü, Shaogang. 1987. "Confucius As an Atheist." In *Proceedings of studies of Confucius,* ed. Zhonghua Institute of the Study of Confucius, 184–205. Beijing: Education Science Publishing House.

Mu, Zongsan. 1997. *The characteristics of Chinese philosophy.* Shanghai: Shanghai Ancient Books Publishing House.

Needham, Joseph. 1990. *Science and civilisation in China: Volume II, History of scientific thought,* trans. He Zhaowu et al. Beijing and Shanghai: Science Press and Shanghai Ancient Books Publishing House.

Onozawa, Seiichi. 1990. The concept of *Ch'i* in the academia of states of Chi and Lu. In *The thought of Ch'i: The development of concept of nature and conception of human in China,* ed. Onozawa Seiichi *et al,* trans. Li Qing, 29–75. *Shanghai: Shanghai People's Publishing House.*

Pang, Pu. 2003. *A discussion of theory of trichotomy.* Shanghai: Shanghai Ancient Books Publishing House.

Schwartz, Benjamin I. 2004. *The world of thought in ancient China,.* trans. Cheng Gang. Nanjing: Jiangsu People's Publishing House.

Sivin, Nathan. 1995. The myth of the naturalists. In *Medicine, philosophy, and religion in ancient China: Researches and reflections,* ch. IV, 1–33. Aldershot: Ashgate Publishing.

Strassberg, Richard E., ed. and trans. 2002. *A Chinese bestiary: Strange creatures from the guideways through mountains and seas (Shan Hai Jing).* Berkeley: University of California Press.

Strong, S., and J. Strong. 1973. A post-cultural revolution look at Buddhism. *China Quarterly* no. 54: 321–330.

Studies of China's Politics Reform. 2007. To build a modernized, democratic and law-based country: The General Theory of the Study Report of China's Politics Reform. *Review of Economic Research* no. 31: 27–56.

Waley, Arthur, trans. 1998. *The analects.* Beijing: Foreign Language Teaching and Research Press.

Wan, Pingjin, ed. *Lin Yutang's literature on Chinese and Western culture.* Shanghai: Shanghai Academy of Social Sciences Press.

Wang, Bing, comp. 1963. *Inner canon of the Yellow Emperor: Basic questions (Huang-ti Nei Ching Su Wen).* Beijing: People's Medical Publishing House.

Wang, Defu, Qiang Zhenxin, and Zhou Zongxin, ed. 1996. *A Chinese-English dictionary of idioms.* Chengdu: Sichuan People's Publishing House.

Wang, Shishun, trans. 1982. *The Translation and Annotation of the Book of History.* Chengdu: Sichuan People's Publishing House.

Wang, Yousan. 1999. Several problems about the study of the history of Chinese atheism. *Studies in World Religions* no. 4: 1–5.

Watson, James L. 1988. The structure of Chinese funerary rites: Elementary forms, ritual sequence, and the primacy of performance. In *Death ritual in late imperial and modern China*, ed. James L. Watson and Evelyn S. Rawski, 3–19. Berkeley: University of California Press.

Wikimedia Foundation. 2008. New culture movement. Wikipedia Encyclopedia. http://en.wikipedia.org/wiki/New_Culture_Movement (accessed September 2, 2009).

Williams, Robert, trans. 1869. *The Nichomachean ethics of Aristotle: Newly translated into English by Robert Williams*. London: Longmans, Green and Company.

Wu, Ni. 1997. The generation of private schools in Ancient China and the characters of private schools in the pre-Qin period. *Journal of Southwest China Normal University (Philosophy and Social Sciences Edition)* no. 1: 54–59.

Xu, Yuangao, comp. 2002. *The annotation and explication of discussions of the states* (Revised Version). Beijing: Zhonghua Book Company.

Ya, Hanzhang, and Wang Yousan, ed. 1992. *The history of atheism in China*. Beijing: China Social Sciences Press.

Yang, Bojun, trans. 1980. *The translation and annotation of analects of Confucius*. Beijing: Zhonghua Book Company.

Yang, Ch'ing-k'un. 2007. *Religion in Chinese society: A study of contemporary social functions of religion and some of their historical factors*, trans. Fan Lizhu et al. Shanghai: Shanghai People's Publishing House.

Yang, Lien-sheng. 1976. The concept of *Pao* as a basis for social relations in China. In *Chinese thought and institutions*, ed. John K. Fairbank, trans. Liu Renmi, Duan Changguo, and Zhang Yongtang, 349–372. Taipei: Linking Publishing Company.

Yuan, Ke, comp. 1985. *The dictionary of Chinese mythology and folklore*. Shanghai: Shanghai Lexicographical Publishing House.

Zeng, Zhenyu. 2001. *An investigation on philosophy of Qi theories of China*. Ji'nan: Shandong University Press.

Zhao, Yunxi. 2003. Fan Tzen: A distinguished atheist. *Journal of Tianzhong* 18 (6): 102–104.

Zhou, Zhenfu, trans. 1991. *The translation and annotation of Book of Changes*. Beijing: Zhonghua Book Company.

Zhu, Qianzhi, comp. 1984. *The collation and explanation of Lao-tze*. Beijing: Zhonghua Book Company.

Index

About the Editor and Contributors

EDITOR

Phil Zuckerman is an associate professor of sociology at Pitzer College. He is the author of *Society Without God: What the Least Religious Nations Can Tell Us about Contentment* (2008) and *Invitation to the Sociology of Religion* (2003), and he is currently on the editorial board of the journal *Sociology of Religion*. He lives in Southern California with his wife and three children.

CONTRIBUTORS

Bob Altemeyer earned his bachelor's degree from Yale University in 1962 and his Ph.D. from Carnegie-Mellon University in 1966. He taught for two years at Doane College in Nebraska and was at the University of Manitoba in Winnipeg, Canada, from 1968 to 2008, when he retired. He is the author of numerous scholarly articles and books, including *Atheists: A Groundbreaking Study of America's Nonbelievers*, with Bruce Hunsberger (Prometheus, 2006).

Samuel Bagg graduated from Yale in 2009 with a degree in ethics, politics, and economics, for which he concentrated in social theory. He grew up in Durham, North Carolina, where he first became interested in the social science of atheism because of conversations with his religious peers. Academically, he is primarily interested in the relationship of religion—or its absence—to civil society and national identity.

Jack David Eller is assistant professor of anthropology at the Community College of Denver. He has conducted fieldwork on Australian

Aboriginal religion among the Warlpiri people of central Australia and is the author of *Introducing Anthropology of Religion* (Routledge 2007). He has also published a number of articles on atheism and secularism, as well as two books: *Natural Atheism* and *Atheism Advanced: Further Thoughts of a Freethinker*, both with American Atheist Press.

Loek Halman is an associate professor of sociology in the department of sociology of the faculty of social and behavioral sciences at Tilburg University in the Netherlands. He is secretary to the board of the European Values Study Foundation and codirector of the European Values Study. He has published widely on cross-national and longitudinal comparisons of basic human values and attitudes.

Leontina M. Hormel is assistant professor of sociology in the department of sociology, anthropology, and justice studies at University of Idaho, Moscow. Her research examines the effects of structural adjustment on work, gender, and class relations in Ukraine, and her article on post-Soviet labor migration has been published in *Europe-Asia Studies*. Current projects include examining how everyday activities translate into local efforts of resistance to globalization in the former Soviet Union and in the United States.

Liang Tong, a member of the Chinese Society for the History of Science and Technology, graduated from Sun Yat-sen University with a master's degree in philosophy of science. Liang considers himself a columnist who is interested in the culture, philosophy, and religion of ancient China.

Peter Lüchau is a postdocotoral fellow at the University of Southern Denmark. He has a Ph.D. in sociology of religion from the University of Copenhagen. His main interests are quantitative studies of religion in modern Europe. He is currently involved in both the European Values Study and the International Social Survey Programme 2008—Religion III Survey.

Innaiah Narisetti is the chairman of the Center for Inquiry India. He has written several books in English and Telugu and translated into Telugu books by Paul Kurtz, Richard Dawkins, Christopher Hitches, Sam Harris, Agehananda Bharati, A. B. Shah, and Sib Narayan Ray. His research focuses on child abuse with religion.

Michael K. Roemer is an assistant professor of religious studies at Ball State University in Muncie, Indiana. He received his Ph.D. from the University of Texas at Austin in the sociology of religion (May 2008), and his research and teaching interests include religions of East Asia, rituals and festivals in Japan, and religion, health, and aging. Recent publications include a book chapter in the *Sociology of Religion's Religion and the Social Order* series (2006) and articles in the *Journal for the Scientific Study of Religion* (June 2007) and in the *Review of Religious Research* (March 2009).

Baffour K. Takyi, is an associate professor of sociology and also the director of the University of Akron's Pan African Studies Program. He received his Ph.D. and M.A. from the State University of New York at Albany (SUNY) and his B.A. from the University of Ghana, Legon. His varied research interests include reproductive-related behavior, including the intersection between religion and HIV/AIDS, family dynamics, and immigration. His published works have appeared in such journals as *Journal of Marriage and Family, Social Science and Medicine, Sociological Focus, International Journal of Sociology and Social Policy,* and many others. He is coauthor of *The New African Diaspora in North America: Community Building, and Adaptation* (Lanham, MD: Lexington Books), with Kwadwo Konadu-Agyeman and John Arthur, and *African Families at the Turn of the 21st Century* (Westport, CT: Praeger), with Yaw Oheneba-Sakyi.

David Voas is Simon Professor of Population Studies in the Institute for Social Change at the University of Manchester. He is particularly interested in the social mechanisms of secularization, cross-national comparisons of intergenerational change, and related topics. His work has been published in *Sociology*, the *British Journal of Sociology, American Sociological Review, Population and Development Review,* and elsewhere. He is setting up an online center for British data on religion, with the support of the United Kingdom funding councils.

Kwasi Yirenkyi is a full professor in the religious studies department, Indiana University of Pennsylvania. He received his Ph.D. in religious studies and sociology of religion from the University of Pittsburgh in 1984. His varied research interests and publications are in church and political development, the charismatic churches, the church and modernization, and African ethics, personhood, and development.